REGNUM PRACTITIONER SERIES

The Jephthah Inheritance

Practitioner Series Preface

While we delight to serve the academic community, our mission is to enable the global church to engage more readily in God's mission in its very diverse contexts. To do this we seek to bring practitioners and academics together. Our desire is that this series will bridge the gap that sometimes exists between, on the one hand, Christian leaders and mission practitioners and, on the other, Christian researchers..

Never before have I heard these enormously complicated issues of family separations for the sake of God told through the lens of Jephthah's story. But the bigger surprise came as I read this account to see how masterfully Andrew Lane used the specifics of this story to challenge each of us to take a deeper look at our own relationship with God.

Ruth van Reken
Author of *Third Culture Kids: Growing Up Among Worlds* (with David Pollock), and *Letters Never Sent*, International Speaker on TCK issues and co-founder of Families in Global Transition

These are stories that need to be told. Andrew is offering us a beautiful piece of art as he is weaving together these emotion-filled stories with reminders of how we as humans, in our search to honour God, stopped listening to both ourselves, our children and even God. It is a gift to each one of us, to receive and reflect upon.

Ulrika Ernvik, MSW, Licensed Psychotherapist and author, originator and developer of SafetyStories®, MK, mom of five MKs, and MK counsellor

An impressive book, which will help and comfort many people, in particular those who have suffered as mission kids. Its contents are of great value in discussing the policy of mission organisations with regard to the children of missionaries.

Dr Freek Bakker, Department of Philosophy and Religious Studies, Utrecht University, and author of a book in Dutch on the experiences of Dutch MKs

I had some real eye-opening moments as I read this that made me understand myself – and others – better. I have an extensive library of Christian books around inner healing, but Andrew has brought out some fresh revelations in this book.

Merle Williams, retired publishing editor, counsellor and MK

This book is astonishingly good. Andrew has written carefully, conclusively with irrefutable logic and the wisdom given him by his wrestling with the difficulties he has overcome as a child of missionary parents working in Asia. Beginning with a powerful scriptural exegesis which reaches a convincing climax, compellingly and logically stated, he follows this with stories that are beautifully told, with power and love, illustrating the complexity of missionary child/parent relationships. This book is going to be seen as definitive on these topics.

John Chenoweth, MB, BS FRCOG, FRANZCOG. Editor and publisher of *Sent: Reflections on Missions, Boarding School and Childhood*

The Jephthah Inheritance

Reflections on the sacrifice of the church's children on the altar of evangelism

Andrew Lane

First published 2023 by Regnum Books International

Regnum is an imprint of the Oxford Centre for Mission Studies
St. Philip and St. James Church
Woodstock Road
Oxford OX2 6HR, UK
www.regnumbooks.net

British Library Cataloguing in Publication Data
A catalogue record for this book is available from the British Library

ISBN: 979-8-8898-3323-9
eBook ISBN: 979-8-8898-3324-6

Photo by Dimitri Altiparmakis.
Photo is of the author outside the gates of his mission school.

Typeset by Words by Design

The author can be contacted on jti.sacrifice@gmail.com

This series has been published with the financial support of EMW

Distributed by Fortress Press in the US, Canada, India, and Brazil

Dedicated to the generations of children
whose lives became defined
by their being made the sacrifice on which
their parents' Christian service was founded,
whose voices went unheard for more than a century,
but who today are able to find healing and even, for some,
a new and vibrant relationship with the God
in whose name they were offered.
May these pages offer them some small validation in their pain,
hope for their future and a pathway towards a new faith.

Not to us, Lord, not to us,
but to your name be the praise and glory
because of your love and faithfulness.
Psalm 115:1

This book is written by an adult who as a child was abused by hurting adults; and as an adult ended up hurting others. But, by God's grace, I was able to understand and was truly sorry for the damage I did. I took responsibility and went on a healing journey. This book could not have been written without these experiences. By God's grace and with the support of others, I was given the gift of breaking the chains of shame and pain (Isaiah 61:10).

As a Christian mission publisher, occasionally you receive a manuscript on a subject that you know needs to be addressed. After a frank exploration of the author's past, we remained convinced of the importance of the work.

This book explores the troubling reality that sometimes, like Jephthah, we make sacrifices that God has not asked us to make. This is especially painful when it relates to our children. This book is also hopeful, pointing the way to a journey that may take many years yet can lead to healing. This is the transforming hope held out in the good news of Jesus Christ, our healer.

Some of the contents of this book may be disturbing for some readers. If you have been affected by issues raised in this book we encourage you to seek professional help.

Contents

List of Abbreviations

MK: Missionary Kid – Anyone brought up on the mission field, even if now an adult.

TCK: Third Culture Kid – Anyone who grew up in a culture not that of their parents.

Foreword

On the surface, it is possible to read this book simply as a thesis about why children should or should not be sent to boarding school at a young age. As a missionary child myself who boarded a small, single engine Cessna at age six to fly off to boarding school three hundred miles from home, I understand with every emotional fibre in me the specifics of this story.

For me, the question wasn't whether or not my parents loved me as I prepared to go. I had long anticipated leaving for boarding school as a rite of passage which proved I was 'getting big.' After all, it was what every child in my missionary community did at that age. Initially, I felt excited. Only as the airplane taxied off and I saw my parents and brothers standing on the tarmac waving at me with no way back, did I begin to realize this was no small thing. When the lights went out that night at boarding school without goodnight kisses from my parents, I felt the deepest loneliness I had ever known. Silent tears drenched my pillow and I didn't know if I could live without them. How could that be possible when I felt my heart squeezing to breaking point?

So, yes, the boarding school story is real. And I have heard many justify the sacrifice of family unity entailed for both parents and children because of service to God through other stories from Scripture. After all, Hannah left her much loved child, Samuel, in the temple from young childhood onward to thank God for breaking the curse of her barrenness. Jochebed, mother of Moses, risked everything when she placed him in a basket in the Nile river and allowed the Egyptian princess to raise him as a surrogate son. Abraham obeyed God's edict that he sacrifice his son of promise in faith that God would still keep his word to make Abraham a great nation.

Never before, however, have I heard these enormously complicated issues of family separations for the sake of God told through the lens of Jephthah's story. To be honest, Jephthah's story itself has always been a complex one to me. I generally read it quickly and move on, assuming there is no real way to understand it.

But the bigger surprise for me came as I read this particular account to see how masterfully Andrew Lane used the specifics of this story to challenge each of us to take a deeper look at our own relationship with God. What are the assumptions we may unconsciously make that are not necessarily true? How do these affect our interactions with God? Is it really possible that in our heartfelt efforts to love and serve him, we can begin to go our own way rather than God's? Can it be true that what seems so right and noble to us may not be God's way at all? Do we, in fact, understand not only that we are saved by grace, but what it means to live in grace for our lifetime after that initial moment of salvation?

These, and countless others, are the important questions that are suddenly square before the reader. Some of them as seen through this lens of Jephthah's story may, at least initially, make us feel uncomfortable. Could we be as misguided as it appears Jephthah may have been in his zeal to serve God? Have we created 'sufferings' of our own making rather than these being God's requirements for us?

For all who read the pages ahead, the invitation is open for us to take a closer look at our assumptions of what it means to follow Jesus and dare to wonder: Is his yoke easier than we have believed and his burden lighter than we have experienced? Is his grace truly sufficient in all circumstances? Does God indeed have something more to offer than we dared to believe before?

I invite you to dare to think anew about your God story as you take a fresh look at Jephthah's story. It will likely be both a challenge and a blessing for you, as it was for me.

Ruth van Reken
Author of *Third Culture Kids: Growing Up Among Worlds* (with David Pollock), and *Letters Never Sent*, International Speaker on TCK issues and co-founder of Families in Global Transition.

The Return

I was in my mid-fifties before I dared to return to my secondary boarding school. A friend had a working relationship with the school and she had offered to arrange with the Headmaster to show me around the newly developed site. But it had taken me almost two years to pluck up the courage to do so.

The Head met us under the archway at the entrance to the school and led us to his study – a room that held many memories for me, none of them pleasant. He could see that I was anxious and gently questioned me about my time at the school, bringing out the records of my years there and listening in some awe as I related what it had been like half a century earlier. Much had changed, fortunately, but he had little or no idea about most of what I was telling him.

Then, he asked me if I would like to visit the building where my dormitory had been to see how it had changed and what improvements had been made. I agreed, though not without some reluctance, and my friend and I followed him the hundred or so metres over to the imposing, red-brick Victorian building in which I had spent some of the most terrifying years of my young life. We paused in the stairwell as I related the story we had all been told within an hour of our arrival of the boy that had died there, a victim of bullying, and the Head stood open-mouthed and aghast as I spoke.

Next, it was up the stairs to the first landing, where we stood outside a room that had been my dormitory and had held untold terrors for me in my early teenage years.

'Are you OK?' the Headmaster asked me. It was then that I realised I was visibly shaking, my body rebelling at the signals my subconscious mind was sending that screamed 'danger,' even after all those years. But I could barely speak. Even as I write, I can still feel the fear and anxiety bubbling below the surface.

Here was the place where this Goody Two-Shoes, a painfully innocent little Christian boy, the much-loved yet abandoned child of godly missionaries, had been ravaged in body, mind and spirit and left to cope alone and unsupported in the name of Christ and His gospel.

My companions were shaken at my visceral response to being there and gently ushered me away. And I was destroyed. Again.

Introduction

> We were all of us born into a very broken world, a world at war. Every heart is wounded. *John Eldredge* (1)

As I approached my fifties, a casual observer might have felt, looking at my life, that I had it good. Married for almost thirty years, with two wonderful sons, I had a steady, well-paid job, lived in a comfortable house in a beautiful part of the world, my mortgage was paid off, my parents were both still alive and I could reflect on some limited success as a musician and writer. More than that, I had been a popular and effective teacher and a regular preacher and worship leader in my church, with a history of music direction, youth leadership and small group pastoring. Closer examination would have revealed a litany of bad choices and a degree of brokenness that placed all this in a quite different perspective. Nonetheless, I had come through some difficult times with my sanity just about intact and a certain hard-won stability evident, at least on the surface.

But appearances can be deceptive – and in my case, they really were. In fact, they were so far from the truth as to be, frankly, opposite to it. I was deeply unhappy and profoundly unfulfilled, and had even begun to look at ways in which I might end my life with minimum distress to my family. But the contradictory nature of my existence was not lost on me and I began to examine the reasons for my depression. It didn't take me long to put my finger on the root causes.

My childhood had been spent in Asia, the eldest of three children of a Christian missionary couple who had given their lives and, as I later came to understand, their children to the service of the gospel, taking the good news of Jesus to the unreached eight thousand miles away from their home in the UK. In some ways, it was an idyllic childhood, spent in a tropical paradise, my days filled with exotic and brightly-coloured birds and flowers and with the potential around every corner that we might come across a cobra or a python, or even a tiger in the road. I loved the sense of adventure and excitement, the people and the food, the jungle, the heat, the smells, the monsoon storms and sunsets, the palm trees and the butterflies …. You get the idea.

But there was another side to my childhood. Expatriate life in the 1960s was not an easy affair and bringing up children was fraught with difficult choices. For a missionary couple on a salary that kept them barely above the poverty line education options for their children were extremely limited. There were local schools, some of them having reasonable enough standards. But this would have meant being educated in the local language, almost certainly at some expense to their mother tongue, thus limiting prospects for tertiary education back home and, consequently, job prospects. Then there were the international schools, intended for expatriate families but largely following a US curriculum, which again was less than ideal for a family expecting to return to Britain at some point. And anyway, these were few and far between, only to be found in the big cities and prohibitively expensive, so an option only in the most limited sense.

The society of which my parents were members solved this education conundrum by establishing a mission school that it ran at its own expense for its members' children. Effectively, then, this was a free education provision tailored to the needs of its children and staffed by Christian missionaries who would understand the particular needs of the children in their care. An elegant solution, you might think.

Of course, none of these options was without its downside and the particular drawback of the mission school was that there was only one school to serve the children of missionaries over an extremely wide area, covering several thousand square miles. This dictated that the establishment be a boarding school and meant that, for most, the time and expense involved in having their children attend the school was significant. For a number of children, it was a three-day journey from their home, involving perhaps half a day's walk, a bus ride, an overnight train and finally a taxi ride of several hours' duration. Clearly, this was not something that could or should be undertaken more often than was necessary so, as a result, the school operated just two terms annually, each with a half-term break that the children spent at school. This meant that each school term approached four-and-a-half months' duration – a very long time indeed for a young child to be separated from their parents and siblings.

The school covered the range of primary education, which had two significant implications. Firstly, it meant that children left their family home to board at five, occasionally six if home leave coincided with the child turning five, and in a few instances at just four years old. Secondly, it meant that once a child reached the age at which secondary education was a requirement it had to take place in the sending country, meaning the child was sent back to the homeland of their parents to another boarding school whilst the family remained on the mission field, with the child returning to their family only every two years or so for a brief summer holiday.

And so it was that at just five years old I was sent away to boarding school to begin a life away from my family, a separation that would continue until I left school at eighteen. And, whilst in many ways there was an aspect of privilege and enjoyment to this kind of education, there were also, unbeknownst to my parents or the mission at the time, deeply damaging aspects that had brought me to the depths of my despair as I moved towards my fiftieth year. A midlife crisis, by any other name, to be sure. So, not uncommon, or even different from that of many of my contemporaries at work or within my social circle. But it was one that had its roots in perhaps an unusual place, and with quite other implications than the issues being faced by my peers. Clearly, this was not something that would be mitigated by buying an expensive red sports car, or any of the other standardly-perceived coping options!

As I reflected on my upbringing, I realised that the defining characteristic of my youth was a semi-awareness of a deep, inconsolable and abiding pain, a sense of grief, rejection and abandonment that could not be assuaged by the love of my wife or children, or even the newly regained relationship I now had with my parents. It was a pain so immense that, at the time, I had been overwhelmed and completely unable to face it. And so, as we are wont to do, I had put it away, deep in the recesses of my heart, safely under lock and key. If I couldn't see it or hear its lamenting voice, I would not feel it, my five-year-old subconscious reasoned, if reasoning it was. And if I didn't feel it, I would be okay.

The trouble is, emotional pain won't be ignored. Oh, it will sit quietly for a while, locked in its drawer, safely behind cupboard doors in a room we never enter. But, in time, it begins to shuffle and scratch around. It festers and ferments and grows. It whispers, then chunters, and finally screams to be let out. What was once just a nagging sore becomes a throbbing, pulsating, searing agony of an open wound that will not, cannot be ignored. It flows in a relentless tide of poison through every part of our being, triggering extreme emotional responses to tiny provocations, firing up intense and uncontrolled anger in response to innocent slights, and oozing an ugly pus of vengeful despair into our words and expressions.

It was this unacknowledged, unexpressed and unresolved pain, this overwhelming sense of rejection and abandonment, this unbearable burden of grief whose full force I was now feeling as it bubbled out of its hiding place. And I had to find a way of dealing with it before it killed me, if only by my own hand.

Once I had identified the source of my pain, the way ahead was clear to me. I had to return to that school in Asia and face my ghosts. Deep within me was a hopelessly hurt little boy whose emotional growth towards maturity had been thwarted at five years old. Taken – dare I acknowledge, sent – from my loving home, I had entered an existence in which love was no longer present, at least in the ways and to the extent that such a young child needs to experience it. I was bereft, alone in my fear, unable at so young an age to rationalise at all this inexpressible sense of rejection. I was unlovable. What other explanation could there be for this sudden separation, this terrifying exile? Worse than that, I was bad. My parents had explained to me that my going away was God's will, that He needed me to go away to school so that Mummy and Daddy could do God's work. And God would be there for me to comfort me in my sadness.

But God wasn't there, I wasn't comforted and I felt such a weight of sadness that, night after night, I sobbed myself to sleep, burying my face in my pillow so the other boys would not hear me. So, my five-year-old brain reasoned, if this was what God wanted and I was unhappy, I must be bad for wanting the opposite. Very bad. Hence the hiding of my grief. I could not let anyone know I was sad or they would find out how bad I was. If the other boys saw me crying, they would tease me, which was bad enough. But if the staff knew, they would tell my parents. Then the teachers would be angry, my mum and dad would be angry, the mission would be angry and God would be angry. Such was the toxic burden I carried alone as a five-year-old, and which now was working its way out of my heart after five decades of suppression and concealment.

> Unless their emotional distress can be shared with and validated by attuned adults, children's necessary developmental narcissism disposes them to take everything personally. It is natural that they should believe that when bad things happen – when life hurts them, when the environment is stressed, the parents unhappy or ill – it is because they are culpable, unworthy, defective. *Gabor Maté* (2)

Thus began a new phase of my life as I journeyed back to my childhood, revisiting places and memories I had not allowed myself to visit even in my thoughts in the intervening years. Many of the memories were desperately sad and difficult, but alongside them were some good and precious ones that had been lost to me under the cloak of abandonment and grief that had smothered my soul and which now, happily, returned to provide a welcome perspective.

> To deny true sorrow is also to deny true joy. *Brian Zahnd* (3)

The story of that trip and its consequences are for another time, though I will touch on them later. Many truths were uncovered and are still being revealed as I journey on. But one overriding question bugged me. Why did they do it? What was their thinking? What were the circumstances that allowed my godly, loving and generally wise parents to hand me over aged five for the rest of my childhood and teenage years into the care of complete strangers, some of whom lacked any kind of qualification or suitability to care for children and none of whom could replace the love and security that I had known up until that point? Even allowing for the fact that it was only in more recent years that the extent of the damage their decision caused had fully come to light, why would any couple have children believing that God required them to be separated and live apart after just five short years? And what kind of God required this of his servants anyway? Did I want to believe in such a cruelly demanding deity?

These are not easy questions to answer and, even insofar as it is possible to suggest answers, the issues undergirding them are complex and personal. But difficult doesn't mean impossible and, as I began to talk not just with my own parents but with those of many of my contemporaries, as well as current mission leaders, TCK experts and professional psychologists and counsellors, one name began to stand out from Scripture.

Jephthah. A minor character in the Old Testament, to be sure, but one whose very inclusion invites consideration as to why his story is there. In the following chapters, I will endeavour to match some of the truths of Jephthah's story to the events of my own life, and that of many others who share my experience. We will look at the decisions Jephthah made and the reasons behind them in seeking to discover something of what lay behind the choice of our parents to dedicate themselves so wholeheartedly to the cause of evangelism that they sacrificed their own children. It is my hope that, as I examine these issues, I may do so with grace and compassion, seeking not to judge but to understand, knowing that had I found myself in the same position my parents did a generation ago, I likely would have done as they, but also in the fervent hope that in highlighting these issues, this is one area of mission history that need not be repeated.

For the most part, I will not be naming missions, since each has its virtues and problems and this is not an exercise in judgment so much as an attempt at understanding. In the same vein, I have not used the actual names of those whose stories I share and I have occasionally combined elements of more than one person's story, partly to facilitate the disguising of their identity and partly for the sake of brevity. This, not just to protect the subject of the account, but also those whose featuring in their story does not perhaps show them in their best light. I reiterate – this is not an exercise in throwing stones but in uncovering a long-hidden truth, seeking a new understanding and assisting those who yet journey out of the traumas of their childhood towards some degree of resolution.

These are stories of good, even godly men and women who made choices that impacted in a profoundly negative way on their children. Such choices were made without malice, often without any possible means of understanding their impact or far-reaching effects. But it is also true that inherent in their outworking were attitudes of colonialism, elitism, entitlement, racism and white privilege (not to mention a good dose of bad theology) to which those of us who carry any trace of them are almost always blind. So, lest any of my words should appear judgmental or unmerciful, let me state from the start concerning the actions of past generations: 'There, but for the grace of God, went I.'

All Scripture quotes are from the New International Version unless otherwise stated.

I have also quoted many theologians, philosophers, psychologists and writers whose wisdom and knowledge far exceed my own, but who have, through those virtues, aided my understanding and informed my own writing. In doing so, I am not necessarily validating their personal beliefs, but only the truth of the words I have quoted as they pertain to the subject in hand. The truth is always the truth, whoever speaks it. And so to Jephthah.

Jephthah's Story

> Satan does not tempt you so much to the "hot sins" like greed, lust and gross ambition. They are too obviously evil and will eventually show themselves as such. Instead Satan tempts you to do proper, defensible and often admired things, but for cold, malicious or self-centred reasons. *Richard Rohr* (1)

Even those with a more than nodding acquaintance with the Bible could be forgiven for not knowing the story of Jephthah. It occupies just two and a half chapters in the Old Testament and recounts two battles in which Jephthah led his tribe to victory. So, who was he and what is his relevance to the issue under consideration here? His story can be found in Judges 10, 11 and 12.

Jephthah lived during the time of the judges in Israel. Following their escape from slavery in Egypt, the Israelites were led first by Joshua, Moses' nominated heir, and then by a succession of leaders known as judges – men and women of faith (if not always as we would define it), who were obedient to God and were raised up in order to lead the nation as it fended off the various invading forces that sought to take back the promised land from them. There was a pattern here that was repeated over and over in those early days of Israel's history. The people would forget God and begin to worship the false gods of the surrounding nations. God would then allow one of these nations to be successful in defeating Israel, who would then remember God and turn back to him for help. God would then raise up a judge to lead the Israelites in battle and grant them victory. Then, a period of relative peace would follow, at least until such time as the Israelites forgot God again and the whole pattern would repeat itself.

Jephthah appears towards the end of this sequence, sometime after Gideon and just before Samson, both of whose stories are much better known. He was, we are told, 'a mighty warrior.' His father was called Gilead and his mother was a prostitute. As often happened in such instances, once Gilead married and had other sons, they drove Jephthah out of the family home and declared that he would receive none of his father's inheritance. Jephthah fled to another land where 'a gang of scoundrels gathered around him and followed him' (Judges 11:3). Meanwhile, the Ammonites had settled in the tribal lands of Gilead, intent upon war, and a discussion ensued as to who might lead the Gileadites should the need arise for them to fight the invaders.

In time, Jephthah was summoned by the tribal elders, chosen for his warrior status, and offered the position of commander if he would lead them into battle against the Ammonites. In addition, he was promised that he would become the leader of the people of Gilead if he were successful. Jephthah accepted and a process of negotiation between him and the Ammonite leaders followed, but failed. We are then told that 'the spirit of the Lord came upon Jephthah' and he began an advance towards the Ammonite armies. And in Judges 11:30-39 we read the following:

> Jephthah made a vow to the Lord: "If you give the Ammonites into my hands, whatever comes out of the door of my house to meet me when I return in triumph from the Ammonites will be the Lord's, and I will sacrifice it as a burnt offering."
>
> Then Jephthah went over to fight the Ammonites, and the Lord gave them into his hands. He devastated twenty towns from Aroer to the vicinity of Minnith, as far as Abel Keramim. Thus Israel subdued Ammon.
>
> When Jephthah returned to his home in Mizpah, who should come out to meet him but his daughter, dancing to the sound of timbrels! She was an only child. Except for her he had neither son nor daughter. When he saw her, he tore his clothes and cried, "Oh no, my daughter! You have brought me down and I am devastated. I have made a vow to the Lord that I cannot break."
>
> "My father," she replied, "you have given your word to the Lord. Do to me just as you promised, now that the Lord has avenged you of your enemies, the Ammonites. But grant me this one request," she said. "Give me two months to roam the hills and weep with my friends, because I will never marry."
>
> "You may go," he said. And he let her go for two months. She and her friends went into the hills and wept because she would never marry. After the two months, she returned to her father, and he did to her as he had vowed. And she was a virgin.

There is a little more that follows, but this is the part of Jephthah's story for which he is remembered and it is the part that concerns us now. So let's sum up what we know. Jephthah is a fighting man, possibly a bit of a thug, who lives in exile and surrounds himself with men of the kind that perhaps nice young ladies would not wish to take home to meet their mother. When the area where he grew up is threatened by another tribe, the leaders go to Jephthah and ask him to lead them into battle. Flattered by the attention and tempted by the prize, he agrees to return home and lead his nation into war. He is on a promise and that promise is the closest thing to kingship that existed in Israel at the time. Confident of success, he establishes how the land lies and, when his brief diplomatic approach is ignored, he sets off into battle. But, before doing so, he makes a vow. If God gives him victory in this battle, he will sacrifice to God the first thing that comes out of his house upon his return. The battle is won, Jephthah returns home and the first thing that comes out of his house is his daughter, his only child. Nevertheless, he fulfils his vow and his daughter is duly sacrificed. Though no specifics are given as to how, his promise to God was to present her as a burnt offering. (Some believe that her sacrifice was accomplished by shutting her away, thus preventing her from marrying, which, in Israelite society at the time, was seen as a disgrace, perhaps even a punishment from God. This is based on the reference to Jephthah's daughter remaining a virgin, but has no further support than that simple presupposition.)

It's a bizarre tale and one that it is tempting to gloss over. After all, the Bible is full of stories that are difficult to understand and we can't be expected to grapple with all of them, can we? But here's the thing. It's there. The story is there in the Bible, a book that claims to be the infallible word of God.

> All Scripture is God-breathed and is useful for teaching, rebuking, correcting *and* training in righteousness, so that the servant of God may be thoroughly equipped for every good work. 2 Timothy 3:16–17.

In other words, everything in Scripture has a purpose and a message from which those who seek to live their lives in relationship with and obedient service to God may glean information useful to the fulfilment of that desire. So, as with everything else in the Bible, it merits us at least asking the questions, 'Why is it there?' and 'What are we to learn from this account?' Let's look a little more closely at these events.

The inclusion of Jephthah's story in the book of Judges authenticates his position as one accepted by God to lead Israel. (Note that he was not *chosen* by God as such, but by the leaders of his tribe. Nevertheless, God accepted him as their chosen leader.) We know very few details, but what little we do know suggests that he perhaps would not fulfil our criteria for what we might call a good man. He was a strong man and a fine soldier, that much is clear. But he kept dubious company and the comment that he was surrounded by scoundrels suggests that his moral standards were perhaps not of the highest. So, he fits nicely into the line of Old Testament heroes whose character flaws and criminal records nonetheless did not disqualify them from being blessed and used by God. Noah, Abraham and Moses feature near the start of this list, each guilty of offences that would have seen them imprisoned and excoriated by today's western society, but with a faith that God honoured and used mightily to bless them and His people. It's a list that will go on to include, amongst others, the murdering and adulterous David; the impetuous and flaky motormouth we know as Peter; and that zealous pursuer and exterminator of the early Christian church, Paul. Hope for us all, then!

On the other hand, ejected from the family home and forced into exile, his childhood and upbringing were coloured with rejection and tragedy. In other words, he was a broken man, just as we all are broken. He grew up in an atmosphere of shame, perhaps always knowing that in time his place in the family would be questioned and that any inheritance was out of the question. Even before his banishment, he must have feared that such a time would come. And, despite his fearsome reputation as a fighting man, we are not told that he resisted this rejection, as was seemingly within his power to do. So, he was a chosen man, but a broken one, who could be forgiven for feeling that God had not been with him during his early life.

But suddenly all that changes and he becomes the focus of attention for his home community. He is brought back and invited to lead them into battle. And here's the first surprise. We might expect that a man of his reputation, a tough warrior with a thuggish following, might jump at the opportunity of a skirmish or two. But instead, he chooses a diplomatic approach, sending messages to the Ammonite king outlining his thinking as to why the Ammonites should step back from conflict. He explains in Judges 11:14–27 that God had given the Gileadites the land and invites the Ammonites to be satisfied with what their own god had given them. In doing so, he demonstrates that he is a man of faith, crediting God with having given the Gileadites their land and finishing up by saying, 'Let the Lord, the Judge, decide the dispute this day between the Israelites and the Ammonites.' Here is a man of genuine faith. He believes God gave the land to his people and, by implication, that God will help them to retain it. He knows who God is and trusts Him to save His people.

At this point we are told that 'the Spirit of the Lord came upon Jephthah.' Meaning that in the story we have heard so far, Jephthah was acting on his own initiative and purely from such faith as he had. But now he was one anointed by God for the purposes of the battle that lay ahead. So, broken as he was, scarred by the rejections of his youth and with good reason, on the face of it, to feel let down by God, Jephthah nonetheless retained sufficient faith for him to ignore his instincts to launch into battle at least long enough to allow for an attempt at finding a diplomatic solution. And now God's seal of approval rested upon Jephthah as he received His spirit for the battle ahead.

What follows might well have excited our interest no more than the very similar accounts of the victories of the other judges – Gideon, Deborah, Samson et al. It is a tale that readers of the Old Testament have become familiar with. The people drift away from God, God uses a neighbouring power to subdue them, the people turn back to God, God raises up a leader, that leader is given victory in battle, peace and order are restored and the people resume a relationship with God. End of story. Until the next time.

But suddenly this story takes an awkward turn. Jephthah makes a vow. If he is granted victory, he will sacrifice to God the first thing that comes out of his house upon his return. In itself, this is not an unusual thing for a man of his time to do. Making a vow was common practice and sacrifice was the standard method of thanking God or showing penitence for sins committed. The entire religious economy was predicated upon it, not just for the Israelites, but in all the religions of the many heathen tribes that bordered and at times overlapped the promised land. There was just one difference. The heathen tribes were partial to human sacrifice, even children, to appease their gods, notably Molech, a god of the Canaanites. But Israel was required to draw the line at animals. In Leviticus 18:21 we hear Moses declaring amongst God's laws for living in the promised land, 'Do not sacrifice your children ....' This command is repeated later with attendant punishments to be enacted in the event of this law being broken.

So, in declaring that he will offer a sacrifice in thanks for the expected victory in battle, Jephthah is making a vow that would have raised no eyebrows amongst those present. And, on the face of it, his intention is to sacrifice an animal, so there would seem to be no question of a child or any other human sacrifice. It was common for animals to live under the same roof as their owners and to wander in and out of the house. So, Jephthah's presumed expectation, that the first thing to come out of his house upon his return would be an animal, is not as unlikely as it might seem to modern, western cultural thinking, as we will see.

We are not told the specifics of the ending to this story. And there has been much debate over the years amongst considerably greater minds than mine as to whether Jephthah's daughter met a grisly end or was just shut away in seclusion, given to God in the sense that she would never marry and would have to endure the disgrace inherent to her culture of dying a virgin. The original Hebrew includes a word that may be translated as *'and'* or *'or'*, which in part leads to this doubt. So, one reading of the passage is 'whatever comes out of the door of my house to meet me when I return in triumph from the Ammonites will be the LORD's, AND I will sacrifice it as a burnt offering.' Another reading of the same passage is 'whatever comes out of the door of my house to meet me when I return in triumph from the Ammonites will be the LORD's, OR I will sacrifice it as a burnt offering.' This second interpretation leaves room for Jephthah to either dedicate this 'whatever' to God, in the case of a woman, securing her purity by maintaining her virginity, OR, in the case of an animal, sacrifice it as a burnt offering.

Such ambiguity in interpretation casts some doubt on Jephthah's expectations as to what might actually occur upon his return and how he might be obliged to deal with that occurrence. What is beyond doubt is that Jephthah did not expect his daughter to be the first one through the door. Miles Van Pelt, a Professor of Old Testament and Biblical Languages, additionally suggests the following point.

> We must understand that he did not expect some type of animal or household pet to burst forth from the house upon his return. We know this to be true for a couple of reasons. First, in 11:31, the verb "to meet" is always used for people, never for a person encountering an animal. Second, in the ancient world, when men returned from battle, women would customarily come forth in procession in order to participate in celebratory dancing (cf. Ex. 15:20; Jud. 5:28; 1 Sam. 18:6). Given the cultural context in which these events transpired, Jephthah likely assumed that a woman would come out from the house to meet him, perhaps a servant girl or, even better, his mother-in-law, but certainly not an animal. A better translation for 11:31 would include "whoever comes out," not "whatever comes out." (2)

Other academic theologians beg to differ, arguing that Jephthah had the burnt offering of an animal in mind when he made his vow and that it was a rash promise born of ignorance and pride. He never even considered the possibility, some feel, that an actual person might become the sacrificial victim. But we cannot be sure what exactly Jephthah's expectations were. And, either way, the consequences of his vow proved extremely costly both for him and his daughter.

For myself, the fact that the specific outcome is unclear suggests two things. Firstly, that whether Jephthah sacrificed his daughter by burning her on an altar or secluding her away from society to remain as a pure and unsullied virgin for the rest of her days is, to us, somewhat immaterial. Sure, being turned into a burnt offering would have been an unimaginably horrendous experience. But who is to say that if she was somehow put away in seclusion, she didn't reach a point in the agony of her perpetual solitude and maidenhood when she wished she had been killed at the outset and a swift end had been put to her suffering?

Secondly, it suggests that we don't need to know. It may be interesting to speculate but, as with most issues of biblical interpretation, it is not an issue on which our faith depends and so it is not anything we should become hung up on. For the purposes of giving the matter our fullest consideration, let's assume for now that Jephthah's expectation was that an animal would emerge from his house and take our discussion from there.

Jephthah's status as an illegitimate child meant he was not allowed to enter the place of worship. In Deuteronomy 23:2 we read, 'No-one of illegitimate birth … may enter the assembly of the Lord.' So, if Jephthah was to offer a sacrifice at all, he was obliged to invite a priest to come to him and offer the sacrifice at a chosen location, likely to be at or near his home. Just taking an animal to Shiloh for it to be sacrificed was not an option, since any such sacrifice would have to take place at the sanctuary, where Jephthah was not permitted to go. This may go some way towards explaining why Jephthah mentions his house, since that was where any sacrifice would necessarily happen.

But why might Jephthah expect an animal to be coming out of his house in the first place? Why does he talk about animals emerging from his house and not grazing in a field or overnighting in a byre or barn? Kenneth Bailey, in his invaluable resource *Jesus Through Middle Eastern Eyes*, explains.

> Simple village homes in Palestine often had but two rooms. One was exclusively for guests. That room could be attached to the end of the house or be a "prophet's chamber" on the roof, as in the story of Elijah (1 Kings 17:19). The main room was a "family room" where the entire family cooked, ate, slept and lived. The end of the room, next to the door, was either a few feet lower than the rest of the floor or blocked off with heavy timbers. Each night into that designated area, the family cow, donkey and a few sheep would be driven. And every morning those same animals were taken out and tied up in the courtyard of the house. The animal stall would then be cleaned for the day.
>
> The story of Jephthah in Judges 11 … assumes the same kind of one-room home. Most likely he returned early in the morning and fully expected one of the animals to come bounding out of the room in which they had been cramped together all night. The reader is obliged to assume that it never crossed his mind that a member of his family would step out first. (3)

This last assertion of Bailey's needs to be set alongside that of Miles Van Pelt quoted above. Bailey was also an expert in the language and texts of the Torah and yet he reaches a quite opposite conclusion in his understanding of this story, despite, it is fair to assume, having the same knowledge available to him. So, as the saying goes, 'You pays your money and you takes your choice.' (As an aside, it is interesting to note that the kind of home Bailey describes may well have provided the context in which Luke describes the birth of Jesus. Between the family area and the animals' enclosure, there was often a sunken area carved out of the stone or wood into which was placed food for the animals – a manger, in fact.)

Jephthah appears to be taking a gamble. But as far as he is concerned, that gamble only concerns which of his livestock he will lose to the sacrifice. Willing as he is to make this gesture of thanksgiving, he would appear not to have thought it through. And the consequences are to be devastating.

One further observation is merited at this point. Jephthah's vow is made *after,* we are told, the Spirit of the Lord came on him. It would therefore be easy enough to claim that this vow was made at the prompting of God's Spirit, as indeed some have done. Two points should be made in respect of this possibility. The first is that the presence of the Holy Spirit in our lives does not render us incapable of sin, as every Christian can testify, particularly the sin of thought and action that is independent of any consulting of God and His will. We may have God's Spirit in us and still make the most appalling decisions out of our own pride, complacency or desire to control our lives, free from any obligation or even awareness of how God's kingdom may, according to Him, be brought about on earth as it is in heaven. This was the sin of Eden. The second point is that it goes entirely against everything that Scripture reveals to us about the character of the God who *is* love that He would 'inspire' Jephthah to make a decision that was to result in the untimely and horrific death of his daughter. So we may understand that, although the Spirit of the Lord had been given to Jephthah prior to him making his ill-thought-out vow, in making that vow Jephthah was not acting at the Spirit's prompting, but of his own free will and out of his own thinking. This is crucial to our understanding of the subject under discussion.

Why is this story in the Bible? What are we to understand from it being there? After all, there are several other accounts of judges leading Israel to victory in battle. Some of them, it might be considered, include details that bring significantly greater glory to God for the manner in which that victory was achieved. As we have noted, we have no details of Jephthah's battle at all. The victory is merely mentioned in passing. And it is Jephthah's vow and its hideous consequences that take centre stage.

So what are we to understand and take from this account?

A Good Idea Is Not Necessarily a God Idea

> The human spirit will not even begin to try to surrender self-will as long as all seems to be well with it. Now error and sin both have this property, that the deeper they are the less their victim suspects their existence; they are masked evil. *CS Lewis* (1)

Standard Christian theology has it that, ultimately, every error of a person's ways has its beginnings in an assertion of independence from God, the desire to go it alone, imagining that we know best and so acting out of our own wisdom rather than God's leading. It is the sin of Adam and Eve in the Garden of Eden and it remains man's sin today. We were created to be in relationship with God, which means we are intended to live in communion *and communication* with him at all times. I believe this is what Paul meant when he encouraged the church in Ephesus to:

> *[P]ray* in the Spirit on all occasions with *all* kinds of prayers and requests. (Ephesians 6:18)

Essentially, he is saying, 'Stay in touch, check in at every opportunity so that you can know God's mind and seek His will.' It's telling us to live out 'May your will be done on earth as it is in heaven.' Which, by the way, is not just us allowing God to have His way, but is on our part an intentional setting aside of our own will and desires. Because the moment we choose to do or say anything independently of God, we separate ourselves from Him, declaring that we have no need of Him, scorning His will for our lives, rejecting the purposes of His kingdom and asserting that we know best. On one level, such separation is both the fullest and the only definition of sin and all other sins stem from this.

Actively choosing to be separated from God and acting independently of Him, not just ignoring His will for our lives but refusing to search out that will, is also one definition of hell. Of all the sayings of Jesus, perhaps the most stunning in its implications for the outworking of Christian life is found in John 5:19. Responding to the opposition of the Jewish leaders to his claim to be the Son of God, He said:

> Very truly I tell you, the Son can do nothing by himself: He can only do what he sees the Father doing, because whatever the Father does the Son does also.

If we are to take this alongside the many injunctions by Jesus and others at various places in the New Testament that indicate Jesus's life is intended to be a template for our own, the questions we need to answer here are, 'How can we possibly justify living in any other way? If this was how Jesus lived, what possible reasons could we have for trying to live otherwise?' Jesus never did anything without first checking in with the Father and asking, 'What are you doing in this situation and please may I join you and become part of that work?' And neither should we.

It is one of the basest deceits of the evil one that it is at moments of contentment or success in our lives that we are most vulnerable to falling into that sin. In the glow of these moments, it is much too easy for us to imagine that the reasons we feel so good about life are because *we* have made a success of it. So we start to make plans to build on our success or increase our happiness, forgetting that:

> Every good and perfect gift is from above…. (James 1:17)

But, as CS Lewis remarks:

> [E]rror and sin both have this property, that the deeper they are the less their victim suspects their existence; they are masked evil. (2)

Since our propensity to do things our own way has its roots way back in that first deceit of Adam and Eve, that belief that we can possess equal knowledge with God and therefore may do as we please, this is indeed an error that lies deep within us, one of which Paul warns us in Galatians 5:17.

> For the flesh desires what is contrary to the spirit and the spirit what is contrary to the flesh. They are in conflict with each other, so that you are not to do whatever you want.

By its very nature, it is an error that we are often unaware we are entering into. The more so when we profess a faith in God and have offered ourselves to His service. And, we tell ourselves, we have received the Holy Spirit. Surely, we are doing a good thing. We are being obedient to God and have sacrificed a considerable amount in following Him and seeking to bring others into His kingdom. Our desires, our instincts are to do good. This project, this event, this meeting, this act of service, this sacrifice must therefore also be a good thing; and because it is a good thing and we are good people it must be a good idea and God will bless it. How can it not be good when it is intended for good? How can it be bad when we mean it for good and are working so hard, praying so hard, giving so much to make it work for good? It is but a short step from this mode of thought to convincing ourselves that it was actually God's idea in the first place. But it is masked evil and it stalks the halls of Christian service.

So, what seemed to Jephthah like a good idea at the time, and may even seem to us today a small matter undeserving of its disastrous consequences, was in fact Jephthah going his own way, turning away from God and asserting his right to do what he deemed best without consulting God, who was about to give him a spectacular victory. It may have been a good idea, but it was not a God idea. God did not require the vow that Jephthah made. He didn't even require the animal sacrifice, let alone a human one, and Jephthah's gesture was made independently of the Spirit with which he had been anointed. This lies at the heart of the issue we are considering here – promises we make to God that He does not require us to make.

Note here that, although Jephthah makes his vow after being filled with God's Spirit, some time appears to pass between the two events. As has already been pointed out, it should not be understood that because God's Spirit had come upon Jephthah his vow was of God. There is plenty of evidence both in Scripture and over the history of the Christian church of men and women anointed with the Spirit of God making bad choices that clearly fell outside of His will. Having God's Spirit within us is not an insurance against wrongdoing. We retain the freedom from God to listen to His Spirit or go our own way. Choosing to remain under the Spirit's anointing is a moment by moment act of the will.

So, Jephthah's idea appears, on the face of it, to have a good deal of merit. 'If you give me victory, I will give back to you something of value to me as a mark of my gratitude.' It's right up there with, 'If you will increase the church's income this year, we will build a new one down the road that will bring in even more new converts.' Or, 'If you will bless us with a child, we will give him back to you and dedicate his life to your service.' The history of the church is littered with prayer meetings, evangelistic missions, pot luck suppers, parties of young people visiting orphanages in Africa, monthly leaflet deliveries and the like, all of which were thoroughly well-meaning, good ideas, but most of which were OUR good ideas and nothing to do with what God was doing to bring about His kingdom on earth. Remember Peter's determination to protect Jesus from death in Matthew 16? It brought him the sternest of rebukes from Jesus. A good idea, not a God idea. The Christian life that is based on asking God to bless what we have decided to do off our own back is not just one of frustration and disappointment, it is one of independence, which means a turning away from God. And that is sin. Just because God is able to ensure that 'all things work together for good' (Romans 8:28) doesn't mean He wouldn't rather He didn't have to if we would just listen to what He was saying and doing in the first place.

Because, 'Everything that does not come from faith is sin,' as we read later in Romans 14:23. And, as Papa says to Mackenzie in William Paul Young's *The Shack*:

> Declaring independence will result in evil because apart from me, you can only draw upon yourself. That is death because you have separated yourself from me: Life. (3)

Grace Overlooked

> The power of grace flows most fully when human will chooses to act in harmony with divine will. *Gerald May* (4)

The doctrine of grace lies at the heart of the Christian faith. It teaches that there is nothing we can do to earn the love or favour of God, but that His love and favour are offered to us anyway, unconditionally, and for no better reason than that He wants to give it. We don't have to do anything in advance to ensure that it will be given to us and we don't have to do anything in response in order to pay for it. Sure, if we understand the value, not to mention the personal cost to Jesus, of what we are being offered, our hearts will want to respond, which is our 'true and proper worship,' or what older translations call our 'reasonable service' (Romans 12:1). Grace is God saying to us, 'I don't have to give you this, I just want to. You haven't earned it because there is nothing you could do to earn it, but have it anyway because I love you. Just take it and enjoy!'

For many, grace is just a little too good to be true. Most of us are unfamiliar with perfect, unconditional love and have grown up expecting that we will only get what we deserve. And, since we know ourselves to be sinful, what we believe we deserve often doesn't amount to very much. So the idea that someone wants to give us something we deeply desire but don't deserve, often, in our own minds, *really* don't deserve, is hard for us to accept. We feel bad, because we don't deserve it. How can we accept such an overwhelming gift of love? We actually feel uncomfortable in doing so. We live in a world that tells us, 'I can't accept that from you unless you let me give you something in return.' We have a mindset of, 'I don't take charity.' We live within the lie that tells us, 'You will only receive in this life what you work for.' And work hard, at that.

Jephthah has overlooked grace as he prepares for battle. (The word 'grace' does not appear in the Old Testament, but the concept is present throughout.) He has failed to understand not only that his victory is assured, because otherwise why had God brought him to this point, never mind anointed him with His Spirit, but also that he need not, indeed, cannot do anything to earn that victory. This victory is to be a gift of grace. Jephthah has done nothing to deserve it – far from it. It's not even just for him. Sure, he will be blessed, as indeed he believes, but, as usual, God's intentions are much wider than the limits of Jephthah's imagination. It's about God once more protecting His people and saving them, not because they have been good, because they haven't, or because they worshipped Him, because they didn't, turning to other gods, but because He loves them. Just that – and only that!

So Jephthah cannot secure victory by promising to offer a sacrifice. And God doesn't want him to try. If victory is to be his, God will grant it without a sacrifice. It is his for the taking, an unconditional gift of grace. God just wants Jephthah to accept that gift and understand that this is how life could be for him and his people. It will be, if only he and they will trust God and worship Him alone. But here, on the eve of the greatest moment of his life, a voice speaks into Jephthah's heart, suggesting to him that he is not good enough to merit the favour of victory and that perhaps he can secure that favour by promising God something in return. Is this his faith failing him at the last moment? Is it a misplaced attempt to flaunt his religiosity in front of his followers? Is it the arrogance of the thuggish street fighter about to assume the role of spiritual leader of his people and clumsily trying to establish his suitability for the role? Is it the voices of the fear and shame of his childhood of rejection, telling him he is not good enough and that he needs some kind of insurance against God changing His mind? Any and all of these may be true – and are likely to be recognisable from our own experience.

Whatever the truth behind Jephthah's vow, it is easy enough to recognise the doubts that may have assailed him as our own when we place our faith on the line. For sure, Jephthah does not believe that he is really wanted at this party. He has overlooked the grace of God that brought him to this place to begin with and now he feels the need to promise to bring along something extra that everybody will enjoy. At least if the party is a flop, he cannot be accused of not having contributed to its success in some way.

Selective Obedience

> If the offering is a burnt offering from the herd, you are to offer a male without defect. (Leviticus 1:3)

The Torah, the Jewish book of the law, speaks of several types of sacrifice that God required of His people. Some were mandatory, such as the sin offering, given to atone for sins committed and as a plea for cleansing from those sins. Others were voluntary, such as the peace offering, which was an act of thanksgiving or worship. Some involved the sacrificing of animals as burnt offerings, others were grain offerings, the fruits of the field, offered in the form of cakes or bread. These sacrifices are outlined in the book of Leviticus and the rules surrounding their offering are detailed and specific. There are subtle variations that the person offering the sacrifice was obliged to observe and the observation of these details was a mark of an individual's seriousness of intent. Offering a sacrifice that was partial or was presented in a half-hearted or slapdash way was not acceptable to God, as we see in the story of Cain and Abel in Genesis 4.

One of the consistencies that runs through these instructions, though, is that any animal offered in sacrifice to God should be male and without blemish. This was a way of ensuring that what was being offered to God was the best. A male animal was more valuable to its owner, so to sacrifice it was a more costly and therefore a more meaningful act. It was clear to the Israelites, then, that just offering any old animal from one's herd was not an option. To do so lacked sincerity and was likely to involve minimum cost to the person offering the sacrifice. Such an offering would be regarded as half-hearted and worthless and would not be acceptable to God.

All of this, it is reasonable to suppose, Jephthah knew and understood. The terms and conditions, as it were, for offering a sacrifice would have been firmly branded upon his memory from childhood. So, when he promises to offer the first thing to come out of the door of his house upon his return from battle, his sincerity is immediately called into question. He cannot possibly know what animal will emerge first, and so he cannot possibly guarantee that it will be either male or without blemish. Leaving aside the possibility that all of Jephthah's livestock were male and perfect (which is not only extremely unlikely but would not have constituted good husbandry, since female animals were essential in all kinds of ways to anyone who kept animals), he is playing a kind of game of roulette with his sacrifice. It's a gamble. Sure, he might lose his best bull. But there is also every chance that he might only lose that one-legged chicken that his wife won't let him eat because it's her favourite and she calls it Hoppety. And it is a gamble that Jephthah is content to take. If he loses his prize bull, well, you win some, you lose some. If he only loses the one-legged chicken – result! (Chicken Hoppety for dinner and guess who gets the drumstick!)

So, the trouble here is that this is not a meaningful sacrifice in any sense of the word. It *may* cost Jephthah in a significant way, but, depending on how many animals he keeps in his house overnight, the statistics are probably in his favour. But even if the animal that emerges first is a male without blemish, that is not anything that can be credited to Jephthah because it was not his choice to offer that animal. The sacrifice is intended as a guarantee of and thanksgiving for victory in battle, a mark of Jephthah's gratitude to God for His help. What is God supposed to feel if that gratitude is represented by a one-legged chicken? Is that how grateful Jephthah really was? What transpired is perhaps a mark of how grateful he *should* have been and so, perhaps, was no accident at all.

Even if we suppose that Jephthah's intention all along was to sacrifice the first person who emerged from his house by placing them in virginal seclusion for the rest of their life, the degree of cost to Jephthah is unquantifiable at the point when he makes his vow. Sure, it might turn out to be his daughter, though I think we can assume from his reaction that such a possibility had not crossed his mind. But even if he presumed it to be one of the servants of his household, it would have been unavoidable for him not to have had a preference as to which one it might be. Losing the household cook would have been a greater loss, and therefore a more costly sacrifice than losing the milkmaid, for example.

Jephthah is guilty here of selective obedience. A sacrifice of thanksgiving was something that the community of Gileadites would have expected. Even though we see later in the Old Testament that sacrifices are not at all the way God wants His relationship with His chosen people to go, and that He would much prefer 'a broken and contrite heart,' for example (Psalm 51:16, 17), at this point in their history He has not expressed this, at least not in so many words. And so a sacrifice of thanksgiving may be in order. But an acceptable one, not a half-hearted one. Jephthah knows what is expected of him, but his heart is not in it. And, as is demonstrated throughout Scripture, from Cain and Abel to Ananias and Sapphira, pretence of sacrifice is something God does not tolerate. Mean it or don't do it at all, is the message. But do it for show, do it to enhance your own reputation, do it in any way other than from a sincere and thankful heart, and God, who sees the secrets of our inmost hearts (1 Chronicles 28:9), will respond accordingly. Jephthah wants to be seen to be doing the right thing, but he also wants to choose which of the rules for sacrifice he will obey and which he will ignore. His obedience only goes so far and no further.

Compounding the Felony

> It does not matter how small the sins are provided that their cumulative effect is to edge the man away from the Light and out into the Nothing. *The Screwtape Letters, CS Lewis* (5)

I guess we can all remember an occasion when we have done something we shouldn't have done and then made it worse by trying to cover up our error. Such is pride and the desperate nature of our false selves that we will do almost anything to protect our reputation and prevent those whose approval we seek from finding out who we really are and what we are really like. Confession may be good for the soul, but it goes against our human nature – and admitting our guilt over even small matters can often be a step too far for us.

At the moment that Jephthah's daughter emerges from his house, he realises that he has been guilty of a terrible folly. Jephthah has made a promise he did not need to make, for whatever reasons. He has turned what may have started out as a right desire, to offer his thanks to God for victory over the Ammonites, into a wrong one in an effort to avoid his sacrifice becoming too costly for him. He has gambled with what he imagined was the fate of his livestock, only to find that now his only child is forfeited to God. And he is devastated. He tears his robes in a demonstration of his distress, well recognised within Middle Eastern culture.

Jephthah's dismay is utterly genuine, of course. And yet, even in the midst of his anguish, he is not prepared to admit the folly of his vow and seek a way out of the horrendous situation for which he is responsible. He actually appears to be ignorant of the means to escape the duty and consequences of his promise. Perhaps the fact that he was unable to attend the sanctuary at Shiloh in his youth meant that his understanding of the Torah was slight, and this was not his fault. Ignorance is not a sin, at least until the offer of acquiring knowledge is refused. But, having made the vow and seen the consequences of it, we are not given any sense that he looked for a way out. Might he have gone to the local priest and asked if there was any alternative? Had he done so, he would have been told, 'Yes, there is.' But he never asked. In Leviticus 5:4–6 we read:

> If anyone thoughtlessly takes an oath to do anything, whether good or evil, even though they are unaware of it … they must confess in what way they have sinned. As a penalty for the sin they have committed … they must bring to the Lord a sin offering. And the priest shall make atonement for them for their sin.

So there it is. There was a way out. But Jephthah either was unaware of it or his pride was such that he could not bring himself publicly to admit his error and seek atonement from the priest. Whatever, there is no record of him even considering throwing himself on the mercy of God for the sake of his daughter's life or seeking any kind of way out of his problem. Jephthah's first sin was forgivable, the problem easily solved. But he chose to compound the felony, even at the cost of his daughter's life. Later, Jeremiah highlights this way out by appealing to our understanding of who God is, the criterion that was so lacking in Jephthah's decision, and that of many mission organisations lured into making the same mistake.

> Do not let your mouth lead you into sin. And do not protest to the temple messenger, "My vow was a mistake." Why should God be angry at what you say and destroy the work of your hands? (Lamentations 5:6–7)

Later on in the Old Testament, in 1 Samuel 14:24–45, we read of Saul finding himself in a similar situation; he had vowed to kill any of his soldiers who ate food on a specific day. But Saul's son Jonathan was unaware of the edict and so broke it. When Saul discovered his son's error, he swore to fulfil his vow and kill him. But the men of his army defended Jonathan and persuaded Saul that Jonathan had acted in ignorance rather than defiance. Saul relented and so was saved from repeating Jephthah's error. But it took an act of supreme courage for the men of Saul's army to speak up on Jonathan's behalf. In doing so, they not only saved Jonathan's life, but they also saved Saul from making the terrible and unnecessary sacrifice of his son, which he was seemingly prepared to do.

It is worth noting here that, as with sacrifices, God was not a great fan of oaths and promises, especially when He had never asked for them in the first place. Jesus makes this clear in the Sermon on the Mount in Matthew 5:33–37 when He declares that, never mind not breaking an oath, we should never make one in the first place and that anything beyond a simple yes or no comes from the evil one.

Presumably, since we know about it, Jephthah's vow was made publicly, in the presence of his followers. Word would have spread. And, by the time Jephthah arrived home in triumph, there would have been an expectation that he would fulfil that promise. Human nature being what it is, it's even possible that his men were taking bets amongst themselves as to what the victim of the sacrifice might be. Odds on, it was going to be a sheep, but you never knew. Did anyone give voice to the possibility that the first thing to come out of Jephthah's house might be a person? Could the seed of fear have already been sown in Jephthah's heart? We cannot know. What we do know is that Jephthah now had a reputation to maintain and he was determined to follow through on his vow. He had always been known as a tough, fighting man, even before the battle with the Ammonites. Now he had defeated them in battle, he was the leader of Gilead and he could not afford either to appear weak or to be seen as disobeying the God who had given him victory.

But that was a deceit of his own making. God had not required of Jephthah that he make his vow or that he provide a sacrifice. Both were Jephthah's ideas. But now Jephthah believed that if he didn't fulfil his promise, he would be disobeying God. So not only has he deceived himself that the original vow was a good idea, he knows that for him not to fulfil that vow is itself a sin. In Deuteronomy 23: 21–23 we read:

> If you make a vow to the LORD your God, do not be slow to pay it, for the LORD your God will certainly demand it of you and you will be guilty of sin. But if you refrain from making a vow, you will not be guilty. Whatever your lips utter you must be sure to do, because you made your vow freely to the LORD your God with your own mouth.

But in his own mind, Jephthah had resolved that God wanted this sacrifice, even though the idea was of his own making. And so, perhaps with the Deuteronomy law uppermost in his mind and the Leviticus law forgotten, or just not known to him, rather than swallow his pride and see if perhaps the law might allow him a way out, as indeed it did, Jephthah sacrificed his daughter, ultimately on the altar of his own pride.

'It does not matter how small the sins are provided that their cumulative effect is to edge the man away from the Light and out into the Nothing,' Screwtape reminds the apprentice devil in CS Lewis's *The Screwtape Letters* (See (5)). And for Jephthah, the cumulative effect of his small sins edges him into the darkest of places.

Justification by Fate

> Self-justification, that was the danger – the exhilarating exercise of explaining why my ways are God's ways after all. *Hugh Nibley* (6)

Felonies are seldom compounded just once. Error leads to a lie, which leads to a second lie in order to cover up the first, which leads to a second error, and so it continues. And one of human nature's darkest tendencies is the alacrity with which we snatch at even more error and falsehood in order to protect ourselves from having to reveal that first error or falsehood and so be exposed for the sinners and frauds that we are. Behind that sits one of the greatest deceits of the human heart – that our failures, just as much as our successes, define who we really are in the sight of others and in our own sight. Every step along this road distances us further from the acts of repentance and restitution that allow us to put our original error behind us.

Self-justification is an extremely hard instinct to lay aside. But it becomes almost impossible when others invite us, often unwittingly, to indulge in it. A person already tempted to fall into error is likely to jump into it if given permission by someone else. Even more so if the person they feel might be hurt by their error is the one who gives them permission to go ahead. We tell ourselves it must be OK if they think it is.

Peter's disowning of his master in the courtyard of the High Priest at the trial of Jesus perhaps falls into this category. Each time he is confronted with the suggestion that he is one of Jesus's disciples, the question is put to him in the form of, 'You aren't … are you?' Had he been asked, 'Are you …?' perhaps it would have been easier for him to say yes. But the suggestion implicit in the presumed negative is, 'We don't think you are; we're not sure whether you are or not.' And in that event, it is much easier to confirm the presumption of the questioner, who is almost leading Peter into doing so. Easier or not, the temptation to allow oneself to be led into going along with the presumption is clear.

This is the final piece in the jigsaw of Jephthah's folly. Already believing that his vow of sacrifice was required of him by God, puffed up with pride and looking to take on the mantle not just of warrior hero but spiritual leader as well, and with the voice of shame whispering in his ear that he cannot now go back on his promise as his army and the nation's leaders look on, ignorant of the fact that there is a way out and unwilling to seek such a way, Jephthah's decision is sealed for him by, of all people, the subject of his sacrifice – his own daughter:

> My father … you have given your word to the Lord. Do to me just as you promised. (Judges 11:36)

What are we to make of this? Let's pause for a moment and turn our gaze onto Jephthah's daughter. And let's ask the difficult questions. What in the name of all that is holy possesses her to acquiesce in this way? Is she some kind of saint all of a sudden? Is she mad? Has she been brainwashed in some way that she should be willing to be sacrificed in the name of her father's folly? Can this be explained away by the place of women in the culture of the times as a simple act of familial submission?

Well, don't look at me. We are not told and I don't know the answers any more than you do. But I do think we are meant to consider these questions. And I believe it is reasonable to suggest, both from our own experience and from what we know of human nature, what might have happened here that didn't make it into the written account we have today.

One aspect of the Bible's accounts, be they Old or New Testament, is that often what we are told are the barest facts. It is fair to assume that behind these stories are countless conversations, small actions and activities of normal day-to-day life that are intended to be taken as read. To have included them all would have been to produce a tome the size of Andorra and a profoundly deep reluctance on the part of anyone to read it. As John remarks at the end of his gospel – kind of!

So, for example, when we are told in Matthew 4:18–20 of the occasion when Jesus called Peter and Andrew to follow him and we read, 'At once they left their nets and followed Him,' are we meant to believe that Peter just upped and went without any kind of conversation with his wife as to what he was doing and what the implications might be for his family? Culturally, it may be supposed that the decision was his and she was obliged to go along with it, but the idea that he just abandoned his fishing business without at least bringing someone else in to take care of it and disappeared for the next three years without a word is faintly ridiculous, even if it does feed our overstimulated sense of evangelical zeal and heroic sacrifice. God may call us to follow him, but he does not expect us to leave our intelligence, compassion and all sense of pragmatism behind. In fact, we still find Peter living at home on the occasion when Jesus heals his mother-in-law in chapter 8 of Matthew's gospel, so some consideration of what was meant by 'they left their nets and followed him' is required here.

We may presume, then, that between the shocking emergence of Jephthah's daughter from the house and her statement of acceptance of her fate, there was a brief passage of time and some doubtless animated conversations. It is not reasonable to suggest that the young lady emerged from the house, delighted at her father's safe return and looking forward to greeting him, to immediately understand the implications of what then took place. Jephthah doesn't even explain his vow to her. He merely expresses his distress. 'I am devastated. I have made a vow to the Lord that I cannot break.' We might expect the girl to invite some explanation of this. 'Come again? What vow? And what does it have to do with me?' Instead, we are told that she said, 'You have given your word. Do to me just as you promised.' None of this is natural or normal in any shape or form.

Once we have understood that the flow of the story as it appears in the Bible is a severely edited one, we may then consider what might have taken place in the time between Jephthah's return and his daughter coming to terms with her fate. (This is not an attempt to add to Scripture, merely to interpret it in an effort to understand it more fully. The difference is critical.) It is reasonable to suggest that there was a conversation in which Jephthah explained his rash oath, and his daughter considered her response. Given the patriarchal culture at that time, did she actually have an option? If Jephthah said he was going to sacrifice his daughter, then sacrificed she would be. So is her acceptance of her fate nothing more than an expression of a daughter's perceived duty in the face of what for her is a *fait accompli*? It would seem that she received an opportunity to consider the matter, since she requests 'two months to roam the hills and weep with my friends, because I will never marry.' This does give weight to the argument that her sacrifice was one of virginal seclusion rather than death, but it is not an irrevocable one.

Has Jephthah argued his case here? Has he perhaps suggested that his own reputation amongst the Gileadites, not to mention his standing before God, rests upon his willingness to fulfil his vow? Has he hinted to his daughter, or even stated outright, that for her to resist his will in the matter would reflect badly on them both and thus bring shame upon the family? Is there a mother in the picture who has had her say? Or is his daughter so signed up to Jephthah's understanding of God and desire to serve Him that she believes this is a good and right outcome? All we can really say is that, within the limits of her understanding and taking into account the pressure she very likely felt from her father to conform to his will and to the cultural pressures of the time, Jephthah's daughter reconciles herself to her fate. This does not make it a good thing, or even a worthy thing. It may have been a virtuous and humble submission to her father and what she perceived to be the will of God. But it may also have been the acquiescence of a young girl who knew no better than what she had been told by her father, and felt helpless to avoid her fate – a position many MKs will identify with.

One further point needs to be made here. In Exodus 22:28 we read God saying to the Israelites, 'You shall give me the firstborn amongst your sons.' Later, Ezekiel will refer to this requirement using the phrase 'the firstborn of your womb,' which could be taken to mean that firstborn daughters are also consecrated to God – whatever that means. But 'sacrificed' remained an option, at least until God spoke directly of his abomination of child and other human sacrifice. In his book *The Death and Resurrection of the Beloved Son*,(7) Jon D Levenson, Professor of Jewish Studies at the Harvard Divinity School (at the time of writing), makes a case for child sacrifice having been a legitimate aspect of God's relationship with His people in the very earliest days of His covenant with Israel. This places the story of the Akedah* in a different light to the traditional and widely held 21st century, western interpretation. Professor Levenson is also quick to point out God's subsequent rejection of child sacrifice and His provision that an animal may replace the firstborn son. But his point is that, for a while at least, the mindset of the Israelites was that the giving back, the consecrating, of the 'firstborn of your womb,' was understood by God's people to be a legitimate and literal requirement on the part of YHWH. If that were so, the acquiescence of Jephthah's daughter becomes something more than a resignation to her fate and takes on a dimension of consecration that she may have understood to be, in some respects, a privilege. But we will return to the subject of child sacrifice in the Old Testament later.

It is a terrifying story, and not just because it involves the quite unnecessary ending of a life, whatever that meant in actuality for Jephthah's daughter. It is

* Akedah means 'the binding' and refers to the binding by Abraham of Isaac to the altar on which he was prepared to sacrifice his son (Genesis 22).

terrifying because it is our story too. How many times have we determined to do something because we deemed it a good idea, with sound spiritual motives and some merit, but decided upon independently of God? And how many times have we compounded that error by persuading ourselves that if we do not see our plan through to the end we will somehow be letting God down and inviting his disappointment, maybe even his judgment? And all the while God was sat by our side with his head in his hands, pleading with us to just pause a moment and talk it through with him. But our pride would not let us.

Jephthah's story reflects a case not so much of a bad man as of a man who made some bad choices, perhaps. (I have that particular T-shirt, by the way, if anyone wants to borrow it!) But it is a salutary tale. Why is it there?

Because, like the parables Jesus told, it contains identifiers for us to recognise that Jephthah's sin is our sin too.

One final observation. Perhaps rather surprisingly, Jephthah appears in the pantheon of heroes of faith listed in Hebrews 11:32. Faith, it seems, trumps everything else. Jephthah stands almost unnoticed in a catalogue of rogues and charlatans guilty of all kinds of sexual sins from adultery to prostitution as well as murder, culpable homicide, nepotism, deceit, betrayal and cowardice. Even child sacrifice, it seems, does not disqualify a man or woman from being lauded for their faith in the pages of Holy Scripture. (I use 'child' in the sense of offspring as opposed to infant. We cannot know the age of Jephthah's daughter but her response to events would suggest she was a young adult at the very least.) Pursuing the truths about the character and nature of God that lie behind Jephthah's appearance in this list is not the purpose of our discourse here. Suffice to say that what it suggests to us about God's view of sin, the value He places upon our faith in Him and the extent of His desire to forgive and restore each of us to Himself merits our mature and considered reflection.

I ought also to mention that I do not believe that the absence of any condemnation of Jephthah in Scripture can be taken to mean that God was OK with what he did. There are many examples of bad choices made by characters in the Bible upon which no comment or judgment is made and we are required to view such choices in the wider context of what is revealed to us throughout Scripture concerning the character of God. Again, I am indebted to Jon D Levenson for pointing out that the Moabite King Mesha in 2 Kings 3:27 sacrificed his son in an effort to turn the tide of a battle that he was losing against the Israelites – and it worked. The tide did indeed turn and Mesha's sacrifice was seemingly vindicated.

In summary, what we recognise in the story of Jephthah is the ease with which those who are chosen and even anointed by God can slip into a mode of independent thinking where we presume to make decisions and choices to which we attach God's *de facto* blessing and approval. Being a Christian, serving God, even in the most public and spectacular ways, does not inure us to the folly of our own thinking. It is the easiest thing in the world to listen to the voices of deceit which tell us that our good ideas are in fact God's ideas and may therefore be pursued and acted upon with impunity. And once we have set off down that path, other sins crowd in on us – our unwillingness to seek help, our blindness to alternative paths, our pride that will not allow us to back down or admit that we were wrong. And, lest we should imagine that such well-meaning choices as to how we serve God are of relative insignificance, here in the life of Jephthah is an example of a life lost; a child sacrificed on the altar of folly and pride.

The days of Jephthah were barbaric times in human history, as much of the Old Testament bears witness to. Thankfully, for the most part, the world has moved on – only, it hasn't. I am not talking about the extreme practices of minority, extremist cliques, nor of uneducated tribal groups with little or no exposure to the outside world. I am talking about the Christian church which, in the personages (and parsonages) of many of its pastors and missionaries, continues to this day, in rather too many instances, to make decisions and choices which place service to God and obedience to unsolicited promises above all kinds of other priorities and commitments. Amongst them is the care and nurture of their children, thus technically sacrificing them in the cause of their ministry.

Of course, this is different to the taking of a life. And I am not suggesting that children are being literally sacrificed in the way that, on the surface of it, may have been the fate of Jephthah's daughter. No doubt, given the potential for evil that lies within the human heart, and the occasional excesses of certain extreme cults, examples of such could be found even in recent history if one looked hard enough. But they are as irrelevant to this discussion as any other despicable perpetration of man's inhumanity to man.

It is unreasonable to go any further because the sacrifices that have been and continue to be made by many in the name of evangelism and service to God fall only just short of this ultimate denouement. And, if the fate of Jephthah's daughter was indeed to be put away and end her life in seclusion, there is little or no distinction to be made. In fact, in a small number of tragic cases, the lives of some children *have* ended as a result of the impact on them of their parents' sacrifice, albeit at their own hands or as a result of desperate choices brought on by neglect and the sense of rejection and abandonment these children felt.

Such is the tunnel vision of many pastors, church leaders and missionaries that the education, happiness and nurture of their own children are pitched at a lower level of priority than their calling and those to whom they feel called. All the New Testament teaching on commitment to family and nurture of children, implied or spoken, lies forgotten amongst the accounts of heroic deeds of sacrifice and commitment to God's work. As a result, many children of dedicated, honest, committed Christian parents have grown and are growing up with huge issues of self-worth, and suffer from poor mental health as well as, ironically, an inability to own the faith of their parents. After all, why would they believe in a so-called God of love who required that they be sacrificed in the name of service to Him? Especially when this love has not only been absent from their own experience but also has resulted in their removal and dispatch from an environment of family love, often at a very young age. Their image of God as their father remains locked into the often distant, mainly absent face of their earthly father. And it is a face into which they can no longer bring themselves to look.

It might be said that the story of Jephthah, brief and distinctive as it is, is insufficient precedent on which to base the argument I am making here. Except that, as I have said, it is there and it is there for a reason. We ignore it at our peril. Moreover, it does not stand alone. Saul's promise that almost cost the life of his son Jonathan and Hannah's promise that sacrificed Samuel into the service of God are further examples of promises made to God that He did not require. Taken together, we can see their outcomes reflected in the lives of many MKs; a few did lose their lives, either through physical death or a life of psychological seclusion born of the loneliness and rejection of their abandonment; some were rescued from the intentions of their parents by wise and caring colleagues concerned for the fate of these children or by the parents themselves recognising the damage they were doing; others seem to have had the hand on their lives of the One who works everything together for good (Romans 8:28).

These are the children of Jephthah's inheritance, born to God's servants, sons and daughters of the anointed ones, but sacrificed in the name of that service, heirs to the legacy of a man of faith who placed service to God and obedience to his oath (as distinct from obedience to God) above even the life of his only daughter.

Suffer the Little Children

> Humans tend to experience no greater distress than in relationships of intentional, unqualified abandonment. *Curt Thompson* (1)

There are three moments from my childhood which defined for me my place on my parents' list of priorities. I entered the world into a loving, nurturing and protecting family and for the first five years knew the security and warmth of that surrounding. My mother was attentive and affectionate, a smiling and ever-engaging presence, affirming her love for me at every opportunity and ensuring that I began and ended each day in a place of safety and assurance. She made a special effort to teach me to love beauty and, together with my father, developed in me a love of music that would be a major joy to me in the years that lay ahead. My father, though a little more distant, nonetheless involved himself in my upbringing as best he could, no more nor less than any father with a busy job and responsibilities that took him out of the house for much of the day. It was a happy and secure home and I knew I was deeply loved.

And then, quite suddenly, the trapdoor of my life fell open and I was plunged into a bewildering and terrifying darkness, beyond the reach of my parents' love and without the security and assurance upon which I had come to depend. At five years old I was sent away to boarding school. Not without some preparation, as my parents sat me down and explained why it was necessary for me to go to school far away. They told me that they needed to do God's work and that I would share in that by going to school far away in the mountains so that they could serve God fully. They explained that God would be with me and would comfort me if I was sad, but that the school was a happy place and it wouldn't be long before I was home for the holidays and we could all be together again. And, inasmuch as I was able to at five, I understood and accepted my fate. I believed their words and held onto them with all my might, even as I fell into that all-consuming darkness and it wrapped itself around me.

Well-meaning though their words had been, the truth of those first days and weeks at boarding school was far from how they had described it to me. It was a beautiful location, high in the mountains, deep in the rainforest, secluded and quiet, with a stream that trickled and burbled through the grounds, monkeys in the trees that hooted in the dawn and a staff of dedicated and mostly caring young Christians. There was much to enjoy, a high standard of teaching and a community of children all of whom shared my own experience.

But my grief was inconsolable. Night after night, I buried my face in my pillow and sobbed myself to sleep. The sense of rejection and abandonment was overwhelming. And with it came a new emotion – a fear of the night. Bedtimes had always been precious to me. One of my parents would read me a story, and both would come to wish me a good night's rest. My mother would smooth her hand across my forehead and kiss me, one of them would pray and I would be tucked in, happy, safe and secure. Then, in the morning, they would be there to smile me into the day, help me choose my clothes and we would share breakfast together around the kitchen table, always with a sense of joyful anticipation as to what the day might hold.

Now, all that was gone, and with it the atmosphere of love and sense of security that had enveloped me for all of my life up until that point. I was hopelessly unhappy, grief-stricken at my loss, beyond lonely and beyond comfort. My parents' promise that God would be with me and would comfort me if I was sad was not coming to pass. Lying in the darkness each night with the terrifying sound of wild dogs howling in the jungle outside my dormitory window, I was completely unable to reconcile myself to this new way of life. For the first time, though my five-year-old brain was not yet developed to the point where I could express it in such words, I felt betrayed, bewildered and let down.

The second defining moment came five years later. Now a seasoned boarder, I had developed coping strategies that had enabled me to at least survive the awfulness of the separation that I continued to feel. They weren't appropriate, or even above the level of my subconscious but they worked, mostly by blocking out the grief and pain and making extreme decisions about the ways in which I could afford to live and think. For example, looking back, I can see that I had resolved not to allow myself to become close to anyone, reasoning that those I came to love always got taken away from me. So what was the point? The pain of such losses was too great, so I wouldn't go there in the first place.

Now, at ten years old, the family was returning home for a year of leave. It was an opportunity to live a normal life together as a family. I was still of primary school age, now with two younger siblings, and we would all be able to attend the same local school together, walk out of the house in the morning alongside each other and return home each afternoon to share our day with our mother and enjoy having one another around for the evenings and weekends. I was not as close to my parents as I once had been – another coping strategy to minimise the pain of the constant separations. But this was an opportunity to deepen our relationship before they returned to the mission field at the end of their leave, when I would have to remain behind at secondary boarding school.

And then the bomb fell. I would not be attending the local primary school, but would be sent to my new secondary boarding school from the start of our leave. A year early, so a year younger than my classmates, but worse than that, to spend the entire term time of our year of leave away from the family again. The explanation, garnered years later from my father, was that my parents wanted to see me settled into the new boarding school before they returned to the field. But, to me, no reason could possibly justify the loss of a precious year of normal family life together. Once again, I felt angry and betrayed.

The third defining moment came during that first year at my secondary boarding school. It was not a happy place. Founded for the purpose of educating street orphans, it had an entry requirement that meant only children who needed a boarding education were entitled to attend. This meant that alongside a smattering of children from families like mine – missionaries, serving military and diplomats – the majority of children had been placed in the school by social services, who deemed that they needed to be removed from their family homes for a variety of reasons, none of them good. It was a dysfunctional, aggressive, bullying environment, ruled by fear. And, for a sensitive young boy, already a year younger than any of the other children, and straight out of the refined atmosphere of a Christian mission school, it was another terrifying and bewildering transition.

I hated it with a passion and yearned for the rare days on which we were allowed to be taken out by our parents. These were called Exeat Sundays and they happened once every half term. On these days, we were obliged to attend a service in the school chapel, after which we were free to leave the school until the evening roll call at around six o'clock. Almost every one of over four hundred and fifty children at the school took advantage of these exeat days and we would crowd onto the front drive of the school, outside the main administrative block, waiting for parents or family friends to drive up and whisk us off for a roast lunch and maybe a nice tea somewhere in the surrounding countryside. A decent meal was a major part of the deal, since the school food was .... I don't have the words.

On the particular day in question, I joined the rest of the school community on the front drive excitedly awaiting the arrival of my parents. It was to be a day of freedom, of joy, an escape from the constant fear and intimidation that was now my lot and an opportunity to feel safe and loved with my family around me. So, greatly anticipated.

But they didn't come. Gradually, the number of children on the drive dwindled until, finally, I was the only one left. Occasionally, a member of staff would walk past, some would even smile. But no-one asked why I was still there or offered to ring my family to find out what had happened. No-one even spoke to me. I dared not leave my post in case they came and could not find me. And, in the days long before mobile phones, my only way to contact home was to walk to the red telephone kiosk at the bottom of the library steps and make a reverse charge call. But suppose they came whilst I was away?

Lunchtime came and went, and still I sat on the wall, hoping, waiting, fearing the worst. It was perhaps the longest afternoon of my life. As six o'clock approached and the cars began to return the other children to the school, their smiles betraying the pleasures of their day, their pockets and bags filled with fresh stocks of biscuits, chocolate and nuts given by parents mindful of hungry, growing youngsters for whom the uninteresting and overcooked school meals were completely inadequate, I finally accepted that my parents were not going to come. My mind was awash with anxiety and grief. Had they been in an accident, perhaps? Were they lying sick at home with no-one to help them? Or … had they just forgotten me?

I dragged my unwilling feet off the drive and made my way to the telephone kiosk to call home. By now, it almost didn't matter what the reason was. There was nothing they could tell me that would be good news. But it was the worst possible news. They had indeed forgotten me, forgotten that it was an Exeat Sunday and, worse, they had invited some of the new missionary candidates to their home for the day. This most important day of the whole half term – for me, at least – had been in my diary from the very start of term. But it had not been in theirs, it seemed. Their focus had been on the new missionaries and in making sure that they felt encouraged and affirmed as they prepared to leave for their designated fields for the first time. Nothing wrong with that. It was a perfectly laudable action; caring, nurturing, loving even. But caring, nurturing and loving of strangers. And their son had been forgotten, buried under the busyness of service to God and their zeal for evangelism.

That was the day I died inside. I had just about survived the effects of separation from my family at five years old. Even when sent away again at the start of my parents' leave, I had reconciled myself to their decision, though barely. But this … this proved the extent to which I was unlovable, bad even. Worthless, undeserving even of one day in the almost two months of that long and exacting half term. I had kept my hopes alive by sheer resilience and determination. Surely, a time would come when I might be allowed to feel that I was as important as their work, their calling. But now I knew that day would never arrive.

There were no tears. I was beyond tears. A poisonous cocktail of emotions flooded through me as I trudged back into the common room where the excited voices of my classmates were exchanging delighted tales of their day out. So this was what God wanted for me, was it? Well, I was a good boy and I would not allow this to stop me from believing in His goodness. Flying in the face of all reason, I clung onto hope with the last remnants of such strength as I had, oblivious to what it was going to cost me in the long term. The trouble was, I believed in what my parents were doing. And I understood that such commitment and dedication meant a degree of sacrifice. I hadn't understood that I would be that sacrifice, of course, though that was now becoming clear. But this was how it was. This was what God required of me.

I was ten years old, already with half a lifetime of neglect behind me. And my image of God was becoming increasingly distorted.

* * *

My own story is far from unique. But was it wrong and unreasonable for my parents to place their commitment to God in so high a place that I was left to feel neglected and abandoned? And why is it that some Christians seem to hear the words of Jesus, 'Suffer the little children … ' and fail to complete the sentence, seemingly imagining that this archaic expression, which actually just means 'allow the children to come to me,' is permission for them to seek the suffering of their children, presumably for their own good? What does the Bible have to say about the care and nurture of our children?

Well, one answer is, 'Not a great deal, actually' which might surprise you. On the other hand, the Bible makes no claims to be a childcare manual and, of course, different cultures over time and around the world have held significantly differing ideas as to what constitutes good childcare. For example, the practice in China of binding a young girl's feet so that they did not grow and remained small was seen as a sign of both beauty and status, despite the crippling effects suffered by these children once they reached adulthood. The parents of these children believed they were doing their daughters a favour and did not set out to damage them. They deemed the practice to be good childcare. Today, we would suggest that this was far from good practice and, indeed, it was outlawed in China in 1912. But there have been practices in childcare all over the world since time began that parents thought were a sign that they nurtured their children but which were, in fact, seriously damaging to their physical or mental health.

Clearly, the Bible was never going to come up with an exhaustive list of dos and don'ts to cover the vagaries of a multitude of cultural practices over millennia. So it doesn't try to. But there is perhaps another obvious reason why Scripture does not outline what constitutes good childcare. It can be found in Matthew 7:9–11, in a conversation Jesus has on the subject of the goodness of God:

> Which of you, if your son asks for bread, will give him a stone? Or if he asks for a fish, will give him a snake? If you, then, though you are evil, know how to give good gifts to your children, how much more will your Father in heaven give good gifts to those who ask him!

In other words, 'Look, guys. I don't have to tell you how to look after your children, do I? You know. You care for them because you love them. You protect them and nurture them and make sure that they have what they need in life. Well, if you understand that, ignorant and sinful as you are, just think how much more God knows when it comes to giving you what you need, if you will only ask Him.' So this is an issue where Jesus steers clear of patronising people by telling them what their instincts and experiences have already taught them. It is unnecessary for Him to lay down rules about caring for children because it kind of goes without saying. There is a list of things that really don't require a sermon. And loving and caring for your children are pretty close to the top of that list.

Jesus's teaching here echoes a well-known passage in Isaiah concerning the restoration of Israel:

> Can a mother forget the baby at her breast and have no compassion on the child she has borne? Though she may forget, I will not forget you! (Isaiah 49:15)

The suggestion here seems to be that for a mother to forget her child or have no compassion for it is so unlikely as to be ridiculous. But even though that may occasionally happen, it's never going to be the case that God forgets or neglects us.

On the other hand, the subject of how to raise children does feature from time to time, and it falls into two categories. In the Old Testament, the importance of training and disciplining a child is the primary focus. In the New Testament, children are mainly used as an example of simplicity and innocence and held up as a model for trust and faith. A sample of Old Testament verses that mention children or childcare gives us the following:

> Whoever spares the rod hates their children, but the one who loves their children is careful to discipline them. (Proverbs 13:24)

(Not licence to hit children, of course, as cultural norms in the context of the Middle East a millennia before Christ should not necessarily be reckoned as appropriate for 21st century living. The principle of discipline is the thing here, not the literal outworking of it.)

> Start children off on the way they should go and even when they are old they will not turn from it. (Proverbs 22:6)

The book of Proverbs contains a number of similar verses, all pertaining to the virtues of disciplining children and lamenting the consequences of not doing so. And that's about it. Except for one account which affirms my earlier assertion that the Scriptural approach to childcare is that some things really don't need to be spelled out. And that takes us back to the book of Judges.

In Judges 13, following closely on from the story of Jephthah, though passing lightly over the reign of three others, we come to one of the fullest and most detailed of all the accounts of the judges: that of Samson. Samson's story begins in almost messianic fashion, with the appearance of an angel to the woman who was to become Samson's mother. The angel tells the woman, who is never named, that, though she is childless, she will soon give birth to a son who will 'take the lead in delivering Israel from the hands of the Philistines' (Judges 13:5). She relates this encounter to her husband, Manoah, who proceeds to do a rather surprising thing. He asks God – actually, we are told that he begs God – to let the angel return so that he can teach the couple how to bring the boy up.

> Let the man of God you sent to us come again to teach us how to bring the boy up who is to be born.

The angel returns and the following exchange ensues.

> "Are you the man who talked to my wife?"
>
> "I am," he said.

> So Manoah asked him, "When your words are fulfilled, what is to be the rule that governs the boy's life and work?"
>
> The angel of the Lord answered, "Your wife must do all that I have told her. She must not eat anything that comes from the grapevine, nor drink any wine or other fermented drink nor eat anything unclean. She must do everything I have commanded her" Judges 13:11–14

So, Manoah has asked the angel – in effect, he has asked God – to help him and his wife know how to raise the child they are to have, perhaps since they have been childless and lack experience in that area. What's more, the angel is there at Manoah's request, a quite specific request, that he teach them how to bring the boy up. But, instead of talking about how to raise the child, the angel issues instructions to the mother as to how to look after herself during her pregnancy. Keep off the wine and follow the law as regards which foods are clean and which are unclean. Today, he might have included advice not to overdo the tuna because of its mercury content and encouraged her to take folic acid tablets regularly. But as to how the child should be raised, apart from an instruction that they are never to shave his head because he is to be brought up as a Nazirite, nothing. Not even a word about sparing the rod and spoiling the child.

Why not? Could it be because God trusts the couple to raise the child sensibly and lovingly and this is something they really don't need to be told? The absence of any kind of list of instructions in the Bible on the raising of children would suggest that this might be the case.

Recent research also suggests that the angel – or God, if you like – knew a lot more about the science behind intrauterine development than we know today. The psychiatrist Thomas Verny, a pioneer in the study of intrauterine influences on emotional health, has written:

> *Before the event of birth, before we have even had a glimmer of sight or* sound *in the womb, we record the experience and history of our lives in our cells.* (2)

And the physician and author Gabor Maté writes:

> *Beyond brain substance levels, there is evidence suggesting that maternal mind states during pregnancy and postpartum shape the very structure of the infant's developing brain.* (3)

In other words, 'Here's what you don't know: look after the mother during her pregnancy and all will be well with the child. Once he is born, God has given you all the instinctual knowledge you need to raise him.'

In the New Testament, we might expect matters to be somewhat different. After all, there is some pretty specific teaching on marriage. But, although children are mentioned in passing amongst this teaching, there is little beyond Paul's instruction in Ephesians, a version of which also appears in Colossians.

> Fathers, do not exasperate your children: instead, bring them up in the training and instruction of the Lord. (Ephesians 6:4)

> Fathers, do not embitter your children, or they will become discouraged. (Colossians 3:21)

(Interesting that fathers are singled out as being liable to exasperate or embitter their children, but it's not the subject under discussion just now. Perhaps food for thought, though.)

Almost every other reference to children in the New Testament centres around Jesus's use of them as an example, commenting on their innocence and simple trust and exhorting His followers to be childlike in their relationship with God. Here is just one example.

> Jesus called the children to Him and said, "Let the little children come to me, and do not hinder them, for the kingdom of God belongs to such as these. Truly I tell you, anyone who will not receive the kingdom of God like a little child will never enter it." (Luke 18:16–17)

Clearly, children are precious to Jesus, but He is using them as a teaching tool here, whilst nevertheless welcoming and accepting them, and He has no comment on how they should be raised. And this is not to say that children are more precious to Jesus, by the way. There is no evidence of this that I can find and, more importantly, everything we know about the character and nature of God tells us resoundingly that His love is equally available and given to all.

There is one other comment made by Jesus that demands our attention here, if only to clarify its meaning. In Luke 17:1-3 we read:

> Jesus said to his disciples, "Things that cause people to stumble are bound to come, but woe to anyone through whom they come. It would be better for them to be thrown into the sea with a millstone around their neck than to cause one of these little ones to stumble. So watch yourselves."

Matthew also quotes these words, but places them in the context of Jesus encouraging the children to come to Him. Even so, Matthew seems to be clear that Jesus is not just talking about children, but is warning against causing any of His followers to stumble. So, in Matthew's account, we read:

> If anyone causes one of these little ones – those who believe in me – to stumble, it would be better for them to have a large millstone hung around their neck and to be drowned in the depths of the sea. Woe to the world because of the things that cause people to stumble! Such things must come, but woe to the person through whom they come. (Matthew 18:6–7)

So, although it is common for this passage to be understood as referring to those who lead children astray, it would seem that Jesus is using the phrase 'little ones' to refer to all God's children – his believers and followers. The Greek word here translated as 'little' is mikros. And the same word is used earlier in Matthew, where we read:

> If anyone gives even a cup of cold water to one of these little ones who is my disciple, truly I tell you, that person will certainly not lose their reward. (Matthew 10:42)

So it would seem that the Bible is content to offer a few words of encouragement to those bringing up children, with just a firm and repeated injunction to be sure to discipline them well and instruct them in the ways of the Lord. It then leaves the rest to common sense, giving us a degree of freedom, but respecting our God-given parenting instincts.

Of course, we will all doubtless be aware of instances in our communities when children have been neglected or abused in the most horrific ways, sometimes resulting in a slow and torturous death. But this is not generally about people not understanding how to raise their children so much as broken and abused people who have lost sight of any sense of what is good and true and so visit upon others the evil that oftentimes was visited upon them. It's not that they don't know how to care for their children, although in rare cases that may be true. Rather, that they choose to take another path and deliberately seek to deprive and punish the youngsters in their care, consumed and blinded by the darkness in their soul.

There is another reason why the Bible doesn't feel it necessary to provide instructions on raising and caring for children. It's because a great deal of what the Bible tells us is about the fatherhood of God. In other words, God doesn't need to *tell* us how to do something when He is willing to *show* us how to do it. As John teaches in his first letter:

> Dear children, let us not love with words or speech but with actions and in truth.

That's 1 John 3:18, reminding us that actions speak louder than words. So, it is in His parenting of us and His demonstration of what it means for Him to love us as a father that we find our standards as He examples and models them to us. And that is what we will look at next.

But first, here is Hope's story.

Hope's Story

Hope was born into a missionary family, her parents called to work in Asia. To this end, they had left their own parents and set up home halfway around the world in a small, rural community. Much of their initial time on the mission field was spent learning the language and acquiring the cultural understanding and sensitivity necessary to earn the respect of those amongst whom they lived. And so, after a while, they became accepted and settled and were able to communicate well enough to begin sharing their reasons for being there, and a small community of believers was formed.

Hope began life in that community, and the little town surrounded by jungle and tin mines became her home. There was a papaya tree in the garden, and pink and red hibiscus flowered above the thick, stubbly grass that skirted the small house. Brahminy kites could often be seen soaring overhead or perched in the branches of the rain trees by the road, and brightly-coloured snakes slept under the bushes. The heat was intense, though it rained at around five o'clock most days, hurling great drops from the sky like darts which bounced high off the concrete and tarmac and thundered onto the corrugated iron roof with a deafening roar.

Hope loved the rain; it lowered the temperature considerably. Often she would run into her room, climb into bed and pull the sheet that was its only covering tightly up around her chin and just listen, her eyes bright with the pleasure of it. Sometimes, she would even run out into it, arms flung wide, her tiny figure whirling through the torrent as she squealed with delight. But the rain wouldn't last and all too soon the sun returned to steam the roads and pavements and dry out the little girl in no time at all.

Then, wonderful aromas would begin to emerge from the kitchen and it would be time for Hope to return inside for the evening meal and family prayers before she was tucked into bed as darkness fell and the crickets and cicadas sang her to sleep. Life was happy for the bright-eyed five-year-old, playing with the children of friends and neighbours, and acquiring a fluency in the local language that meant her parents were soon playing catch-up. But all that was about to change.

One day, Hope's parents began to talk to her about going to school. She already knew about this, of course, because some of her friends had begun attending the local kindergarten and it sounded like fun. But Hope would not be going to the village kindergarten with her friends. She was to be sent away. Far away. Two hundred and fifty miles up into the hills of the north country where she would be with the children of other missionary families. Her parents did their best to make it sound like a big adventure and they told her that she would be happy and well looked after. But to Hope, going anywhere without Mummy and Daddy was frightening and it made her sad. After all, she was just five years old.

When the day finally arrived, Hope's father had a conference to attend in the city, so he wasn't even there to say goodbye. But her mother packed a small suitcase for her and drove her to the station to put her onto the train where the other children who would accompany her were already partway through their journey. The track was long and straight and the train could be seen from some distance away, billowing smoke into the humid air as it rattled towards them. Hope felt a tightening in her chest which she didn't understand and it suddenly became difficult to breathe. But her mother had told her that Jesus needed her to go away to school so that Mummy and Daddy could serve Him better. She would be sad for a while, but God would look after her. So she was determined to be brave and fought back the tears as her mother crouched to embrace her for one final time and then helped her up the steps into the carriage.

A tall, bespectacled lady in a floral print frock stood at the top of the steps and took Hope's hand as she climbed up, smiling encouragement.

'There's a good girl. You must be Hope. I am Miss Martin and I am going to be your teacher.'

Hope looked up into the smiling face and wondered what the strange lady was so happy about. She smelled of Nivea cream and mothballs and had her hair loosely tied up in a bun that hung slightly to the left, giving her a lopsided appearance.

'Now, wave to Mummy and we'll go inside and find you a seat.'

Hope turned dejectedly and lifted her tiny hand slowly in a reluctant wave as her mother beamed up at her.

'Goodbye, darling. You're going to have a wonderful time. And we'll all be together again at Christmas,' she enthused.

Hope wasn't exactly sure how long it was until Christmas, but she knew it was only August because her father had just had a birthday, so she suspected it wasn't any time soon. She forced a smile and turned back into the train, accepting the proffered hand of her teacher and allowing herself to be led inside the carriage. Soon she was settled into a seat next to a small, red-headed boy with freckles and a bored expression who, she was told, was called Raymond. He would be her friend, Hope was assured. But Raymond just grunted and turned to look out of the window as the train let out a long whistle and began to chug out of the station.

Hope was on the wrong side of the train to see her mother clearly. And anyway, she was too small to see out of the window properly. But she just caught a glimpse of her mother waving both arms and smiling broadly as the train pulled away.

Why was Mummy so happy when she felt so sad, she thought to herself? And why weren't the other children sad like she was? After all, they had all just done the same thing as she had, leaving their parents on a train platform somewhere down the line, not really understanding when they might see them again. Hope felt bewildered.

Why had Mummy been so happy? And why hadn't Daddy even been there? Perhaps they were glad to see her go. Hope thought back a few days to when she had got cross and thrown her teddy across the room because she didn't want to have a bath. Was she being punished for losing her temper? Was this what happened to little girls when they were naughty? Was God cross with her too because she had been so bad?

Well, she wasn't going to cry, however bad she felt. She was five now and she didn't want to be called a cry-baby. None of the other children were crying so she wouldn't either. Hope reached into her bag and fished out the box of snacks her mother had prepared for the journey, pausing before she opened it. Somehow, it seemed like her last connection with home, for now at least. Suddenly, Miss Martin snatched the box from her hands and declared, 'I think it would be nice to share these with the other children, don't you?' That was when the tears began. And by the time the box was returned to Hope, it was empty.

The journey was long and hot and Hope felt dirty and tired by the time the train reached its destination. But even then, there was a three hour drive before the school would be reached and the ordeal would be over – this part of it, at least. The children were piled into a fleet of taxis, some without a supervising adult, and crushed together along the back seat to save on the expense. Then began the long, slow journey up into the heart of the mountains on narrow, winding roads that were no more than a succession of hairpin bends. Often, they would find themselves behind a timber lorry, belching a thick, black, diesel-fuelled smoke that lingered in their clothes and hair and caused waves of nausea. It was too much for Raymond, who vomited into his lap and then cried at the shame of it, necessitating a brief stop whilst Miss Martin cleared him up. But the car stank for the rest of the journey and Hope was sure she too would be sick before they reached the top of the mountain.

They were held up again, this time for more than an hour, when they came across a small landslide that made the road impassable until the fresh, red earth could be cleared. This at least gave the children a chance to stretch their legs a little and blow the diesel fumes from their lungs as they wandered along the steep banks that led up into the jungle, picking at ferns and probing at monkey cups. And then it was back into the cars and on towards the school.

By the time they arrived, Hope had fallen gratefully asleep, her head resting on the shoulder of another child, and she woke with a start when the taxi came to a halt outside the school buildings. For a few seconds, she was unsure where she was and looked around uncertainly, her blinking eyes failing to register anything familiar. The cool mountain air felt strange on her skin and she shivered. Then reality returned and she was suddenly overwhelmed with such a deep and all-consuming sense of loss that she could no longer contain her tears and she sobbed inconsolably as she was helped from the taxi.

Gentle hands led her away into this new world that was now to be her home. But there were no kindnesses that could console the little girl at her loss, nor drive the fear from her eyes as she lay on the bed in her dormitory wracked with sobs, drained now of tears, though her chest still heaved with the pain of her bereavement. She cried into her pillow so that the other children wouldn't hear her, bewildered, alone and terribly afraid.

Hope's life changed forever on that day. At five years old, taken from her home and parents, nothing would ever be the same. She was destined to spend the rest of her childhood in boarding schools, away from the loving home environment she had known so briefly, and forced to find her own way in the world. Confused, frightened and bereaved, she would be forced to grow up almost overnight, and find ways of coping and surviving in an unfamiliar environment without the security of a safe adult to give her the love that every child needs and deserves if they are to grow into adulthood knowing that they are loved and valued in this world.

She was alone. And that was how it was going to be from now on.

> No conceivable condition exists under which a human being has less agency or fewer options than in infancy and early childhood. The imperative to survive overrides everything, and that survival depends on the maintenance of attachment, at whatever cost to authenticity. *Gabor Maté* (1)

And God Said…

And God said, 'Let there be light.' And it was so.

And God said, 'Let man have dominion over the animals.' And it was so.

And God said, 'This is my beloved son. Listen to him.' And they did.

And God said, 'Send your children away,

So you can devote your lives to telling people about me.' And they did.

Child on the altar, blood on his face.

Hopelessly broken, lost without trace.

Child on the altar, stake through his heart; family taken, driven apart.

Child on the altar, tearless his pain. Given for Jesus, infant now slain.

Child on the altar, exiled in grief; wholly abandoned, shorn of belief.

Child on the altar, child no more. Child forever, bloodied and raw.

And God said …

But the child was not listening anymore.

An Ever-Present Help

> God is our refuge and strength, an ever-present help in trouble. (Psalm 46:1)

The lack of specific instructions in the Bible concerning raising and nurturing children can perhaps be best explained by the fact that the entire sweep of the story of God and His relationship with us is that of a father and His child. Or, to be more accurate, a parent and their child. We read right at the start of the story, in the first chapter of Genesis:

> So God created mankind in His own image, in the image of God He created them: male and female He created them. (Genesis 1:27)

So it is clear from the outset that, if male and female are both created in the image of God, then all that makes a man male and all that makes a woman female is present in the character and person of God. The Bible's use of the word 'father' should not be seen as diminishing the feminine characteristics of God's character or the equal importance of women in His creation so much as a demonstration that God understood that the cultures into which His message was being delivered were of a patriarchal nature. A female god would have been misleading in some instances and downright unacceptable in others. But, sadly, predominantly male interpreters of Scripture have allowed a great deal of misunderstanding to develop about this aspect of the nature of God through the centuries, as well as promoting a considerable abuse of power by men within the hierarchy of the church.

Interestingly, one of the issues that caused so much controversy amongst conservative Christians following the release of William Paul Young's book, *The Shack*, was the fact that the Father God figure in the story is presented, at the start, as a woman. But the reasoning behind the author's choice is no different from the Bible's choice to portray God as male. As the character herself explains to Mack, the somewhat bemused protagonist who was violently abused by his earthly father as a child,

> Mackenzie, I am neither male nor female, even though both genders are derived from my nature. If I choose to appear to you as a man or a woman, it's because I love you. For me to appear to you as a woman and suggest that you call me Papa is simply to mix metaphors, to help you keep from falling so easily back into your religious conditioning.

> Hasn't it always been a problem for you to embrace me as your father? And after what you've been through, you couldn't very well handle a father right now, could you? (1)

And theologian Marcus Borg, writing about female images of God in the Bible says:

> Female images of God suggest something different. God is the one who gave birth to us and all that is. God wills our well-being, as a mother wills the well-being of the children of her womb. God is attached to us with a love that is tender and that will not let us go. And like a mother who sees the children of her womb threatened and oppressed, God can become fierce.
>
> It is also important to realize that male and female metaphors for God are not intrinsically incompatible. God as "father" can be compassionate. This is the point of the parable of The Prodigal Son (Luke 15:11–32). So also in both Old and New Testaments, "the Lord" whom we are to love with all our heart, strength and mind is also compassionate – a word whose semantic associations in Hebrew mean "womb-like". (2)

So, although the Bible speaks of God as Father and uses terms such as Lord and King, as well as non-gender images such as Rock and Consuming Fire, it is important to our full understanding of His nature that we keep in mind that He is beyond gender, but incorporates all the aspects and qualities of both human genders that we love and admire in each other. So, when we talk about God the Father, we are also talking about God the Mother.

What, then, are the characteristics of this God of the Bible that pertain to parenting and offer us a template for how we should raise our own children? Well, the list of verses that begin 'God is … ' is a pretty extensive one. Here are just a few to be going on with, in no particular order.

- Unchanging. (Let's call that consistent, reliable, for the sake of parenting terminology.) 'I the Lord do not change' (Malachi 3:6).
- Gracious. (He loves to give us many things that we don't deserve.) 'For the Lord your God is gracious … ' (2 Chronicles 30:9).
- Merciful. (He is understanding, merciful and forgiving of our weaknesses.) 'For the Lord your God is a merciful God' (Deuteronomy 4:31).
- Patient. (Bearing with us and waiting as we learn from our mistakes.) 'The Lord is slow to anger' (Nahum 1:3).
- Kind. (What older translations call lovingkindness. So, loving, too.) 'I will tell of the kindnesses of the Lord' (Isaiah 63:7).
- Present. (He is always with us, behind us, beside us when we look to Him.) 'When you pass through the waters, I will be with you … ' (Isaiah 43:2).
- Just. (He shows His righteousness and justice in His judgments about us.) 'He is faithful and just … ' (1 John 1:9).

- A source of strength and protection. (He is there for us when we feel vulnerable and need to rely on Him, a place for us to go to and feel safe.) 'He is my mighty rock, my refuge … ' (Psalm 62:7).
- Compassionate. (He demonstrates empathy when we are suffering.) 'He will show compassion, so great is His unfailing love' (Lamentations 3:32).
- Loving. (Not just verbalising love, but being and modelling love for us.) 'And so we know and rely on the love God has for us. God is love.' (1 John 4:16).
- With us. (Identifying with us in our humanity as well as in His divinity.) 'Surely I am with you always, to the very end of the age' (Matthew 28:20).

Nehemiah sums it all up beautifully as he leads the Israelites in a confession of their sins as they approach the fullness of their restoration to Israel and Jerusalem after their exile.

> You are a forgiving God, gracious and compassionate, slow to anger and abounding in love. (Nehemiah 9:17)

The list of the aspects of God's character that speak to us about His fatherhood of us as His children as we seek to parent in His likeness, is considerable and longer than we have time to list here. But sometimes we make this more difficult than it is. Sometimes, the whole thing can be summed up in just a few words. In this instance, three words.

> *God ... is ... love.* (1 John 4:8 and 16)

And everything else flows from there. (Of course, we then have to ask, 'What is love?' and there are as many answers to that as there are people to answer.) But in essence, that is the key. If we love, we are patient. If we love, we are kind. If we love, we are compassionate. If we love, we are reliable. If we love, we will be fair and just. If we love, we are present, we will be there, a constant source of strength and protection in our vulnerability.

It might even be argued that the explanation of marriage given in Genesis…

> That is why a man leaves his father and mother and is united to his wife, and they become one flesh. (Genesis 2:24)

…as well as being a divine mystery, is a pictorial representation of the intention that children are provided with an example of the image of God and of his love that is complete and rounded in a way that a parenting model with a gender bias is not. In other words, the reference to 'one flesh' is not just about the union of a man and a woman in marriage, though it is of course that, but it is also a statement that encapsulates God's desire for each of us that we live in relationship with each other in a way that mirrors the relationships of the Trinity. God is three and God is one. A husband and wife are two and they become one. And, as a couple in relationship with God, they become a trinity – a being that is both three and one. In that relationship, we are better able to convey a sense of the character and nature of God to our children if what they receive from us is the full range of strengths and virtues that we define as male and female but that, as they pertain to God, are just facets of His character. It is a grace that we are not asked or expected to example this alone, but to share that responsibility with another.

This is not in any way to denigrate or undervalue the many parents who are obliged for a wide variety of reasons to raise children on their own. After all, parenting is far from being the only area of human existence in which the actuality for most of us falls well short of God's intentions. Nor is it to suggest any degree of condemnation of those of us who have found love in single sex relationships and have chosen to share our lives with a child and raise them in a loving, nurturing and protecting home. I believe that God honours each of us in our place, understanding what has led us there; rejoicing in those areas of our lives where He sees wholeness and rightness of intent; weeping with us in those areas where we remain broken; and always seeking to challenge, rebuke, remould and heal those areas in which we continue to live in conformity to the world rather than seeking union in relationship with Him. That's all of us, folks! So, God has His standards, intentions and ideals, but these are not accompanied by any illusions concerning our ability to live up to them, though He will never cease challenging us to do so. Meanwhile, He joins us where we are and walks with us on our journey.

For Christians, the complete answer to the question, 'What is love?' is found in Paul's magnificent statement on love in 1 Corinthians 13. There, we learn that love is patient, kind, lacking in envy, not boastful or proud, not denigrating of others, not self-seeking, slow to anger, forgiving, taking no pleasure in wrongdoing but taking joy in the truth, always protecting, always trusting, always hoping and always persevering. We also learn that anything we do, even the most religious, spiritual or apparently Christian acts, are worthless unless we do them in love. This includes any good ideas we might have that we pursue in our zeal for God, but which we haven't actually checked with Him to be part of His purpose or plan; the rash oaths we make; the promises to God that He never required; the attempts to preserve our own reputation – sometimes even God's reputation – by compounding the original felony. All these things are worthless because they are not done in love. They will pass into the trash can of history, as will every aspect of our false selves, those parts of us that are merely images we have projected onto the screen of our lives for others to see and admire.

Additionally, I am going to suggest that we can take Paul's admonishment a small step further. Most of us understand, at least in our minds if not actually in our hearts, that loveless acts are ultimately worthless, even if by His grace God makes something of value out of them. But might it also be true that the love of which Paul speaks pertains not just to our actions themselves, but to the consequences of those actions upon those whom we profess to love? Let me explain.

David was a young pastor – keen, innovative and energetic. Married for almost five years, he had been looking for an opportunity to arrange a weekend away for the church youth group so that he could give them some teaching on relationships and provide a spiritual context for them as they made their way through their early and mid-teens. Phoning various suitable venues, David was offered a weekend in the early summer which corresponded with the start of the half-term week and it seemed perfect to him. The Sunday was also his fifth wedding anniversary, but he was sure his wife would understand and agree that this was a fantastic opportunity to minister to the church's young people that should not be missed. So he went ahead and booked it, paying a substantial returnable deposit which he promised he would not need back, and set about designing a poster to put up in the church the following Sunday to advertise the event.

That afternoon, a member of the church was knocked down by a car and died. David had finished the poster and had just had time to print it out before he was called to the hospital to be with the family of the victim, where he spent the rest of that day alongside them. Naturally, this formed the topic of conversation at the dinner table that evening and the subject of the youth weekend was forgotten for the time being. A pastor's life is full and often frantic, and David found himself in the church office on Sunday morning without having mentioned the weekend to his wife. The poster lay on his desk and he just had time to pin it up on the notice board in the foyer before taking his place for the start of the service.

And so it was that David's wife came to church that day to find a poster by the door telling her that her husband would be away for their wedding anniversary. (A good idea, but not a God idea, and a sacrifice that God had not required.) And she was heartbroken. Later, David would protest that he had intended all along that she come with him and they could teach the young people together, that it was a wonderful opportunity and a really good thing and that some degree of sacrifice was to be expected in his line of work. (A compounding of the felony.) He also 'forgot' to mention that the deposit was returnable, so disinclined was he to alter his plans, instead talking about his commitment to the centre and being reluctant to let them down. (A rash promise which he could break, but was unwilling to because the cost to him was too great.) But the message he had sent to his wife was already written large across her heart. 'My ministry is more important than you.'

And so, an action that in every respect appeared to be a generous, thoughtful idea, one that would bless, teach and encourage many, perhaps even become a seminal moment on their path to adulthood, in part because it was David's idea and not God's and in part because, though it was done out of love for the people he pastored, it was not done in a way that showed love to the one he had committed to love for life, became a cacophonous and unpleasant noise in his marriage. A loud gong or a clanging cymbal that would echo down the halls of their relationship until such time as David understood that his zealous, well-meaning ideas were worthless unless he could carry them out at God's prompting and with a love that encompassed all of those affected by his actions.

So, love – and God IS love – is the alpha and omega. The beginning and the end, the first and the last motive for all that we do. And not just the love we have for those who might be blessed by our actions, but love for those who might be sacrificed in their name by our tunnel vision. If we truly love God more than our reputation as his servants, all these things fall into place. Because God does not lead us down the path of error. He has a way for us to serve Him that blesses those we seek to serve without damaging our relationships with our families or making it harder for them to trust and believe in God themselves.

There is one other aspect of God's character that is necessary for us to understand if all the others are to have any meaning. And that is the truth and reality of His presence – that He is always there, always with us, always available to offer us those consequent aspects of His love. Consequent because His patience is a meaningless attribute to us if He is not there to show us patience. His kindness, His mercy, His grace are irrelevant to us if He is not with us to dispense it. His love does not flow beyond our intellects into the deep recesses of our hearts if He is not present to minister it to us.

And so it is in our earthly relationships as parents and children. As I lay in bed as a five-year-old, far from home, lonely, tearful and afraid, the love my parents had for me was no less than it had been before I had been sent away to school. But it was, in a sense, meaningless, because it was not present, not available to me in any kind of meaningful way. Because, to my infant self, love meant cuddles and smiles, it meant a sense of safety and someone to run to when I was sad or frightened. It meant my mother's hand smoothed across my brow as I prepared for sleep, the goodnight kiss and the sense that all was well and I was OK. Whatever had happened during the day, it was all right now because she was there to make it all right and to reassure me of her love and protection. But now, she wasn't there. And it wasn't OK. I didn't feel safe or protected. If what had happened during that day had hurt or upset me, there was no-one now to make it all right, to explain those events, to validate my feelings and ease me into an untroubled sleep. My parents were not there – that was the truth of my reality. And so their love for me was not a presence, it was a memory, and now an act of faith. Did they still love me or had they forgotten me? They were no longer with me and I was assailed by doubts. Their presence had been removed from my life, and with it their love had also been removed. Worse than that, the memory of the love that had been mine all my life up until that point was what made it so hard to live without that love and that presence now.

Do any of us really believe that a call to ministry or mission work is a call from God to sideline our families? Clearly, since actions speak louder than words – and they really do – some believe it is OK, or at least are willing, to live in ways that deny what they know to be the truth. There are even verses in the Bible they would quote to support this belief, which we will look at in detail in a later chapter. But for now, I believe that the example of God's love for us, the nature of His character as revealed to us in Scripture, His actions towards those He calls His children and the template of relational living, of mutual love, service and delight that we see in the outworking of the Trinity, all suggest to us that both love and presence are essential to our responsibilities and effectiveness as parents.

> God is our refuge and strength, an ever-present help in trouble. (Psalm 46:1)

In fact, God is our strength and refuge *because* He is an ever-present help in trouble. If He is not there, how are we to run to Him? If He is not there, how is His strength of any relevance to us? If He is not there, how is He to help us?

Of course, what God means when he speaks of being ever-present with us is something we need to consider. Obviously, He is not present in a physical or visual way. But even if we are to understand His presence as being the placing of His Spirit in us, as Jesus suggested (John 14:15–31), what does this actually mean in our daily lives? And, if even Jesus at the most vulnerable and abandoned moment of His life cried, 'Why have you abandoned me?' it would imply that, even if God is with us all the time, there are times when our awareness of that presence is withdrawn or hidden from us, for whatever reason.

To sum up, we find our model for parenting in God Himself, who is beyond gender but examples fully all the qualities and virtues pertaining to what we understand as male and female. This model, alongside the general absence of specific instructions in the Bible, suggests that everything we need in order to understand our roles and responsibilities as parents can be found in the nature and character of God. It also suggests that God has instilled in us the necessary instincts and sensibilities for us to parent effectively, and that he finds no need to patronise us beyond a small number of basic instructions which might, to some degree, go against those instincts. So, for many, especially in 21st century western societies, the complex issues surrounding the disciplining of children require reinforcement that discipline is not only good, but necessary if our children are to grow up into healthy and well-adjusted adults. How we outwork that respects the integrity of our individual cultures and is left to us.

The necessary components of good parenting are defined by two essentials: that we love as God has loved us and that we are present for our children, as God is ever-present for us. Our kindness is not complete without our love. Our patience is not a blessing without our love. Our justness is self-serving without our love. And our love can become irrelevant if we are not present to offer it in meaningful ways. Children, especially young children, cannot and should not be expected to rationalise the love of an absent parent. Neither can they be expected to understand a love that sacrifices them on the altar of our ministry, our good works, our best-intended ideas or well-meant projects.

The American charity the National Fatherhood Initiative quoted a US Census Bureau statistic in 2016 which indicated that twenty-four million children in the United States, that's one in three, lived at that time without a father in the home.

(3) Scandalous and distressing as that is, it is extremely unlikely that this figure included the children of pastors and missionaries, whose fathers remain in the family home, but who are largely or completely absent from their children's lives.

I can find nothing in Scripture to suggest that this might be God's will, for us or for our children, and plenty to indicate the contrary. God loves us and demonstrates that by His presence with us. Who are we to imagine that we have a better way?

> Children's sense of security, trust in the world, interrelationships with others and, above all, connection to their authentic emotions hinge on the consistent availability of attuned, non-stressed and emotionally reliable caregivers. *Gabor Maté* (4)

Michael's Story

The time had come for Michael to go to school. The eldest of three siblings, he had grown up in a rural village far from the nearest town, the only home he had ever known a mud hut with dried reeds for roofing. For a year already, he had been helping Gracie, the house-girl, fetch water from the river more than a mile away in a twice daily ritual that had toughened his bare feet on the dusty tracks and given him the deportment of someone from a Swiss finishing school from bringing his small but precious load back to the village, balanced expertly on his head.

But now he was five and the time had come for him to leave the little world that was all he knew. Gracie, with whom he had spent most of every day throughout his young life, had been sent home and now Michael sat outside the hut in the cool of the evening as his parents settled themselves down next to him, their backs pressed up against the walls of their home. It was rare for the little boy to see them both together and he couldn't recall a time when the two of them had actually sat down to talk with him. It made him a little uneasy, as if something bad was about to happen, as indeed it was.

Two days later, at first light, Michael was helped into the back of a Land Rover, his small suitcase tipped over the side next to him as his parents smiled up at their little boy and waved him off to school. He had a brand new hat to fend off the sun and a large water bottle hanging on a strap around his neck. He placed a waxed paper bag beside him on the seat containing some dried fruit and a wrapped peppermint to stave off the hunger pangs until lunch, which would be bought in the next town, two hundred kilometres away. The journey would take all day, with other children picked up along the way. But it would be dark long before they reached the school and the African sun would take its toll on the small frames sprawled over the hard benches in the back of the open vehicle.

Michael wiped his mother's parting kiss from his cheek with the back of his hand and turned his face away as the Land Rover chugged along the dirt road and out of the village. He would not look back now for fear that his courage might crumble. That fateful night, two days earlier, as they had sat together outside their home, Mummy and Daddy had told him that God would be with him, that he had to go to school so far away because God had important work for them to do, so he mustn't be sad. Daddy had even told him, 'Big boys don't cry.' And so he wouldn't. Not now.

He had cried that first night after his parents had revealed what was about to happen. Not because he was to be sent away to school, but because he had wanted to say goodbye to Gracie. But he had been told she had returned to her own village and he might never see her again.

Every day Michael could remember had been spent with the silken-skinned young girl, her big, dark eyes ever watching him play whilst she prepared his next meal or beat his clothes against a rock by the river, often singing in a rich, low voice. As well as her songs, she had taught Michael how to cut the new reeds that made up the roofing of the village huts; how to look out for the tell-tale bubbles that meant a hippo was beneath the muddy water near the fording place; and which leaves growing along the edge of the jungle paths were edible and which were poisonous. A thousand things that meant Michael was as adapted to life in the village as any of his playmates. His sobs had been uncontrollable as he had buried his face in his pillow that night, desperate that his father would not hear him grieving for his beloved Gracie in a way that his young mind could not yet express. He was frightened, too, at the prospect of life without her.

And so, as the Land Rover left the village and gathered pace along the red dirt track, Michael set his gaze towards the north and a future clouded in fear and uncertainty.

* * *

Half a century later, Michael was in the garden when he received the news of his mother's death in a phone call from his sister. It was a very matter-of-fact conversation. Not unexpected and, in some ways, they agreed, a blessed release from the pain and confusion that had dogged her final months.

'I'll let you know when I have the death certificate and then we can talk about arrangements for the funeral.' His sister's voice betrayed no sense of the import of this day. She might have been organising a family trip to the seaside, Michael thought.

He put down the small trowel with which he had been turning over the soil in the narrow flowerbed that ran alongside the patio, tucked his phone into his pocket, wiped his hands on the grass and made his way into the house. His wife Melanie was pouring hot, newly-made jam into jars and didn't look up as he entered the kitchen.

'That was Brenda,' he said. 'Mother died an hour ago.'

Melanie's focus altered not a jot as she continued pouring the jam.

'Well, that's a relief, I suppose,' she said. 'Are you going to have to arrange the funeral or will Brenda and Kevin do it?'

'We'll all talk about what we want. But they will have to deal with the undertaker and vicar. She'll have chosen the hymns herself. I'll probably end up sending out the notifications to her surviving friends. And the mission, of course. Though God alone knows if they will even send someone.' Michael sighed. There were no easy tasks at a time like this, but he didn't want anything to do with any of them, if truth be told.

Melanie paused her pouring and looked up at him. 'Are you OK?'

'Yes, fine. It's not like we were close. Or that I wasn't expecting it. But ….'

Michael's expression took on a quizzical look as unbidden tears began to roll down his cheeks. He watched them from inside his body as if he were quite detached from their meaning. And, in truth, he was surprised. Appalled even, as his tears turned into great sobs that wracked his almost sixty-year-old frame, constricting his chest so that they came in huge gasps and groans.

'Michael! What on earth …?' Melanie was clearly no less surprised than her husband. Suddenly, the jam had lost its thrall and she moved swiftly to her husband and wrapped her arms around him from behind.

'Darling!' She didn't know what else to say.

It seemed like an eternity before the sobbing subsided and an exhausted Michael was able to compose himself enough to speak. They had moved through to the lounge and now sat side by side on the settee.

'Sorry about that,' he said, forcing a smile in the general direction of his wife.

'There's no need to apologise, Michael. Your mother has just died. I just wasn't expecting it, that's all, knowing how … ' Her voice trailed off. Perhaps this wasn't the time to label her husband's relationship with his mother, if that's what you could have called it.

'It wasn't about Mother.' Michael looked straight ahead, just as he had done that day fifty years earlier in the back of the Land Rover.

Melanie paused, clearly struggling to absorb this unexpected revelation. 'OK. So ….' She wasn't even sure what she wanted to ask next, so bewildered was she.

'That was about Gracie.'

Melanie struggled to compose herself. 'Who's Gracie?'

'My mother. My real mother. I mean, not the woman who gave birth to me. But the one I knew as a child. The one who got me up in the morning, helped me to dress, gave me my breakfast … loved me, cared for me. I hardly saw Mother and Dad from one day to the next, so busy were they with language study and evangelistic work. But Gracie … I was with her all the time. She was an African girl from a nearby village. A house-girl, really. But she was all I knew. And I was never allowed to say goodbye.' His voice trailed away.

'Oh, my God, Michael. How did you cope?'

'I didn't know any different. That was just how it was. Mother and Dad were missionaries and Gracie was my mother. She did everything for me, everything with me.'

'But she was … well, black, wasn't she? I mean … didn't you notice?'

'It wasn't important. I was African. Africa was all I knew, the village was all I knew. And Gracie was all I knew when it came to someone caring for me and teaching me, bringing me up. I spoke her language better than English until I was five.'

'So, what happened when you were five?'

'I was sent away to boarding school.' Michael's tears gently flowed again. 'And we were forbidden to speak anything other than English. We were beaten if we did. So, gradually, I lost it.'

Michael fished around for his already sodden handkerchief and blew his nose loudly. 'And when I came back to England to board as a nine-year-old I lost it completely. And forever.'

Melanie thought about this for a moment, her brow furrowed with concern. 'Michael ….' She wasn't sure she knew how to ask her next question. Or even if she should ask it. 'Why have you never spoken about these times before?'

Her husband shook his head sadly. 'Too much,' he mumbled. 'Too painful. Didn't want to go there.'

Melanie stood up and walked over to the window, her arms folded across her chest as if to comfort herself. After a while, she turned. 'And now? I don't understand. Has your mother's passing just brought it all back or … '

'In a way. You see … when I was sent away to boarding school at five, my parents didn't really need Gracie anymore. Oh, she'd done some housework and cooking for them but they had mainly employed her to look after me. So they dismissed her and sent her back to her own village. By the time Brenda and Ian were born, they had found someone else. But ….'

The pain was etched into Michael's face as the years of unexpressed grief continued to find their way out of the deepest recesses of his being where they had lain fermenting for five decades.

'I've blamed the mission, blamed my parents, even blamed God for requiring them to do these things. But to be honest, they're all equally responsible and blaming them doesn't really help. And Gracie, especially … because I never got to say goodbye to her.'

He paused, remembering that night when he had been told that Gracie was gone from his life forever. 'I do remember crying at the time. A lot. At least, I thought so then. But Dad had told me that boys don't cry, so I didn't dare let him see me doing so. And I got it all out of the way into my pillow those first couple of nights. Until now.'

'So you think your actual mother's passing has finally allowed you to grieve properly for Gracie?' Michael nodded, screwing up his face once more as the tears flowed again.

The whole experience had shocked him. He couldn't remember crying since … well, since he was five. Not really crying. And now, here he was with perhaps the bulk of his life behind him sobbing like … like a five-year-old, actually. It was almost like that little boy had come back and inserted himself into his adult body. His grief was raw, immense, inconsolable and new. Yet not new. Surely, it had been there all the time. He had just somehow managed to keep it hidden away under control all this time. But now it had burst its banks. And, as it did so, the seed of an idea began to grow in his mind. An unrealistic, self-indulgent, probably unaffordable, ludicrous idea that no normal, sane, grown man would entertain for more than a second. And yet ….

At work here is a kind of 'false memory syndrome' in reverse: on the conscious level, people often remember only the happy parts of childhood. Even if troubling

> incidents are recalled, the emotional aspects of those events are suppressed. Parental love is legitimately remembered, but the child's feelings of not being understood or supported emotionally are not. *Gabor Maté* (1)

Two months later, Michael boarded a plane bound for Entebbe. He still wasn't sure it was the right thing or the sensible thing at all. But its momentum was irresistible. He was returning home, to the little village that had been his world for those precious, special first five years of his life. More than that, he was going to find Gracie. He didn't even know if she was still alive. But he had to go, had to search her out, speak with her, hold her, let her hold him as she had done so many times when they had sat by the river or outside the village huts, singing in that rich, low voice, weaving grasses expertly together, her big, dark eyes flickering from him to her work and back again.

Perhaps this was his parting gift from the woman who had always struggled to show him affection, spend time with him even, her attention always on the poor lost souls who didn't know Jesus. Perhaps, at last, she was giving him back what he had always longed to have in his life again.

A mother.

> There is nothing more impactful psychologically than facing separation from those we are attached to. The resulting alarm is immense and the pursuit of proximity desperate. The motivation to close the gap becomes all-consuming. *Gordon Neufeld* (2)

From Great Commission to Great Omission

> We know of too many instances when … divine call was used to evade genuine responsibilities. And how many children of pastors, filled with resentment, refuse to darken the door of a church today because to them "the call of God" was nothing but an excuse for their parents to ignore them and indulge in their religious enthusiasms? *Mark Galli* (1)

The issue of those in Christian service neglecting their families is in some ways no different from the examples we see all around us in every kind of work situation. The temptation, the need, even, to throw oneself into one's work, the often considerable demands of jobs that require a person's presence at evening meetings, weekend conferences or week-long business trips is a familiar and perhaps an ever-increasing one. And so the problem of absent parents is not confined to pastors or other full-time Christian workers. But the implications of that absence are different, because the way in which we live our lives tells our children something about the nature of our faith, and thus speaks of the nature of God Himself. And so, whilst a healthy work ethic is something most parents would want to teach their children, as Christians, a life given in love, through love and by love is a higher priority. So, ministers whose vicarage (or whatever) door is always open, who are willing to welcome parishioners, even homeless people, into their kitchen for a cup of tea and a chat, but who are never there when their children come home from school or who seldom have the time to sit and read a bedtime story send a message to those children. And the message is, 'What I am doing for God and those I am doing it with and for are more important than you are.' As a conversation between a couple of Pharisees in Season three, episode eight of *The Chosen*, goes:*

> Pharisee 1: We serve God first, then our families.
>
> Pharisee 2: We serve God first BY serving our families.

Author and humourist Adrian Plass, in his satirical and semi-autobiographical book, *The Sacred Diary of Adrian Plass*, speaks of the glow he feels, as a Christian leader, at being asked to meet with a mother and child who have been abandoned by their husband and father, welcoming the opportunity to minister comfort, only to find when he arrives at the appointed place that it is his own

---

* **The Chosen*, a television series on the life of Jesus produced and directed by Dallas Jenkins, can be found at https://watch.angelstudios.com/thechosen

wife and son who are sitting there. Their protest at his neglect in the cause of his ministry is well made, and it's funny because it's true!

This way of living, and its accompanying testimony – make no mistake, that is what it is – is inevitably magnified for the missionary in full-time service overseas and often results in more extreme manifestations of family neglect. Often, this has meant allowing children to be sent away and separated from their parents. We will look at the specific effects being sent to boarding school at such a young age has on children in due course. But first, we need to consider the motivation of parents to send their children away at all, and the degree of understanding they had in doing so. Clearly, the experiences of Hope and Michael were far from happy; ultimately, they proved to be damaging to such a degree that the consequences were deep, serious and lifelong.

But what possessed these parents to make this choice to be separated from their children, to hand over their care and nurture to people they had never met, to do so when the children were still so very young and in the knowledge that this was how it was going to be thereafter? There are a number of practical factors and we will look at them in detail.

A Lack of Options

For most missionaries – almost all, in fact, during the 19th and major part of the 20th century – education options were extremely limited.

Language was an issue, with the great majority of missionaries speaking a language other than that spoken in the schools available to them. This raised the prospect of their children being educated in ways that were unfamiliar to the parents and risked indoctrination in cultural, political and religious thinking which they were anxious to avoid. It was not uncommon for missionary societies to warn their members specifically against the dangers and problems of their children acquiring the local language and what it might lead to. I have seen a letter which was sent to my own parents stating just that.

The quality of teaching and the syllabus, such as it may have been in African, Asian and South American schools during this period, were not judged to be adequate by most westerners. Missionaries feared that if their child returned to their passport country to attend university they would be hindered by having only qualifications from what were considered third-world countries at the time, or by having UK qualifications for a US university, or vice versa.

The rural, often remote nature of many missionary designations meant that, even if parents had access to what they regarded as an education of sufficient quality for their children, it might involve a three-day walk through difficult terrain just to get there. Such journeys were not only impractical, they were also frequently dangerous, often involving the fording of large rivers, the risk of encountering wild animals or even bandits, and a lack of transport and support services to provide food and accommodation en route.

Homeschooling had serious limitations in the days before the internet, though this is the one alternative that a small number of families chose. But even that had drawbacks, not least the isolation of children from others of their own age, and – this is the one many missions themselves baulked at – the fact that it essentially removed the mother from mission work itself, thus potentially halving the effectiveness of a married couple on the field.

So, choices were very limited, at least until the last quarter of the 20th century when international schools began to spring up and become more affordable to the missionary purse. Then, homeschooling resources, riding on the back of internet availability in the 1990s, also came into their own.

System Pressure

For the most part, resources on the mission field have always been at a premium. Funds were meticulously allocated, partly out of good stewardship and partly because they were generally in short supply. But any mission's greatest resource is its members. And most held the view that, where a married couple was involved, both should serve since both had been called. Any distraction from that service was frowned upon.

This is not to say that women were given equal roles in respect of their involvement in the work. Far from it, in many cases. In fact, until the more enlightened days of the late 20th century, with a small number of exceptions, there was a tendency on the one hand for many missions to send their single women members into places of significant isolation and genuine danger, whilst on the other hand taking exception to wives being involved in their husband's work, insisting that married women serve in an area other than that of their partner. Such is the story of Jean, a qualified doctor who was refused permission to work in the same hospital as her husband on the grounds that it was against the mission's principles for husbands and wives to work together. To be fair, she was told she could take up a position in another hospital. But that hospital was almost two hundred kilometres away! It was a solution that remains breathtaking in its inappropriateness. Jean chose to remain with her husband and children, her medical training and expertise unused, a victim of a religious system that had become self-defeating, dysfunctional and ultimately damaging to its members.

Even so, wives had been called just as their husbands had and there was work to be done. Children were seen by many missions as a distraction from that work and considerable pressure was placed on families to have a local girl care for the preschool children and for those of school age to be dispatched to a boarding school. Such schools were often set up by the missions themselves and most had a good reputation educationally, at least. Chefoo School, set up by the China Inland Mission in the north of China in 1880, boasted that it was 'the best school east of Suez'; Hebron School in Tamil Nadu, India, came into being at the turn of the 19th century, again as a result of protestant missionaries wishing to provide for the education of their children; Dalat International School, originally in

Vietnam and then in Malaysia, was set up by the Christian and Missionary Alliance (C&MA) to provide a North American secondary education for missionaries in South-East Asia; Colegio Monterrey in Costa Rica is a particularly visionary example, on which more later. Other missions made use of schools with a Christian foundation that had been set up to educate the children of European settlers; St Andrew's School in Turi, Kenya, is just such an example. But where a mission had itself established a school, with all the attendant outlay of precious resources, it became important to those missions that all members signed up to their children attending. As a consequence, it was inevitable that anyone who questioned the suitability of this for their own children was frowned upon.

And so the system which had been set up to serve the mission's members began to close in on them. Attendance, in many cases, was all but compulsory and those who showed any unease over sending their children away had it made clear to them that rocking the boat was not an option if they wished to remain in the mission.

That said, in general, it seems that schools established by missions to educate and care for the children of their members provided an excellent education and prepared their students well for their secondary and tertiary experiences in their passport countries later on. Some schools failed some pupils, as will almost always be the case. And, inevitably perhaps, there were occasional serious fall-downs in respect of such matters as discipline, nurture and pastoral care. Mission schools were not immune from issues of physical, emotional, spiritual and sexual abuse, despite being staffed almost entirely by Christians. But this is because Christians are not immune to sin, rather than the schools being bad places per se, even if sometimes the priority given to staffing them appropriately was lamentable. Instances of educationally and/or pastorally unqualified missionaries being drafted in to fill a school vacancy were not as uncommon as might have been wished. Indeed, some of these personnel, despite the shortfall in their appropriateness for the role, were obliged to stay in their position for up to a decade.

That said, there were some schools that failed their children badly. Mamou Alliance Academy, set up by one mission in Guinea, became a focus for some of the worst excesses of mission schools when a number of its alumni forced an inquiry into the behaviour of its staff in the second half of the 20th century. Examples of physical, sexual, emotional and spiritual abuse were detailed by a number of those who had attended the school as children, and their stories are brutal, horrifying and salutary. Initially, the mission concerned closed ranks and it was some years before any degree of culpability was accepted by them for the treatment suffered by too many of its children; eventually, some limited liability was accepted, albeit reluctantly. Out of that tragedy was born the organisation which became known as MK Safety Net, which has helped MKs from many missions seek justice and resolution for the abuse they suffered during their time at mission schools.

A second school, this time in Asia, employed a staff member who was later proved to have abused a significant number of girls placed in his care, though the mission concerned was unable, some felt unwilling, to pursue the staff member to the point of prosecution, despite his own eventual admission of guilt. He was even protected and successfully continued in a pastoral capacity within a second Christian education establishment for some years, even though the institution concerned was aware of his misdemeanours. As I write, those girls continue to deal with the effects of their suffering without the consolation of justice having been served to their abuser; their sense of betrayal by the mission and the church remains visceral.

The Spirit of Sacrifice

Missionary work has always been tough. But, in the early days, it was especially so. Travel was often a matter of weeks or even months, environments were often hostile and the interval between financial support being given and it actually reaching the field was often lengthy. Sometimes it never arrived at all, having been lost or stolen en route. Just the sacrifice of leaving the comforts of home, not to mention friends and family, for a life of comparative danger and poverty was significant, and recognised as such.

An ethos of sacrifice developed around missionary work which meant that, eventually, many felt that if what you were doing didn't cost you something, preferably something significant, it was of little value. Some mission leaders felt it was legitimate to challenge new missionaries with warnings that, fairly enough, were based on experience as to what might lie ahead, but which also contained man-made expectations of what God required from them.

> Some people make a sacrificial and heroic life their whole identity, and end up making everyone else around them sacrifice so that they can be sacrificial and heroic. *Richard Rohr* (2)

One of these requirements was that you gave your children into the care of others, not just for the benefit of their education but also so that you might devote yourselves more fully to the work. This was deemed appropriate to one's calling. After all, it was reasoned, many of those who went before us gave their lives. Surely, being separated from your children for a while paled in comparison. The spectre of Jephthah and his unnecessary and unsolicited oath loomed threateningly over the mission fields of the world.

Was this a legitimate requirement of someone already working in an extreme situation or the emotional blackmail of a dysfunctional, self-serving and closed system? Clearly, both views were taken by different people at different times.

And there is another question that may be asked in this context, unpalatable though some will find it. For some, perhaps more especially the men, it could be asked if sending their children away was truly the sacrifice it appeared to be.

Sadly, especially for some fathers, staying at home and looking after their children would have been the real sacrifice. Trekking through the jungle on their own, facing the dangers inherent to the places and people around them, preaching in the villages, handing out tracts, wrestling with the political, administrative and spiritual issues around them were all things they loved and enjoyed. They were excited by the challenge and revelled in the adventure of it all. There was little or no sacrifice in leaving their homes, their own parents, their secular jobs in a factory or office. They loved their work and – can this really be true? – some loved it more than their families. In actuality, it cost them little to do what they did. It would have cost them a lot more to stay at home nurturing their own children.

Hard to believe? Perhaps. And, clearly, impossible to substantiate, except by personal testimony, since few would admit to such a thing. But please understand I am talking about a small minority here. And not exclusively men, either. Let me take you back to Hope's story.

Some forty-five years after the events already related, Hope was a happily married wife and mother entering her fifties. In her own mind, she had overcome the difficulties of her childhood though she increasingly found herself angry and depressed about her relationship with her parents, which had always been soured by the sense of rejection and abandonment that she had carried over the years. One day, desperate to find a way to resolve her grief at the loss of her relationship with her father she rang him and asked, 'Dad, do you love me?'

'Of course I love you,' came the expected reply. Hope paused for a moment, hardly daring to continue for fear of the answer her next question might elicit.

'But do you love me more than the Indians?'

There was a long silence at the other end of the phone until, finally, Hope replaced the receiver, her worst fears realised in that deafeningly empty quiet.

Some years later, she would stand in awe of the reverence and honour with which Indian Christians flocked to his funeral to pay their respects to a man who had given his all and loved them as his own. And she envied them. For Hope's father had not been able to demonstrate that love to those who actually were his own. For this man, at least, it would seem that his work involved little or no sacrifice on his part. It was his wife and children who made the necessary sacrifices so that he could do what he loved. A work profoundly blessed, make no mistake. But by the grace of God – and at a significant cost to his family.

It Was for the Best

I haven't considered sending my children to boarding school, just as I haven't considered sending them to Siberia. *Sarah Brown*, former boarder, in a *Daily Telegraph* article, May 1992.

A boarding school education has always been looked upon as a privilege and was generally only available to the well off. So, for the average missionary living off a meagre income and often from a humble background in the first place, the opportunity to send their child to board somewhere, and have it paid for, was hard to resist. This was particularly true of the British, where the boarding school tradition was entrenched in the culture, having produced generations of political, military and diplomatic leaders over many years. (Out of a total of fifty-five British prime ministers who have held office at the time of writing, twenty attended one single public school, and nine of those attended the same university college. Only ten of the fifty-five attended a state or non-fee-paying school.)

Clearly, there were obvious attractions. The resources of boarding schools meant staff were better paid thereby attracting the best teachers, at least in theory, and enabling schools to offer extra-curricular opportunities, particularly in the areas of sport, science, music, art and drama, which were simply beyond the purse of state schools. Having the children for twenty-four hours a day also meant boarding schools had time to indulge these subjects. There is no doubt that one consequence of this was that the talents and abilities of the children were nurtured in a way that enabled them to achieve successful careers that might otherwise have been unattainable.

For some parents, a further attraction was the character-building aspect of boarding school, which was reputed to teach independence and creative thinking, and develop character by affording children opportunities to acquire leadership skills through cadet corps, for example, or by participating in intensive sports or arts programmes. It would be 'the making of them,' as was observed by one parent sending her seven-year-old son to boarding school for the first time in an excellent, if heartrending documentary* produced by Nick Duffell, a UK psychotherapist who went on to write a seminal book of the same name and run courses for boarding school survivors. Whilst these advantages are undoubtedly beneficial to many, the cost at which they come in terms of emotional equilibrium and maturity is one of the great hidden tragedies of the boarding school setup – and of today's Christian community.

Author and psychotherapist Joy Schaverien, in her book *Boarding School Syndrome*, highlights some of these issues.

> Ex-boarders commonly present with generalised depression, relationship breakdown, and problems with intimacy or with parenting their children. It became clear that these children had suffered significant bereavements and moreover boarding school was a form of imprisonment. (3)

Nick Duffell, in *The Making of Them*, quotes journalist Katherine Whitehorn in a 1990 Observer article in which she asks:

**The Making of Them* can be found at
https://www.youtube.com/watch?v=2uRr77vju8U&t=2s&ab_channel=MrExboarder

> Why do we call it a tragedy when a child is taken into care and a privilege if he's sent off to prep school? (4)

Later in the book, Duffell himself observes:

> Many people, particularly those who were sent away early, spend a lifetime trying to recover. The 'old guard' tends to consider such people 'life's failures' and, out of fear of being so labelled, many old boarders will have decided neither to talk, or in some cases even think about those days. (5)

Despite this, there were many attractions to parents offered a boarding school education for their children. And, since no-one was really aware of them at the time, few if any of the disadvantages were highlighted. There will even have been some parents who felt their children were better off being technically brought up by trained education experts than suffering at the hands of their own relative ignorance and inexperience. In other words, for some, there was a sense of 'they will do a better job of it than I could ever do.'

Kerry's story highlights this issue. I met Kerry when she was in her mid-forties, suffering from a deep depression that had begun in her teens and grown as she got older, largely untreated and significantly misunderstood by those around her. Sensitive and intelligent, Kerry carried such an unbearable weight of rejection and abandonment as a result of having been sent to boarding school as a six-year-old that now, heading into her middle years, she was almost incapable of dealing with day-to-day living and had made more than one attempt to take her own life.

After many months spent building up her self-confidence and talking through the issues that were so disabling to her mental health, she agreed that we should meet with her parents, from whom she was largely estranged, to talk through and explain some of her feelings with them. Their inability to accept her depression in all its dark reality was a very tangible obstacle to her dealing with her lack of self-worth and ongoing sense of abandonment. (This is not an uncommon position for Christian parents to take, many often feeling that depression is a sin, or at least a failure that can be overcome by 'pulling yourself together' and getting over it and on with it. I recall one parent of a child with a diagnosis of bi-polar disorder, on revealing this to a Christian friend, receiving the response, 'But I thought he was a Christian.')

So we met together and talked through some of the events of Kerry's early life, including the first time she had been sent away to school. In an effort to build up a picture of her parents' thinking and emotions at the time, I suggested to Kerry's mother that the years between Kerry's birth and leaving for school must have been filled with all kinds of fears and doubts as she anticipated having to give her child away. This was her response.

'Not really. I never thought about it. We knew that boarding school would give her the best opportunities, so we were happy that she could go.'

I tried to hide my shock at this reply, fearful that such a hard and unemotional stance would trigger Kerry's already significant feelings of rejection; I hoped that the answer to my next question would compensate somewhat.

'But when it came to actually sending her away and having to say goodbye to her at the station as she left for the first time, that must have been very hard for you.'

'No. We knew it was the best thing.'

I was stunned. But I had one more question to ask.

'But now that you understand how the experience damaged Kerry, would you do things differently if you could have your time over again?'

'No. We trusted God for her care and we would do so again.'

I would like to be able to say that this was a one-off and that I never encountered such a response again but, sadly, I can't. Whether it be from an expertly practised sense of self-denial or a refusal to allow one's true feelings to feature in the practical decision-making process out of an acute desire for self-protection, I cannot say. But some Christian workers seem to exist in a reality that means they are so focused on their mission and calling, they cannot – perhaps dare not – allow anything to deflect them from it. The knowledge that their children are suffering as a result of their actions is just too hard to consider.

This brings us to the question of how informed parents were in making the decision to put their children into a boarding situation. How much did they know, could they have known, that might have made them think twice about whether or not this was right for their child?

The study of child development was a comparatively late addition to the field of psychology, beginning at the end of the 18th century and growing in importance during what might be termed the golden age of missionary work in the 19th and early 20th centuries. But it was the work of John Bowlby and Mary Ainsworth on attachment theory in the 1950s, '60s and '70s that suggested taking children out of their family home at an early age might be crucially damaging to them.

So the answer to our question, 'How much could parents have known?' is 'Little or nothing.' At least until the second half of the 20th century. Even then, it was still a new science and easy to disparage by those who felt that its conclusions undermined their best practices. Even once the ideas surrounding attachment theory began to filter out into the public consciousness, they took a long time to be generally accepted. And in the hothouse reality of the mission world, acceptance of such matters, conflicting with decades of tradition, took much longer. Even half a century on, there are many who refuse to accept that early childhood separation is as damaging as experts suggest.

This ignores the parental instinct and sense of familial responsibility that many might feel is a natural consequence of having a child, perhaps even more so in the context of a Christian family. Clearly, many parents struggled with the conflict created by this instinct for care versus the requirements of the mission to devote themselves to the work of evangelism whilst having others raise their children.

This dichotomy, some might say confusion, was also apparent within the leadership of missions during the 20th century. For example, in an early 1962 presentation to the Overseas Council of one particular mission, their then Medical Officer remarked:

> All too soon, even as early as six years, the child leaves home for school. Then a tie is broken which can never be replaced with exactly the same tension as was its previous characteristic. The relationship between children and parents in later years is related basically to his life in the early years of childhood. (6)

Whether this statement was made out of some knowledge or training received by the Medical Officer or whether this was just the instinct of his life experience we cannot know. But, whilst the Medical Officer recognised the truth of this observation, we note that this understanding did not lead him to act upon it by recommending that boarding be removed as an option. (It should also be noted that in the case of this particular mission, despite six being identified as the age at which children were sent away to school, many children actually attended as young as five and, in a small number of instances, at just four.)

So here we have a medical professional who understands the importance of proper nurture and care of children in their early years, who recognises that separating children from their parents at too young an age creates a no-going-back scenario that will lead to a permanent altering of the parent–child relationship, and yet who still feels that encouraging this separation is legitimate in the service of God. And this flying-in-the-face-of-reality attitude is coming from the person trusted to deliver medical and, in those days, psychological advice in the mission. Furthermore, it is found in an official report to the leadership and deemed sufficiently important to pass on to that mission's members, making it extremely hard for those members to dispute.

Later in the same report, the Medical Officer lists a set of attainments that all children were expected to have reached by the time they attended school for the first time. Understandably perhaps, these included such matters as 'being able to control their natural functions' and 'wash, dress and care for himself.' These are reasonable enough expectations, although it should be noted that one of the effects for many of these very young children of being separated from their parents was prolonged periods of bedwetting, a recognised symptom of acute anxiety, which often then resulted in physical punishment and public humiliation, as we shall see later.

Perhaps less reasonable are the expectations that 'he should know of heathenism and the reason for his parents' life and work,' or 'should know the basic facts of prayer and be able to co-operate with understanding in his parents' work for God.' At five years old, bear in mind. These latter statements clearly demonstrate the priorities of this particular mission, which elsewhere described children as 'a tool for evangelism.' Sadly, this was an attitude that was widely respected amongst other missions at the time, many of which replicated such examples of what they saw as a dedicated approach to mission.

So we see here that although knowledge of child development and the impact of the effects of early childhood separation was scanty, even where it was present, it was largely ignored. There is evidence that it was dismissed on occasions, as witnessed in the testimony of one missionary wife who took the information she had gathered from one of the early child psychology books to her mission, concerned firstly for her own children, but also for the fate of the hundred or so others with whom they shared a boarding school.

So disconcerted were the mission by this rocking of the boat that they flew out the missionary's national director to speak to her on the field – in those days an expensive and very much last resort. The national director listened as she made her case and then turned to her husband and asked, 'What are your thoughts on this?' The husband, who had not read the book, but had listened to his wife's evidence on the matter responded along the lines of, 'Well, I'm not sure there's that much in it.' Whereupon the baffled lady was told, 'In cases like this we go with the husband.' She was instructed to 'lose' the book and not to discuss its contents further with her friends and colleagues, and there the matter ended.

In short, there was little evidence available on the subject of child development, such evidence as was to hand was liable to be cherry-picked to suit the purposes and aims of the mission's structure and system, and anything that might have been seen as an open challenge to the chosen way of doing things was smacked down in no uncertain terms. Thus, parents were left with nowhere to go. The message they received was, 'This is how we do things, it is the will of God and so glorifying to Him; sacrifice is to be expected in the service of God and your children are part of that sacrifice. Oh, and if you can't toe the party line on this or are somehow determined to be awkward about it, don't be surprised if you are cold-shouldered by the rest of the mission community. Questioning the policy of the mission's leadership indicates a disloyalty and lack of faith that will make it hard for you to continue in fellowship in the future.' These latter points remained largely unspoken but were clearly indicated and, indeed, some missionaries did return home, unable to cope with the fracturing of their family that mission service required. Others were told they would not be welcomed back after furlough because they were unable to comply quietly with the formal child policies of their mission. You sacrificed your children or you sacrificed your calling. You accepted Jephthah's inheritance or you left with nothing.

> In the sixteenth century, kings and bankers channelled enormous resources to finance geographical expeditions around the world but not a penny for child psychology. This is because kings and bankers surmised that the discovery of new geographical knowledge would enable them to conquer new lands and set up trade empires, whereas they couldn't see any profit in understanding child psychology.
> *Yuval Noah Harari* (7)

So, we can see that, alongside some very practical issues relating to the availability and quality of education to missionaries, many found themselves trapped in religious systems that had become closed and dysfunctional and which, gradually and almost unnoticed, compiled pharisaical rules which the missions then required their members to follow. For the most part, such pressures were never to be found in writing but were, at least, the implicit, sometimes explicit subject of conversations that left families feeling trapped. Such rules created painfully divided loyalties for parents, eager to serve God to the best of their ability, but understanding too that their role as parents should not only honour God but also preserve and nurture the prospects of their children.

Happily, many missions today have learnt the lessons their predecessors seemed unable to grasp. So we see homeschooling on the increase and use of local day schools, too, as third-world standards of education have risen to match more closely those of missionaries' home countries. But boarding remains an option that is still countenanced by many missions and which, despite huge improvements in the care of children in such establishments, still amounts to neglect, and emotional and spiritual abuse.

In 2016, I wrote a poem called *What Do You Want for Christmas?* and published it on social media on Christmas Day, just for my friends, though these included several with a similar experience to my own. Here it is.

What do you want for Christmas, little boy?
I want my mummy.
Love come down, peace on earth, comfort and joy.
She will give me all these things.
She will care for and hold me, cherish and nurture me. I want my mummy.
That year, I asked for a parent. I was given a child.
What do you want for Christmas, young man?
I still want my mum.
I know I'm supposed to be old enough not to need her any more,
But I've never really had her, so I still do.
I really need some love, some peace of heart, some comfort and joy.
I just want my mum.
Again, that year, I asked for a parent. Again, I was given a child.
What do you want for Christmas, my friend?
Whatever.
A bit of love would be nice. Any kind of love, from anyone.
I've given up on the idea of peace, of comfort or joy.
I just want someone to hold me and mean it. I want someone to love me.
That year, I asked for love. Once more, I was given a child.
What do you want for Christmas, old man?
A child.
A child I can love, bring peace to, give comfort and joy.
A child I can weep with, laugh with, play with, grow with.
A child I can care for and hold, cherish and nurture.
I want a child.

That year, I asked for a child. And I was given a child.
And the child was Him.
And the child was me.
And together we wept and laughed and played and grew.
And we were forever a child.
And we were forever a man.
And we were for ever.

Later that Christmas Day I received a message from a friend working in a city in which there were a number of mission schools. She asked if she might share my poem with a dormitory of girls with whom she had spent some time that day who were very distressed and missing their parents. She felt it might at least demonstrate to them that there were people who understood their sadness.

I was very happy to give her permission, but I asked her, 'What on earth are these children doing still in school, not just during the Christmas holiday, but on Christmas Day itself?'

Her reply was a devastating one. These girls, it seemed, were the daughters of missionaries who were so dedicated to the cause of evangelism that they actually left their children in boarding school for two of the three holidays of each school year. For these parents, having their children home for the school holidays more than once a year would have been an unnecessary distraction to their work. So, the children were left at boarding school whilst their classmates – everyone else, in fact – went home, compounding their misery and distress.

Here is Nick Duffell again, this time quoting journalist George Monbiot, writing in *the Guardian*.

> Having provocatively suggested that "Britain's most overt form of child abuse is mysteriously ignored", he (Monbiot) claims that, "this practice [boarding school] offends no fewer than eleven articles of the UN convention on the rights of the child, which Britain signed in 1991. Yet it attracts scarcely a murmur of concern." (8)

So, it continued. And the denial goes on; in this case, not just of the damage that childhood separation causes, but that the boarding was happening at all. The mission concerned in the above case had assured me personally that there were no children of their missionaries still in boarding school.

> Carl Jung suggested that it is not even so much what happens in the parent–child relationship that has the greatest impact on the child. What is missing in that relationship leaves the greatest scar on the child's personality. Gordon Neufeld (9)

In conclusion, why do Christian missionaries send their children away to boarding school? For many reasons – some of them practical, some of them very personal, some of them because they are under considerable pressure to do so. But ultimately because, for them, obedience to the great commission has led to a great omission. They have forgotten the example of their Heavenly Father, whose promises of His unfailing love for and eternal presence with us is what enables them to serve in the way they do. And they have fallen into a neglect of their children which can be excused in a hundred different ways, but which has untold consequences. We will examine some of those consequences later. But first, here is Marianne's story.

Marianne's Story

Marianne was six when she was sent away to school. A shy, pretty little girl, her parents were new to missionary work and had only recently arrived to complete an orientation course when Marianne was taken to the mission's boarding school for the first time. It was holiday time, but they were anxious to get to their field of work, so they took their little girl to the school so that she could see it before term started and the other children arrived.

The plan was to stay in a nearby hotel for a week then settle Marianne in with the other children when they arrived. But events overtook the couple and, receiving a message that their presence was required at the mission station earlier than expected, they said their hurried goodbyes and left their daughter at the school to await the arrival of the other pupils two days later. The suddenness of her parents' departure took Marianne by surprise. It had been bad enough that they were going to leave her, but she had been bracing herself for the dreaded day and, now that it had come upon her so unexpectedly, she was totally unprepared and understandably distraught.

The school was an empty and lonely place for the little girl and the staff who were there were busy preparing for the approaching term and hadn't the time to spend with Marianne. And the dormitory, which in just a day or two would house another eleven little girls, felt enormous and threatening as darkness fell. Marianne felt terribly alone and afraid as she lay there on her own that first night. She had never been apart from her parents before so this horrible emptiness was a new and distressing experience for her.

Despite all of that, unpleasant as it was, it was not the worst thing. You see, Marianne's parents were from Switzerland. And here, in this Spanish-speaking school, with its exclusively Spanish-speaking staff, Marianne had been left at six years old speaking only Swiss German. She might as well have been on Pluto, so isolated did she feel. Completely unable to express her distress and deep sense of bereavement at being torn from her family so suddenly, she had been cast adrift on a sea of confusion and bewilderment. Even when the other children began to arrive for the start of term, she could only stand silently by as old friends chattered excitedly to one another, unable even to ask what she should be doing or where she should be going. She would wait for the school bell to sound or a whistle to blow and then follow the others as best she could. But sometimes a signal would mean everyone ran in different directions. And several times she stood in statuesque panic, unable to locate anyone she knew from her class or dormitory, completely bemused as to where she should be or even why.

If Marianne wanted someone to pass the jam at tea time, she would have to point, which embarrassed her as her mother had always taught her that pointing was rude. Whilst all the other girls sang the hymns at assembly with enthusiasm, she could only hum the tune, desperately searching the unfamiliar words on the page of the hymn book if one of the girls next to her had been thoughtful enough to find the number for her.

The staff were kind and most of the girls helped Marianne as best they could. And in time she began to pick up words, then phrases, and to slowly overcome the enormous hurdle she had been left to negotiate all by herself. But those early days at the school were a kind of torture that left their mark on the little girl, and it was a long while before her pretty smile and dancing eyes became a familiar sight around the place.

Many years later, returning to the school for the first time since she had left it as an eleven-year-old, all the emotions and terrors of those early days returned; the sense of isolation and fear, the confusion and bewilderment, the sense of bereavement and aloneness. Suddenly, she was a little girl again, following her friends to find out where she should be, feeling overwhelmed with a desire to leave the place and her cauldron of emotions behind. It took huge courage for her not to just run away, as many would have done, but stay and face those fears and the ghosts of her childhood. That same bravery that had seen her through the most difficult time of her life now came to her aid as she reviewed those days and found hope in the strong and courageous woman she had become.

But she would never forget.

> No infant refrains from emoting to the parents precisely what he feels or from signalling when she requires help. The failure to do so later in childhood is a developmentally abnormal adaptation – for some a truly devastating one, which undergirds the woundings that follow. *Gabor Maté* (1)

Justified by Fate

The confusion expressed by Michael in his story over who was responsible for his treatment as a child, is a common experience and a much discussed theme in MK circles. Given the damage that we now know to have been imposed on the children of missionaries separated from their parents so early in life, does responsibility for this damage lie at the door of God, missions, parents or a mixture of all three? This is a question that needs to be asked not in order to apportion blame, but to understand the underlying causes that allowed organisations to inflict untold damage on those children for whose care they were ultimately responsible.

Many MKs brought up on mission fields and sent from the family home at so tender an age now understand that what happened to them was of its time. That is to say, the combination of limited options already discussed, the paucity of information available on child development and the genuine sense of calling felt by men and women of huge courage, commitment and integrity, but blinded by zeal to their duty of care to their members and their families, meant that the decisions made regarding the raising and education of missionary children can perhaps be summed up as 'the best we could do, done in good faith and without the benefit of hindsight or the knowledge available to us today.' And so there is a reluctance to throw stones or apportion blame on the part of many, feeling as they do that maybe, under the same circumstances, they might not have had either the information or the courage to have acted so differently themselves.

> The purpose is not to blame parents or previous generations or spouses but to enable us to discard beliefs that have proved dangerous to our health. *Gabor Maté* (1)

On the other hand, mission policies were often riddled with contradictions that gave mission leaders permission to ignore the hard questions of life balance and simply proceed with what they wanted to do, as previously discussed. In part, this was due to the colonial history of many of the nations that sent missionaries out during the 19th and 20th centuries. Almost all had a record of, as they saw it, taking civilisation to the third world, exporting their own systems of justice, education, medical and social care, and even etiquette. As a result, many missions imposed the standards and cultural norms of their home country onto the locals, often quite unconsciously. Some saw this as part of their mission – to deliver what they understood to be an improved quality of life alongside their evangelistic purpose. In many instances, the consequences of this were disastrous, resulting in the destruction of rich cultures and heritages much older than their own.

One only has to look eighty miles offshore to the west of the British mainland to see how 18th and 19th century missionaries sent from Scotland to the remote islands of the St Kilda archipelago imposed such pharisaical rules upon that unique society that it completely destroyed its cultural heritage of song and dance, both being forbidden in the name of God and decency. It even impacted the economy, forbidding any kind of work either on a Sunday or on those days when a midweek service was held; this in a society where outdoor work, at least, could only be done for six months of the year, meaning every day lost increased the possibility of the community going hungry during the winter months. Losing two or more days a week to Sabbath observance was a significant factor in the ultimate demise of this special community.

This confusion of ideologies is borne out by some statements issued in the past by missions in defence of their policies, which were at best colonial and, in some cases, downright and offensively racist. Christian journalist and writer Mark Galli has commented:

> The nineteenth century mission movement, though strong on evangelism, was sometimes blinded by colonialism and so seemed blind to the verses about serving in love. (2)

References to 'heathen natives,' for example, and warnings against missionaries letting their children associate with them seem to us today self-defeating for emissaries of a loving God to a people lost in their sin. One mission instructed parents not to employ local girls to look after their young children for fear of spiritual and moral corruption whilst simultaneously encouraging mothers to do so in order that they be freed up for language study. And the claim by this same mission in its members' handbook that, 'The final responsibility for the child must ever be the parents' and no-one can dictate for another what is right in these matters,' shows a complete lack of awareness of the power and control they were themselves exercising over their members. Because, whatever the confusions apparent in the policies of some missions in the 19th and 20th centuries, the expectations communicated to the members of those missions were clear and unarguable. The systemic pressure and call to sacrifice already discussed meant many parents felt obliged to act against their instincts in respect of their children's care.

Documents such as the one quoted above, which have come to light in recent years, have exacerbated matters with regard to the mission's role in the upbringing of MKs. Though occasionally encouraging, many have confirmed the worst fears of MKs concerning their mission's priorities when it came to children. The institutional readiness to split up families in the name of service to God, requiring parents to sacrifice their children, as many MKs view it, was the action that spoke louder than any words about the pre-eminence of family life.

Safe Carers

Even the apparently generous provision of a mission school staffed by Christian men and women – which you might expect to have been a secure and happy environment, as indeed many were for much of the time – does not bear close examination when it comes to the appointment of the staff who would effectively raise the children of missionaries in their stead. Often, little priority was given to recruiting trained pastoral staff to work alongside the teachers, resulting in mission members whose calling had been elsewhere being taken out of their field situation to fill in at a mission school. Initially, this was a temporary measure that frequently became permanent as no formal replacement was forthcoming. Sometimes, teaching posts were filled in this way, a consequence being that missions occasionally lost members who had a teaching qualification but had received a different calling and designation. Ultimately, these people became disillusioned with the whole process and simply left the mission. One of the accusations made by the alumni of Mamou Academy was that their mission appointed some of their members onto the staff of the school because they weren't very good at anything else! Such a policy was interpreted as being culpable in the significant abuse suffered by some of the children at the school.

Those missionaries forced into the pastoral care of the school's children felt particularly out of their depth, often having little or no experience of caring for children and little desire to do so. They went out of obedience and, sometimes, because they felt unprepared to argue the issue with senior leaders. Almost always these people were young ladies whilst the mission leaders were rather older men who could be quite stern and foreboding. What were they to do?

Take the case of Maureen, a young nurse who had grown up as an only child and gone to the mission field to work amongst a particular ethnic and language group to whom she felt called. Two years into her language study, a rigorous and difficult foray into one of the world's more complex dialects, she was asked by her mission leaders if she would go to their boarding school to look after a dormitory of five- and six-year-old boys. A vacancy had arisen unexpectedly and she was needed, just for a term or two. Reluctant, but feeling unable to refuse, she agreed. It was twelve years before she would leave the school, and then only because her visa had run out; at this point, she left the mission.

Looking back, Maureen talks about some very special times at the school and she clearly loved her time with the children. But she also talks about the extent to which she felt very exposed due to her total lack of experience with children, her confusion over issues of discipline and the lack of guidance given to her by her heads of school, of which there were five during her time there. She admits to having been completely out of her depth on occasions and making decisions which, in hindsight, were inappropriate and left her and, sadly, some of the children who were in her care, with some significant regrets.

But the point is this. To place a single woman who was an only child and completely inexperienced in any form of childcare in charge of up to a dozen children was not only unfair to the children, but unfair to the lady concerned. No kind of training was ever offered or given, as a result of which mistakes were made which impacted the lives of children already traumatised by being removed from their families, and it left the lady herself in a difficult and invidious situation. Also, the mission permanently lost one of its members from an area of work to which few had been called and to which she never returned, her two years of language study seemingly wasted.

So, in a significant number of missions, not only was the decision made to separate children from their parents, there was also a failure to provide adequately trained staff to act in loco parentis, exacerbating an already fragile situation. In time, this failure to take proper measures to recruit fully trained and appropriate staff within their schools would be deemed culpable in the multiple instances of physical and sexual abuse being uncovered, which had the most widespread and long-lasting consequences. Of course, such issues can be present in any institution, but there is no doubt that some missions made themselves more vulnerable to accusations of failure of duty of care by their blatantly unprofessional and irresponsible approach to appointing staff.

Varied Perspectives

There is no question that many MKs cannot be criticised if they see their mission as largely responsible for the neglect they faced as children and the issues they continue to face as adults. Not all do, by the way. There are many MKs who speak with glowing affection about their childhood and who, on the face of it, seem to have come through the experience with a first-class education not only in terms of their schooling but also in respect of their cultural understanding and worldview. They declare themselves relatively, sometimes completely, unscathed by their experience and grateful for the many opportunities their upbringing afforded them. And, of course, for most MKs it was a childhood of adventure and excitement, often in stunningly beautiful and exotic surroundings, at least as long as they remained on the field, with opportunities contemporaries in their home countries could scarcely conceive. But no-one's experience was anything less than a balance of good, bad and indifferent. For those who acknowledge their woundedness, there is an understanding that in suppressing the bad they also suppressed the good, thus distorting their issues in a way that can be seen as disproportionately traumatic, at least until the healing process is allowed to begin and the good memories can be recovered through the process of facing the painful ones.

As for those who protest that it was all good and they suffered no ill effects, this may possibly be true; probably not even they can truly know. But it may also be that they have just been so successful in suppressing the bad that it has remained completely out of sight. (A child's natural sensitivity is a factor here too.) Some perspective on this is provided later in Mark's story, in which a medical professional attended a gathering intended to offer understanding and healing to those suffering from childhood trauma. His intention was simply to reunite with childhood friends but he was 'hit like a train,' as he described it, becoming utterly overwhelmed with emotions which, up to that point, he hadn't realised were there.

On both sides, there is a need to understand the validity of each person's experience without judgment. Just because someone declares themselves to be unscathed does not mean that they are deceiving themselves any more than it means they actually are unscathed. And just because another is deeply traumatised many years later does not mean that they are weak or self-pitying in any way. These are matters of personal mental health that must be respected – each person having experienced a unique set of circumstances that, taken alongside their character, personality and home environment, moves their experience beyond the rational understanding of others. (One MK who attended a gathering to explore issues of healing wearing a T-shirt bearing the legend 'Get over it,' so clearly of the view that the idea of MK childhood trauma was an overstatement, added significantly to the distress of many of those present.)

> People often make comparisons that unfairly denigrate their own experience. Though you may be justifiably grateful for your lot, the fact that others have suffered 'more than' you does not diminish by one iota your own pain, nor erase its traces in your psyche. Levels of trauma are not to be evaluated, much less graded on a bell curve. *Gabor Maté* (3)

Parental Awareness

And what of the parents? We have already examined the systemic pressures that meant many parents felt any decision was no longer their own but was significantly shaped by their mission's policies. So, undoubtedly, some may feel such circumstances effectively dictated their decision to let their children go and that, in real terms, it was not their choice at all.

The other side of that particular coin is that, with the exception of those who went out to the field single and subsequently married and started a family – though even they did so in knowledge – those who were already married, with or without children, were aware of their mission's policy. They knew that one day, maybe even immediately if their children were already older than four, there would be long separations that would continue to occur for as long as the family remained within the mission or the child was of school age. Their decision to join the mission was inextricably entwined with their choice to relinquish their children to the care of others – strangers, in fact.

That is not to say that parents dealt with the matter easily or without much soul-searching. Many faced the approach of that first relinquishment with an inexpressible dread which caused them to re-evaluate the decision to follow their calling. Many others, whilst still certain in their minds that they were doing the right thing, and the best thing for their child, nevertheless began a journey of bereavement that started some years before their first child left home and continued throughout their lives. The fact that they trusted God for the care of their child did not mitigate their pain of losing them in the least. And when, often many years later, they realised the extent of their child's own grief and hurt (though many parents never did), it tested not only their parent–child relationship but also their relationship with God, who some felt had not honoured the trust they had placed in Him to guard their child's heart and mind. I know of more than one retired missionary who has effectively lost their faith after discovering the true extent of the trauma their child suffered as an MK.

Lindsay E Stone in her dissertation *Missionary Kids and Trauma* cites 2017 research done by JO Kim et al in asserting:

> Missionaries and their children who have lived on the field are at a high risk for experiencing trauma and developing PTSD. (4)

Others, as we saw in Kerry's story, seemed emotionally disconnected from the process and apparently largely unaffected by it. In most cases, some would say in all, this was a self-protecting front, hiding their true feelings – some, because they felt that to reveal them would indicate a lack of faith or resolve; some for fear that they would be perceived as weak; some through an intense desire for privacy; some because they genuinely believed that their choice was the right one and they were oblivious to any potential consequences, which of course made their decision easier; others still, because they knew in their heart that their choices had been wrong and they were simply unable to face up to such a daunting truth.

But, ultimately, each family and each parent made their own decision to send their children away, however reluctantly. And, although some did choose to leave the mission field at the point at which their first child reached school age, they were very much in the minority and were often made to feel that they had let the side down. Meanwhile, for the child, the fact that their parents *chose* to send them away is at best impossibly difficult to understand and at worst a rejection of them as a person. That first separation, even if it was the only separation, broke a cord between parent and child that could never be easily repaired. Others might grow in its place over time but, for many, that original cord that binds a child to its parents from birth was snapped, irrevocably and forever. For there was no escape from the awful truth. 'Mummy and Daddy don't want me anymore.' For any child, the process of growing away or detaching themselves from their parents is always something that must be done by the child, in their own way and at their own pace. To force the breaking of this bond too soon is to create lifelong consequences for that child.

> (For those who know) the pain of a broken family or permanent loss of support from a parent, that sense of abandonment easily casts a shadow on their impressions of God. It makes them feel like orphans. *Brad Jersak* (5)

The accusation of overly emotional language being used in this respect is sometimes levelled at MKs. But anyone who has watched, as I have, a child of five, six or seven – the age is almost immaterial – being literally and forcibly wrenched from their mother's arms on their first day at boarding school and carried hysterically sobbing from her presence will testify that there are no words too strong to describe such a distressing sight.

One of the more shocking revelations that came out of a mission school alumni gathering was the recollection by one woman that she and her friends, instead of playing 'Mummies and Daddies,' used to play 'Orphans and Children's Homes.' These were children of six, seven and eight, whose default play involved them pretending to be who they felt themselves to be – not children of mummies and daddies, but orphans in a children's home.

Even so, it is extremely difficult for some children, particularly perhaps those brought up in the Christian faith, to express their sense of rejection to their parents or even admit that they hold their parents responsible for what happened to them. Nonetheless, in their hearts they know that, whatever other factors were in play – from the biblical imperatives of sacrifice and evangelism to the child policies of individual mission organisations – ultimately, the parents agreed to a separation that was within their power to avoid.

The experience of families being broken up in this way is often spoken of in terms of it being equally difficult for the parent as it was for the child. And it must be acknowledged that for most parents it was devastating and heartbreaking. But it was different in one very important way. For the parent, choosing, allowing – however you may wish to describe it – for their child to be sent away was always something that was in their control, however much they may have felt pressured at the time. Ultimately, they could have said no. The consequences for their lives may well have been extremely hard to deal with but they were adults, capable of making mature decisions, able to rationalise and, one would hope, with support structures to fall back on. Sadly, and almost unbelievably, in many missions this was not actually the case. There was no support structure provided and parents were expected to deal with their problems alone; required to, even. For to betray any kind of perceived weakness in the face of a sacrifice being made by all was to demonstrate what was interpreted as an unacceptable lack of faith. Moreover, they had the reassurance that this was God's will and that He would care for their children and watch over them whilst they were away. There was some comfort for them in this, some hope.

But the children were not in control of the situation. They were alone and frightened, bewildered and often grief-stricken, incapable at that age of rationalisation, or even of understanding what was happening to them. There was no comfort, no hope. Or worse, they found a way to hope, only for that hope to be cruelly and constantly dashed into little pieces as their pain continued year upon year. The consequences for their lives were beyond measuring, beyond understanding by them or their parents, and seemingly unending.

> In all cases, early rejection or perceived rejection leads to distorted, unrealistic thinking. *John White* (6)

What of God?

And so we come to God. Was this separation His idea? Was it something He required of parents, perhaps as a mark of the seriousness of their intent to serve Him? Was the cause of evangelism more important to Him than the value to a child of growing up in a loving family, safe, secure and happy, instead of frightened, alone and bereaved?

The basic premise of evangelical Christian missions has always been The Great Commission – the words of Jesus to His disciples at the moment of His leaving them following His resurrection. It is to be found in Matthew 28:18–20.

> Then Jesus came to them and said, "All authority in heaven and on earth has been given to me. Therefore go and make disciples of all nations, baptizing them in the name of the Father and of the Son and of the Holy Spirit, and teaching them to obey everything I have commanded you. And surely I am with you always, to the very end of the age."

There are perhaps two reasons why these words are central to the Christian faith and experience. Firstly, they are the final words of Jesus. Humanity has always had a fascination with the last words of those leaving us, in whatever way, instinctively understanding that these words carry a weight and import that is beyond the ordinary. Secondly, Jesus has promised His disciples that He will return one day and these are His instructions for what they should do in the intervening time. His use of words such as 'all', 'everything' and 'always' and His use of the phrase 'to the very end of the age' also indicates that these words are not just for those present, but for those who will come after. And so the evangelical church has taken them to apply to all Christians in every age until Christ returns.

Alongside this stands the theology of judgment and salvation.

Man is sinful and 'the wages of sin is death' (Romans 6:23).

Man can only be saved by faith in Christ. In the words of Jesus, 'No-one comes to the Father except through me' (John 14:6).

Anyone who does not believe in Jesus is doomed to eternal punishment, as outlined by Jesus when asked by his disciples to explain his parable of the weeds in Matthew 13:36–43. And this is backed up by Paul in his letter to the Romans, where he says in chapter 10:13–15.

> "Everyone who calls on the name of the Lord will be saved." How, then, can they call on the one they have not believed in? And how can they believe in the one of whom they have not heard? And how can they hear without someone preaching to them? And how can anyone preach unless they are sent? As it is written: "How beautiful are the feet of those who bring good news!"

Further impetus to the cause of evangelical mission is given by the words of Jesus in Matthew 24:14.

> And this gospel of the kingdom will be proclaimed throughout the whole world as a testimony to the nations, and then the end will come.

Taken together, these passages from Scripture form, for many Christians, a template for life. One day, Christ will return – the sooner, the better. Meantime, Jesus has instructed us to spread the good news (gospel) that unless they believe in Him everyone is going to hell; and He won't return until everyone has been told about Him.

At least, that's how simple it is for some, which sometimes overlooks the instruction not just to 'go' and 'tell' but to 'disciple.' This means showing how to live – educate, inform, encourage and example. Even the 'go' imperative has caused much discussion amongst theologians, many of whom understand the word to be an instruction to 'do'. But for others, 'go' meant 'go somewhere else'. Leave your home and family for the sake of the gospel and take the news of Jesus to those who, but for you going, would otherwise never hear. Amongst many other examples, the imagery of Frank Houghton's great missionary hymn, *Facing a Task Unfinished*, that 'unnumbered souls are dying and pass into the night,' has been a powerful motivator for many young Christians who felt called to serve overseas.

So it would seem that there is a strong case for the missionary calling. I would add that if the Christian faith at its heart is about a relationship of love and grace between God and the believer, then it's the most natural thing in the world to want to share one's joy at being in love and talk about it to anyone who will listen – especially if the relationship is one that has changed your life significantly for the better.

But how to deal with the cost that is involved and the arguments that others might put in the way of you going? For example, those who might suggest that leaving your parents just as they reach retirement age or when they are maybe in ill health is a betrayal of family values. Likewise, the idea of having to send your children away to boarding school. Or, an argument many men faced, the cost to women in exposing them to dangerous situations and uncivilised societies, especially in days gone by.

In such instances it was necessary for those who felt a calling to the mission field based on Scripture to counter these arguments from elsewhere in Scripture. It wasn't enough to just quote the Great Commission or other passages concerning evangelising the unreached or even ministering to the poor. They needed precedent for such sacrifices as they themselves were to make – or at least some kind of mitigation.

Scripture as Justification

The precedent when it came to children was found in the story of Hannah and Samuel, which appears in the opening chapter of 1 Samuel. Hannah is one of two wives of a man named Elkanah, whose other wife bears him children whilst Hannah remains barren. One year, as they visit the temple, Hannah is particularly distressed at the shame she carries for her inability to bear a child and she promises God that if He gives her a son she will dedicate him to the Lord's service. In due course she gives birth to a son and names him Samuel, which means 'God has heard'. And we read in verse 24, 'After he was weaned, she took the boy with her, young as he was … and brought him to the house of the Lord at Shiloh.' There, she and her husband left him and we read in chapter 2:11, 'Then Elkanah went home to Ramah, but the boy ministered before the Lord under Eli the priest.'

Samuel went on to be a key figure in the history of Israel and one of the most significant prophets in the whole of the Old Testament. So there it is. Proof positive that if you sacrifice your children in the name of service to God they will be blessed and, more than that, become leading figures in the faith, examples for others to admire and imitate.

Many sons of missionaries had this story read to them in reverent tones as they prepared to go away to boarding school, accompanied by such injunctions as, 'You are our Samuel. God will bless you and make you strong and wise for His service.' And today, as they look back on those times, many of the same sons read those words:

> 'After he was weaned … '
>
> 'young as he was … '
>
> 'she and her husband left him … '
>
> 'Then Elkanah went home to Ramah, but the boy … '

And their anger and resentment burns with a new intensity born of the years of abandonment and hurt, the nights of loneliness and tears, and the loss of their own faith because God did not bless them and make them strong and wise for His service. As far as they are able to tell, God was no more present with them in their isolation and fear than the parents who had sacrificed them in His name.

The second Scripture that every missionary child knows from hearing it repeated time and again in defence of their parents' actions is found in each of the synoptic gospels – Matthew 19:29, Mark 10:29 and Luke 18:29. (Ironically, numerologists will tell you that the number 29 is all about relationships, compassion and co-existence!)

The Matthew passage reads as follows:

> Everyone who has given up houses or brothers or sisters or father or mother or children or property, for my sake, will receive a hundred times as much in return and will inherit eternal life.

Mark adds to this somewhat:

> "Truly I tell you," Jesus replied, "no-one who has left home or brothers or sisters or mother or father or children or fields for me and the gospel will fail to receive a hundred times as much in this present age: homes, brothers, sisters, mothers, children and fields – along with persecutions – and in the age to come eternal life."

And here is Luke's take on it.

> "Truly I tell you," Jesus said to them, "no one who has left home or wife or brothers or sisters or parents or children for the sake of the kingdom of God will fail to receive many times as much in this age, and in the age to come eternal life."

So, some differences in the text each time, but the thrust is the same. Though, it's worth noting at this point that if this text was quoted to a child, they would pick up on the words, 'in this present age' or 'in this age.' A necessary reassurance for a child and no doubt seen as an incentive by parents using these words as backing from God for the separation the child was about to experience. The message is, 'This is God's will and he has promised that you will live happily ever after, albeit there may be some suffering to be endured along the way.'

But again, many MKs look back with sadness and feel that this hasn't been true in their experience. So, why not? Is it some failure on their part to merit the fulfilment of this promise? Or was the context in which the promise was originally made such that it should never have been passed on to young children in this way? Or is God simply not to be trusted to honour such an extravagant assurance, or at least not yet?

These passages stand as central pillars in the missionary's defence of their decision to send their children away, and the failure of each to be proved reliable by their children is central to the loss of faith and enduring cynicism with which many MKs live to this day. (This last passage, quoted with shocking insensitivity by a missionary at one alumni gathering, was met with hoots of derision.)

So, how valid is it to take passages from Scripture like this and use them to justify decisions that will impact others? And it's the others that are important here. After all, if I were to believe that the account of Jesus encouraging Peter to walk on water meant this was something I too could do and step out of a boat into the middle of the sea, it's only me who might drown. But once I take a story which, no less than that of Jephthah, stands in some isolation in the Bible and use it to justify decisions made about the lives of my children and partner, I have to be very sure that I have my theology right. The missionary world is littered with parents who made the decision to send their children away 'in good faith' and 'trusting to the mercies of God' only to find that not only were these children seriously damaged, but that it led to family estrangement and even a rejection of their parents' faith.

So let's look at the passages one by one, starting with Samuel, which raises some interesting questions. Clearly, the logic of taking an example such as this from Scripture and applying it to one's own life and faith three thousand years later is fraught with danger. If Hannah's desire to honour God and sacrifice Samuel to him was a good thing, why then was Jephthah's similar action not? On the face of it, Hannah's actions may be interpreted as selfless and honouring to God. And He did indeed honour them. Whereas Jephthah's promise, whilst it may also have been selfless and honouring to God inasmuch as his expectation was that the first thing to emerge from his house upon his return would be an animal, was ill-thought out, uncalled for and foolish.

Let's compare another similar example: that of Moses. Moses was born at a time of great persecution for the Israelites living in slavery in Egypt and male babies were liable to be killed as a political means of population control, preventing Jewish males becoming so great in number that they would be a threat to the Egyptians in their own land. So Moses' mother hid her child in a waterproof basket which she placed amongst the reeds at the side of the river, hoping to conceal her son until he was old enough to mingle unnoticed amongst the other children. But the child was discovered by the Pharoah's daughter, who took him as her own and raised him in the royal household. Eventually he would become the most iconic of all Israel's leaders, releasing the nation from its bondage and taking them back into the promised land from which they had come in the time of Joseph in order to escape a famine.

Most biblical accounts lack detail and often background as well. But we don't have to consider the wider picture in this case for very long before we realise that, well-meaning as Moses' mother was in hiding her child, her choice to expose her son to the elements on a crocodile and snake-infested river, even under the watchful eye of his older sister, Miriam, was one which today would have had her prosecuted for criminal neglect. Should a Christian mother today consider protecting her infant from danger by placing him in a basket on a crocodile-infested river because Moses' mother did so? I'm not sure anyone in their right mind would suggest so, especially not on the spurious premise that such an action might ensure her son became a national or spiritual leader.

The story of Jephthah stands in sharp contrast to that in Genesis of Abraham and Isaac, where God ultimately prevents Abraham from sacrificing his son and provides a ram in his place. But it does perhaps stand alongside that of Hannah in 1 Samuel 1.

'Young as he was.' What a lifetime of implications and consequences are hidden in those few words. Never again would he know a mother's love. It is another example of someone making a promise to God of a kind that He did not require and that would have huge consequences for the child involved. There are significant differences too, it must be acknowledged, one of which is that God chose to grant Hannah's request for a child, which obliged her to follow through on her promise, as per the provisions of Leviticus we discussed in an earlier chapter. And God did honour Hannah's desire for him to become a man of God, though it must also be acknowledged that he wasn't a great father, perhaps because parenting was never modelled for him in any meaningful way.

But, as Catholic contemplative and theologian Richard Rohr observes in *The Divine Dance*:

> We are not punished FOR our sins, we are punished BY our sins. (7)

In other words, everything we do has implications and consequences and, for the most part, these are not the result of God intervening in order to discipline or punish us. They are simply how the world works. If I do not model good parenting to my children, they will likely grow up not understanding what good parenting entails. That's not God judging me or paying me back for my bad example. It's just what happens, just as if I cross the road without looking and get knocked down by a car that is not God's judgment, but the consequence of my carelessness. Thus, my ending up in hospital with two broken legs and the imprint of a Ford Fiesta on my right shin is not me being punished FOR my sin, but BY my sin.

This has implications for our whole approach to how God deals with us, particularly with regard to how we interpret and understand Scriptures that promise God's protection. We may not play fast and loose with these promises by taking risks with our personal safety just because God has promised somewhere in the Bible to keep us safe. There is an implicit quid pro quo here which requires that for God to fulfil His part of the deal we don't brazenly dare the enemy to destroy us. He has not blessed us with intelligence, common sense and good judgment just so that we can demand impunity in exchange for our foolish behaviour. If I place my head in a lion's mouth to prove the truth of God's promise to keep me safe, I am likely to find that His definition of keeping me safe is to take me instantly to be with Him, even as the lion gives thanks for his dinner! The well-publicised 2017 example of an African pastor who summoned his congregation to the banks of a crocodile-infested river for the express purpose of increasing their faith by walking on the water at God's instruction, only to meet an immediate and grisly, if not entirely unpredictable end, is a salutary and tragic example of such folly. The name of the river? Crocodile River! Hmm ....

Similarly, understanding the context of God's promises in the Bible and acknowledging what the words actually say, as opposed to what we would like them to say, will avoid us becoming disappointed because we think God has said something that He actually never intended us to believe. Our fault, not His. For example, a much-quoted verse that has brought comfort to many Christians is Jeremiah 29:9.

> 'I know the plans I have for you,' declares the Lord. 'Plans to prosper you and not to harm you.'

This promise is given through Jeremiah to the Jews who have been exiled in Babylon. So the context is not one of joy and peace; inasmuch as it is one of hope, it is of hope for a distant future. This is God saying, 'I know you feel like this is the end and your lives are over, but I do have a plan. Actually, most of you won't see that plan come to fruition because you will die in exile. But for your children, there is hope. Some of them will return. Meanwhile, I'm still in charge and I will bless you with a measure of prosperity where you are, even though, at the moment, this looks like an unmitigated disaster.' In fact, the reason why only *some* Jews did return eventually to Jerusalem was that many chose not to, so flourishing were their lives and businesses in their new home. So when we offer this verse to comfort someone and encourage them that God is in control, it's important that we understand that, despite its ultimate truth, the original promise was given into a situation of utter devastation and hopelessness. 'The light shines in the darkness ....'

It's also important to note that it is a prophecy rather than a promise – and not even a promise in the terms that we might hope it to be. 'I know the plans I have for you' does not mean that these plans will come to fruition. God doesn't actually say that they will. He is saying, 'I know what I intend to happen here, and what I intend is to bless you.' But He does not say that what He has planned *will* happen, only that He *intends* it to happen. Whether or not it does actually happen is going to be dependent upon the Israelites returning to God and seeking Him. Because God works tirelessly not to violate our free will and always lets us decide things for ourselves; because He submits to our choices and respects our decision to live so much of our lives without Him, we have the power to thwart His plans. He knows the plans He has, but if we don't co-operate with those plans, they will not come to fruition. Yes, He wants to bless us:

> "Test me in this," says the *Lord* Almighty, "and see if I will not throw open the floodgates of heaven and pour out so much blessing that there will not be room enough to store it." (Malachi 3:10)

If we seek His will for our lives and engage with Him in His work of bringing about His kingdom, He will provide all that we need:

> God's work done in God's way will never lack God's supply. *James Hudson Taylor* (8)

But if what we are doing is the result of our own good ideas and not a result of His leading, we can claim all the promises we want and they will not make a jot of difference, save for the grace and mercy of God in not judging us as we deserve, due to our folly in imagining that we can do anything of worth without Him. (Note, too, that the Malachi verse is part of God's encouragement to His people to honour the full amount of their tithe; it is not just a random promise of blessing, but God's promise to fulfil His part of a covenant when we fulfil ours.)

> It is funny how mortals always picture us as putting things into their minds: in reality our best work is done by keeping things out. *CS Lewis* (9)

So, what do we believe? How much do we dare to believe? Are the examples of God blessing others in times past down to the fact that those people were somehow better, more holy, more deserving than we are? Or is it a matter of context – that promise was for then and God doesn't work like that these days? Does God really want to bless us? Are we really deserving of grace? (Think about that last one for a moment!)

The question of how we are to understand the passages about blessings that will come to those who give up family and home for the service of God has been an equally powerful and commonly invoked defence by those sending their children away into the care of others. We have already examined the fact that a proper understanding of who God is and how He works is a prerequisite for obeying His will as opposed to following 'the devices and desires of our own heart'. Who Jesus has called us to be in Him trumps any exciting ideas we might have manufactured out of our own ambition as regards vocation – serving Him rather than serving ourselves, and doing so under His banner.

> Values must precede vision. Values connect you to the Vine. *Brad Jersak* (10)

So, when we study Jesus's words in Matthew 19:29 about leaving 'houses or brothers or sisters or father or mother or wife or children or fields for my sake,' as with almost everything that Jesus said, we find its truest meaning when we consider it in context. Of course, some of the words of Jesus stand alone in the strength and essence of their truth. But others, and I suggest this is one of those, are best understood within the framework of Christ's teaching in that moment.

Here, the context is a conversation Jesus has had with the man described as the rich young ruler. The man's question is how he may get eternal life and, having asserted that he has been obedient to God's law and asked if there is anything else he must do, Jesus tells him to sell his possessions and give to the poor. What goes almost unnoticed in Jesus's instruction, however, is how he begins the sentence; 'If you want to be perfect ....' We are reminded of His words from the Sermon on the Mount, 'Be perfect, as your Heavenly Father is perfect.' This is Jesus's contemporary rendering of the Levitican mantra, 'Be holy, as I am holy,' which underpins the giving of the law. The young man claims to have done all that has been asked of him in the Torah and challenges Jesus to raise the bar. Ever willing to do just that, Jesus replies, 'All right, then, if you want to be perfect, here's what you must do. Sell your possessions and give to the poor.' We are told that the young man went away sad because he had great wealth.

This prompts a discussion amongst the disciples about the cost of following Jesus, and Peter asks, 'We have left everything to follow you! What then will there be for us?' And that is where Jesus speaks about leaving the people and things we love and what our reward will be. So the context appears to fit the missionary calling – those who leave home and family to serve God will receive many times over what they have given up. (There is a school of thought that suggests Jesus may be referring here to the necessity of young people to break away from their family homes and ties and move out into the world to live under the rule and guiding of God, and that such a life of submission and obedience cannot necessarily be fully accomplished whilst living under one's parents' roof. But whatever the merits of this possibility, it does not invalidate Jesus's use of the word 'everyone.')

All good so far, then. But did you spot the temptation contained in this passage? 'If you want to be perfect … ' These are words that excite and challenge many Christians. On one level, rightly so. Jesus has challenged us to be perfect. The trouble is that any degree of perfection we may attain, just as with any degree of righteousness, is only attainable through our having the humility to accept and understand that such attainment is only achievable in and through Christ and His grace, 'lest anyone should boast' (Ephesians 2:8–9). But when our pride and ambition get the better of us, we imagine that, like the children of Israel in the wilderness, our best route to perfection is through sacrifice. And such is the level of our excitement and ambition, we are in danger of sacrificing more than God has asked us to give Him. In other words, though God requires our hearts and our lives in service and obedience to Him, He does not and never has required that we sacrifice the hearts and lives of others, least of all our children. Like Jephthah, we strike out on our own and promise Him something He has never asked us to give. And at the end of the road lies a broken child, placed on the altar of pride and ambition in the name of Christian service. No wonder God told His people:

> I hate, I despise your religious festivals. Even though you bring me burnt offerings, I will not accept them. Though you bring me choice fellowship offerings, I will have no regard for them. Away with the noise of your songs. I will not listen to the music of your harps. (Amos 5:21–23)

and:

> I desire mercy, not sacrifice, and acknowledgment of God rather than burnt offerings. (Hosea 6:6)

You see, there is a phrase here that may not be overlooked, nor its implications ignored. 'Everyone who has given up' is not the same thing as 'Everyone who has had taken away from them.' In other words, whilst this promise might be true for those who choose to follow Jesus and serve Him and in doing so give up their home and family, it does not promise that their children will be similarly recompensed. Now, we could talk here about the principle of 'covering' intrinsic in Jewish society of the time, which meant, for example, that when a husband or father was converted to a new faith his wife, children and even his servants also took on that faith. The royal official whose son is healed by Jesus in John 4 is just such an example, as is the Philippian jailer in Acts 16. However, Jesus is moving people on from Old Testament principles into a faith that is a fulfilment of the law, which He Himself sums up in His words, again from the Sermon on the Mount: 'So, in everything, do to others as you would have them do to you, for this sums up the law and the prophets.' To this we might add that there is a time when a promise is made that *is* 'to you and to your children,' though also 'to those who are afar off, whom God shall call to Himself.' This is Peter's assertion that the Holy Spirit is available to everyone in Acts 2:39. This gives the absence of such a promise from the words of Jesus an even greater significance.

Once again, we are faced with a verse which can be interpreted according to what we want it to mean unless and until we are prepared to take a closer look at what Jesus actually said. John's gospel ends with such a reminder, since it would seem that some had taken Jesus's words to Peter, 'If I want him (John) to remain alive until I return, what is that to you?' to mean that John would not die. It seems likely that John had died at this point, since the final chapter of his gospel has all the hallmarks of an add-on, thus it was causing a problem for some believers who felt that a promise Jesus had made had not been fulfilled. It was felt necessary to explain that what some believed was true was not actually what Jesus had said. We can wish whatever we like into the promises of God, but that does not endow them with the truth that we want to believe.

Another powerful passage evoked by those in God's service to justify prioritising their work over their children appears in Matthew 10:37, where Jesus says:

> Anyone who loves their father or mother more than me is not worthy of me; anyone who loves their son or daughter more than me is not worthy of me.

But here, again, it is important for us to hear exactly what Jesus said and not what we have interpreted it to mean. He is talking about relationship, because relationship is what He is all about and He desires us to be in complete, intimate and everlasting relationship with Him. He does not say that being in relationship with Him gives us permission to neglect our earthly relationships or responsibilities to our families. We can love God more than we love our wives or our children, even our own lives. But one of the ways we do that is to love those He has given to us as He Himself loves them and to example His love, as Paul encourages in Ephesians 5:25.

> Husbands, love your wives just as Christ loved the church, and gave Himself up for her.

We do not become worthy of Jesus by abandoning our children into the care of others or marginalising our partners so that they are not a part of our ministry.

Jesus encourages our belief that a relationship with Him, the Father and the Spirit should be our primary focus in all areas of our lives; but this does not and cannot come at the expense of our loved ones. Many of us live with a dualistic tendency in our thought processes which we carry over into our interpretation of Scripture. For some, loving Jesus more than we love our families means focusing on him to the exclusion of our families – either we love God completely or we love our families completely, but we can't do both. As a result, the experience of many MKs was that they came third or fourth or fifth on the list of priorities, perhaps particularly when it came to their fathers, as we saw in Hope's story. But this is not what Jesus was saying. The fact is, if we love Jesus first, He will lead us to love our partners and children even better and more fully than we do now. It's not about pushing them out to make room for Jesus. Just as Jesus chided his disciples for trying to keep children from him (Matthew 19:14), so He desires for us to bring our children into the lap of our ministry and demonstrate to them how to show the love of Jesus to all, and not to some at the expense of their own. 'Suffer the little children' does not mean 'Let the little children suffer'!

Here, then, are a number of passages that have been used by missions over the years to justify what they do and why they do it. And, in essence, there can be no question as to the fundamental validity of their position.

The Great Commission is an instruction from Jesus to go into all the world and preach the gospel, making disciples of all nations. Those who hear and accept this call are unquestionably right to do so, though how far and when they should go bears equally serious consideration, especially when doing so threatens to jeopardise the physical and mental health, and the safety and faith prospects of children.

Hannah's offering of her son, Samuel, back to God is a humble act of gratitude which is honouring to Him and blesses her son. Likewise, we may offer our children to God for His blessing, but not at the expense of their proper nurture and growth, or indeed of their mental health or personal faith.

We are right to take comfort and claim the truth of the promise expressed in the words of Jesus that anyone who gives up their home and family will receive an overabundance in like manner in time; but we may not assume that this blessing will be given to those on whose behalf we make such sacrifices. 'Left' in this context seems to have a connotation of 'moving on once we have fulfilled our responsibilities' rather than 'abandoning'.

We are to love God above everything, but not at the expense of anyone, least of all those whom God has given us that we might care for them.

What has called the interpretation of these Scriptures into question has been the failure to properly consider the full meaning and import of these passages. In an effort to throw themselves enthusiastically and self-sacrificially into the service of God, some have over-interpreted them and made promises and sacrifices in the style of Jephthah which God never asked nor required of them, to the grave detriment of their families.

> Why would people go to the mission field and die in some developing country and yet not demonstrate affection and love for their own family members? Why would a successful preacher give all of his time to the ministry and yet neglect or even abuse his wife and children? Because they are trying to earn love and acceptance by their actions. They are trying to earn God's approval because they don't truly understand his love. *Jack Frost* (11)

Yes, Jesus instructed us to go; but go now? Go overseas? Go whilst our children are too young to be separated from us?

> The Jesus who leaves family and friends to preach and heal relative strangers is the same one who stayed at home until he was thirty, long past the age when young men of that day did so. *Mark Galli* (12)

Yes, what Hannah did in giving Samuel back to God was a good, humble and honouring thing to do and we may not be in error in doing likewise; but take him and leave him? Take him after he was weaned? Remove all parental love, safety and protection from him?

> It's one thing to make sacrifices for your own life, but was it fair to make them for our children's futures too? *Pete Greig* (13)

Yes, there is a promise that we will be blessed if we obey God's call to share His gospel in the world; but is that promise also for our children? Should we ignore the fact that, though we have been called, they haven't, at least not yet? Do the blessings we are to receive trump the trauma we are causing to our children?

> If ever the book which I am not going to write is written, it must be the full confession by Christendom of Christendom's specific contribution to the sum of human cruelty and treachery. Large areas of 'the World' will not hear us till we have publicly disowned much of our past. Why should they? We have shouted the name of Christ and enacted the service of Moloch. *CS Lewis* (14)

(Hmm .... Still a fan of the great man, then?)

Yes, we should love God above everyone and everything. But does He intend that we do not love our children adequately as well? Does He only give us enough love for Him so that there is none left over for our family? Are we accurately modelling God's love to those to whom we have been sent when we send our children away and make those people our priority?

> If you who set yourselves to explain the theory of Christianity had set yourselves instead to do the will of the master, the one object for which the gospel was preached to you, how different would now be the condition of that portion of the world with which you come into contact?! *George MacDonald* (15)

Anna's Story

Anna was thirty-four when I first met her, a vibrant, independent woman with a successful career and a ready smile that lit up the room the moment she entered it. Always immaculately dressed, she radiated a confidence and affability that masked her deep-seated insecurity well, at least until she began to reminisce about her childhood. Then her countenance would cloud over, her eyes narrow and darken and her voice descend to a grey monotone as she recalled her early years at a mission boarding school.

She recalled waking up towards the end of one school holiday to see her mother exiting her bedroom, a wet patch on the pillow where her mother had been weeping over her. The same thing happened the following night, only this time Anna became aware of her mother's presence beside her bed, woken by the tears that now fell onto her cheek as she slept. Not daring to open her eyes, and frightened by this overt display of her mother's own grief at their imminent separation, she kept her eyes closed and waited until her mother had left the room. It was the same every night during that final week before Anna left for school. But the little girl remained still and silent each night until her mother departed – and they never once spoke about it, either then or later.

Once at the school, Anna developed night terrors and would wake sobbing from her sleep, clutching her pillow for comfort, terrified by the dreams that had woken her, but even more afraid of the reaction that awaited her from the lady into whose pastoral care she had been placed. Woken by Anna's weeping, this woman would enter the dormitory angry and scowling and drag the little girl by one arm into her room. There she would be thoroughly reprimanded for her selfishness in waking the other girls and spanked for her naughtiness before being returned to bed. In the morning, the mattress would again be wet, but this time not with the little girl's tears. Again she would be spanked, told off in front of the other girls and the mattress hung in the playground to dry, where it would remain throughout the children's breaks for all to see. Needless to say, whose mattress it was could not be kept a secret and Anna's trauma, leaked unknowingly from her body whilst she slept, would be flaunted before the entire school, and frequently mocked.

Anna's story, related to her contemporaries almost thirty years after the events had taken place, was greeted with stunned silence. Probably, some present had joined in the mockery at the time, blind then to the humiliation in which they had participated, now chastened by the cruelty of their ignorance. The bedwetting was to be expected, and Anna was far from being alone in her martyrdom to this particular symptom of her distress. But it was the behaviour of the adult that was really shocking. That a Christian woman, called to serve God and willing to travel halfway around the world in order to do so (if she had been called and not just co-opted) should display such a lack of empathy, even of basic sensitivity, as to punish a child for having a nightmare and then beat her again when she wet the bed was genuinely shocking.

> Children have virtually no capacity for biological self-regulation; their internal biological states – heart rates, hormone levels, nervous system activity – depend completely on their relationship with caregiving grown-ups. *Gabor Maté* (1)

Anna herself was more generous in her assessment of her experience. Aware of the shortcomings in the mission's staffing policy for their school, she speculated that probably the woman concerned had not been called to her role and lacked any real training or experience in carrying it out. She did not blame the person so much as the system that had failed the missionary almost as much as the child in her care. She deplored the presumption that being a Christian was sufficient qualification to place someone at a school where the physical, emotional and spiritual welfare of a number of children would be their personal responsibility. And she lamented the complacency and lack of awareness that allowed such a person to remain in her position despite the very visible signs that she was not equipped for the post and that her children, far from being cared for, were suffering under her auspices.

One of her audience remarked, 'That's why I am not a Christian. If being a believer still allows you to treat children like that, I want nothing to do with it.' But Anna had her own take on her experience, concluding, 'I felt like that as well to begin with. But I came to see that who this woman was is not who Jesus is and I should not judge Him by her witness. I didn't want to throw out God's baby with her bathwater. And I'm glad I didn't, because God has proved Himself to be loving and compassionate and faithful to me in ways that she never could have been and simply didn't understand.' Such is grace.

Father, But Not Far Enough

The issue of the number of children born to missionaries who have been lost to Christ because of their childhood experiences at the hands of missions who prioritised evangelism over the care of their own children is the elephant in the room when reflecting on an otherwise largely worthy history. It is a legacy of trauma born of bad theology, insensitive and often heavy-handed pastoring and, frankly, a distorted image of who God is and what he requires of His followers. The same can be said of many in full-time ministry at home.

> Only two things can cause parents to forsake a child: the necessity of love for the child's sake or the demands of freedom for the parents' own sake. *Brad Jersak* (1)

The freedom that parents sought, or at least, in many cases, missions sought on the parents' behalf, was the freedom to carry out their mission work unencumbered by the responsibility of caring for their children. There was a certain irrefutable logic to this, if only in human or commercial terms. From the missions' point of view, the value of a married couple who had committed themselves to working with them overseas was beyond measuring – and the investment that missions made in them as assets, to put it bluntly, was incalculable. Very often, a couple might be the only missionaries in quite a large area so, technically, the only Christian witnesses available to several hundred thousand people. It was quite simply not reasonable to place a couple into such a situation and then write off fifty per cent of that asset to childcare, especially when the additional financial investment in training and language study was taken into consideration. It was a waste of valuable resources and it made accepting couples onto the mission field an unaffordable luxury.

But there are two problems with this 'calculation'. The first is that it *is* a calculation – a business equation, and one that omits the possibilities of God redeeming such situations for His purposes. The second is that, as has been previously mentioned, in many of the cultures in which missionaries were working, foreigners coming into the community to share the message of a God of love and then sending their children away did not attract the members of that community to God, it repelled and appalled them.

I once asked a church leader in Asia what the response had been within his community when they saw missionaries coming to them preaching about a God of love and then sending their children away to boarding schools for such long periods. His answer struck at the heart of the mission's policies. 'To be honest, it was a rank bad witness,' he said. 'We would never do such a thing in our culture and it probably set back the cause of evangelism twenty or thirty years in our country.' This from a man who had worked humbly and loyally hand in glove with just such a mission for almost half a century. His support of and dedication to the work of that mission was undeniable; his judgment of the damage they had done by their failure to match their lives to their message, unequivocal.

It was never God's intention that we survey the wondrous cross one-eyed. Serving God is an eyes wide open calling. If we have good news to share, then the power of that good news lies first in the way that we example it in our lives, not in the words we speak or the literature we hand out. In many nations, there is no greater witness than that of a loving family, caring for and nurturing its children, demonstrating the fatherhood of God in a way that is irresistible and, in its own way, makes words superfluous.

Imagine receiving a letter telling you that you had been left a luxury, five-bedroomed house in ten acres of land with a swimming pool and private vineyard attached and all you had to do was take up occupancy and it would be yours for life, only to discover that it was built near the summit of Vesuvius. The initial excitement and appeal would be rapidly counteracted by the disappointment experienced in discovering that the best news ever was actually attended by a risk so substantial that it went against all your wisdom and best instincts, and was therefore beyond reasonable consideration. That is what many felt when faced with missionary families who preached love but seemed completely unable to understand that breaking up their families and sending their children away into the care of complete strangers was an offence to local culture and traditions, and a violation of the very virtues and beliefs of which these people spoke. This blatant double standard on the part of westerners in African, Asian and South American nations, in particular, was viewed with deep suspicion of the kind described by Jomo Kenyatta, President of Kenya for almost fifteen years in the 1960s and '70s, who famously said:

> When the missionaries came to Africa they had the Bible and we had the land. They said, 'Let us pray.' We closed our eyes. When we opened them, we had the Bible and they had the land. (2)

Obviously, Kenyatta's comment is targeting the inherent hypocrisy in the kind of mission work that was seen on occasions to be a Trojan horse for colonial land grabs, to which Kenya was undoubtedly subject once its natural assets were uncovered, rather than the double standards of its spiritual message. But hypocrisy and double standards are what they are, whatever their context, and the point is well made. The actions of the messenger that contradicted the words of the message were inevitably the source of mistrust faced by many missionaries in the communities to which they were sent. And if you can't trust the messenger, you won't trust the message.

> You have to trust the messenger before you can trust the message, and that seems to be the Jesus Christ strategy. Too often, we have substituted the messenger for the message. As a result, we have spent a great deal of time worshipping the messenger and trying to get other people to do the same. Too often, this obsession became a pious substitute for actually following what He taught – and He did ask us several times to follow Him, and never once to worship Him. *Richard Rohr* (3)

Did some missions lose sight of the message in amongst their pride and enthusiasm for the work? It would not be surprising if, for some at least, the certainty that they were 'doing a good thing,' maybe even 'doing the greatest thing,' in being obedient to the call of God clouded their objectivity as to the means and consequences of certain aspects of that work. The perception that being a missionary is the ultimate vocation in the service of God and that, as such, missionaries are beyond criticism or reproach was a discernible one in some quarters. If that led to a degree of complacency when it came to any form of self-assessment regarding the logistics and outworking of mission policy, that would perhaps be understandable.

But, the fact is, it did not seem to occur to most mission leaders that what they were asking of their members was contrary to the teachings they so keenly communicated; and the objects of their missionary enterprise, the local people themselves, were far too polite and deferential in most cases to point out the extent of the discrepancy.

> Preaching means more than handing over a tradition; it is rather the careful and sensitive articulation of what is happening in the community so that those who listen can say: 'You say what I suspected, you express what I vaguely felt, you bring to the fore what I fearfully kept in the back of my mind. Yes, yes – you say who we are, you recognise our condition.' *Henri Nouwen* (4)

Of course, every mission throughout history can point to its successes, be they measured in terms of converts, church plants or enduring Christian communities that continue to thrive today. That all of these societies did what they felt called to do, for better or worse, cannot be doubted. Unfortunately, it is also true that they did not serve their children well and many of those children suffered hugely; and for most if not all of their lives as a result, they were unable to share the faith of their parents, and were traumatised to the point of clinical depression, profound dysfunctionality in their relationships and even suicide.

In part, this was because, like Jephthah, missions compounded the original felony of early childhood separation when these children reached secondary school age. Up to that point, most had at least been schooled in an institution founded by the mission for the express purpose of educating the children of its own missionaries. Now, these same children were returned home to complete their schooling; driven into exile, separated from their families not just by a few hundred miles, but by several thousand, two or three continents and multiple time zones, sometimes for more than a year at a time. For many, this was the straw that broke the camel's back.

> Even when not mistreated, being left in the care of strangers is traumatic .... A shell is formed to protect the vulnerable self from emotion that cannot be processed. Whilst appearing to conform to the system, a form of unconscious splitting is acquired as a means of keeping the true self hidden .... The child then makes no emotional demands but also no longer recognises the need for intimacy. The self begins to become inaccessible. *Joy Schaverien* (5)

Herein lies one of the hidden tragedies of the MKs' experience. By failing to understand the true nature of who God is, missions created a situation for their members' children in which they were unable to discover the true nature of who *they* were, their identities hidden beneath a mask of pretence necessary for them to survive in an alien and unsafe environment. We will explore this, together with the particular traumas and abuses of the secondary school experience, later. For now, we must uncover the remaining element that underpinned the theology of missions in the past which disguised for them the full nature of the God of relationship, love and compassion in whom they believed, but whom they perhaps did not fully know, even to the extent that such a knowledge is possible to obtain in this life. (I say this from a heart of pain and grief rather than one of judgment, for none of us can know what we do not know until that thing is made known to us.)

That element is contained in the doctrine of penal substitutionary atonement – the concept that the death of Jesus in place of us was also Him receiving the punishment that was due to us and that God, in His wrath, abandoned Jesus to His suffering on the cross. I do not propose to outline that doctrine here, since it has been well discussed in many other places by many who are better qualified than I to explain its intricacies. Suffice it to say that I believe the Bible is clear that Jesus died the death that we deserve for our sins, even though He Himself was sinless, and therefore His death was indeed substitutionary. Where the predominant interpretation of penal substitutionary atonement undermines or distorts the truth of the character of God is when the death of Jesus is seen as something God required in order to satisfy His wrath and need for vengeance, rather than the most wonderful offering to us from the Father and the Son of love and grace mutually given. In other words, Jesus's death was not something that was required by an angry and vengeful Father, but something that we, mankind, required out of our own thirst for vengeance and violence. As Brian Zahnd has put it:

> Jesus sacrificed Himself to the love of God manifest in forgiveness, not to the wrath of God for the satisfaction of vengeance. It was not God who required the violent death of Jesus but human civilization.(6)

Richard Rohr sums up the problem that exists within this theory.

> Why would God need a "blood sacrifice" before God could love what God had created? Is God that needy, unloving, rule-bound, and unforgiving? Once you say it, you see it creates a nonsensical theological notion that is very hard to defend. What would God ask of me if God demands violent blood sacrifice from God's only Son? A violent theory of redemption legitimated punitive and violent problem-solving all the way down— from papacy to parenting. *Richard Rohr* (7)

Bringing up children to believe that they were 'sinners in the hands of an angry God,' as the 18th century revivalist and preacher Jonathan Edwards famously put it, was to so distort the truth of the loving Father, who they needed more than ever, as to destroy not only their hope and faith that there might be someone somewhere who would love them and not abandon them, but also to destroy any lingering hope that they might be lovable in themselves. After all, since these children understood themselves to have been abandoned by their earthly fathers in the name of a loving God, all that remained was that this God might love them in the ways they wanted their human parents to love them. Instead, what they were given was an image of a God who had abandoned His son to a violent and cruel death and then turned away in disgust because He was too holy to look upon sin. So distorted and one-sided was this presentation of a judgmental God who was angry with our sin, over against a loving God whose wrath was the manifestation of His desire to restore us back into relationship with Him, that I vividly recall being taught to memorise Romans 3:23, 'All have sinned and fall short of God's glory', and only much later discovering, to my surprise, the following verse that continued that same sentence, 'and all are justified freely by His grace through the redemption that came by Christ Jesus.' So, perhaps it is not surprising that the reaction of many of these children was as William Paul Young once described it in an online discussion about his book *Lies We Believe About God*:

> The God that I grew up with, I couldn't trust Him. Anybody that would beat the hell out of his own son to be right with other people .... How can you trust someone who you don't know loves you? (8)

Once again, the children of those messengers of the gospel who were sufficiently dedicated to its propagation to leave homes and families for its sake, though taught at their mother's knee that God is love and He will love, protect and guide them through the time of separation, are also presented with an image of a God whose first thought is to judge and punish them. In effect, to threaten to send them away from His love, just as their fathers had done. A God who is too holy to look at us, who abandons, then turns away from the suffering of His Son in His darkest hour and leaves Him to die alone and in agony. This is difficult enough to contend with for an adult; but for a child still at primary school, an impossible circle to square and one which left many MKs bewildered, frustrated and, ultimately, quite unable to take up the faith of their parents. Thus, the missions' ledger of souls won for Christ did not stand alone, but alongside a debit column listing the names of these missionaries' children, who had turned their backs on this apparently unfeeling God, overcome with cynicism and resentment, wounded, sometimes fatally, by the contradiction they recognised in the teaching they received. As one former MK has written:

> How could we believe in a God who allows the best man that ever lived to be hounded to death on a cross? Is that all that God cares about our humanity and its search after God, after truth and righteousness and peace? Put Jesus Christ a man on the cross, and put God in heaven, like some distant god imprisoned in his own lonely, abstract deity, and you cannot believe in him, in a god such that he is monstrously unconcerned with our life, and who does not even lift a finger to help Jesus. *TF Torrance* (9)

The mindset that led many mission leaders to value suffering and sacrifice over love and compassion led them to present God with the same unbalanced nature, forgetting that they were created in God's image. Instead, they were creating God in their image, as we are all wont to do at times. That mixture of distorted priorities and an interpretation of Scripture that, in their minds, supported their position was a lethal cocktail that poisoned the hearts and minds of their children.

The issue of God abandoning Jesus on the cross because He was too holy to look on the sin that Jesus was taking on Himself is a classic example of the dangers of a literal interpretation of Scripture. The idea of God being unable to look on our sin comes from a single verse in Habakkuk 1, where we read, 'Your eyes are too pure to look on evil.' Taken in isolation and out of context, this gave some theologians cause to declare that God had abandoned Jesus on the cross for this very reason. Jesus was taking upon Himself the sins of the world, as prophesied in Isaiah 53:6. '[A]nd the Lord has laid on Him the iniquity of us all.' The trouble is, we cannot take any Scripture in isolation and hope to understand it properly. Context is everything, whether it is the context of the passage, as with this verse in Habakkuk, or the context of the whole of Scripture and what it teaches us about the nature and character of God. The full quote, in Habakkuk 1:13, goes like this.

> Your eyes are too pure to look on evil; you cannot tolerate wrongdoing. Why then do you tolerate the treacherous? Why are you silent while the wicked swallow up those more righteous than themselves?

The whole of this passage, like Psalm 37, is discussing why the wicked prosper, and why God does not seem to judge them now for their evil ways. It is the prophet's complaint to God that He does not seem to act when people behave in evil ways, but lets them go unpunished. But he is not declaring that God's eyes 'are too pure to look on evil.' His statement is rhetorical sarcasm, if you like. And he goes on to affirm that God sees the treachery and wickedness of these people, so clearly He does look on their evil; He just isn't doing anything about it. Habakkuk's complaint might be paraphrased thus:

'So, you are too holy to look at man's sin, are you? But you know it's going on, so why do you tolerate it? You see this treachery, this wickedness, so you must be looking at it. But why are you putting up with it? Why are you letting them get away with it?'

A similarly literal interpretation of Jesus's words on the cross, 'My God, my God, why have you abandoned me?', added fuel to this particular fire. Jesus had declared from His own mouth that God had abandoned Him, therefore God must have been absent from the events of the crucifixion, must have turned away and left His Son to suffer and die alone.

No! Emphatically not! For two very clear and important reasons.

Firstly, we know that God is love. Not that He loves, but that He *is* love. Therefore, He cannot *not* love. He *is* love. It is His nature, the very essence of His being. It is what moved Him to create us – so that He could love us and be in relationship with us. He existed in relationship with the Son and the Spirit before the creation of the world, as we see from Genesis 1 and as is affirmed in John 1, where John asserts that Jesus, the Word, was with God in the beginning. He was with God and He was God. And the Spirit brooded over the face of the deep. There it is – Father, Son and Spirit – the Trinity, already present and in relationship with each other, and creating man to be in relationship with them/Him. The whole of Scripture thereafter is about God's ceaseless efforts to bring us into the fulness of that relationship and mankind's resistance to those efforts. It is the unstated but intrinsically implicit truth of who God is that He is that relationship, because He is love. Therefore, there is no part of God that is capable of turning His back on His beloved Son at the point of that Son's greatest torment and suffering. It just could not and did not happen. The Mirror Bible translation of 2 Corinthians 5:19 puts it this way:

> God was present in Christ when He reconciled the total cosmos to Himself.

God was *in* Christ. He was not absent from Him. He had not abandoned Him. Jesus Himself had said, as recorded in John 16:32:

> You will leave me all alone. Yet I am not alone because my Father is with me.

In effect, He is telling His disciples, 'It's going to look and maybe even sound like even my Father has left me. But that won't be the truth.' Why not? Because His Father *is* love. He is not capable of abandoning His Son. That's not who He is.

So, why did Jesus indicate from the cross that God had abandoned Him? Did He not mean what He said? Why would He say something that wasn't true? Why would He say something that could be so badly misunderstood?

If I said to you, 'Jingle bells, jingle bells' you are likely to hear in your own mind what follows: 'jingle all the way.' It's a well-known song and someone quoting the opening line to us triggers our memory of what follows. When Jesus said, 'My God, my God, why have you abandoned me?' he was, in effect, quoting the opening line of a well-known song. A psalm, actually – Psalm 22 – which is a stunningly accurate prophetic poem describing not just some of the actual events of the crucifixion of Jesus, but also the physical effects on the one being crucified. (Notwithstanding the fact that Jesus is presented as speaking this line in Aramaic, though it was written in Hebrew, I believe its origin would have been clear to his listeners.) A thousand years before Christ, and six hundred years before crucifixion was even invented, David itemises the specific tortures produced by this most barbaric form of execution. Jesus must have read it from behind the sofa! It was for Him then as it is for us now – a graphic and detailed representation of what He was going to suffer.

Season two, episode four of Dallas Jenkins' epic TV film masterpiece, *The Chosen*, shows Jesus passing by a scene of crucifixion as He enters Jerusalem one day, pausing to look up into the faces of the men hanging there. Nothing is said, but Jonathan Roumie, as Jesus, conveys masterfully the thoughts that must have assailed Jesus on the many occasions that He witnessed such a spectacle. 'That will be me one day.'

So, Jesus is not literally asking why God has abandoned Him. He quotes the opening line of this psalm in order to communicate two things. He knows that those listening will recognise the words and that in quoting them, He will trigger their memories of what follows. He is telling them, 'All this was prophesied. This is not a mistake. This is not a surprise. God knew and I knew that this was going to happen and it is all part of our plan of salvation.' His words were not meant to discourage those who heard them, because their response was not meant to be, 'Oh, no – He has lost His faith and this is the end.' Their response was meant to be to recall the words of the psalm that followed His cry and sing them through to the point where it says in verse 24:

> *For He has not despised or scorned the suffering of the afflicted one; He has not hidden His face from Him but has listened to His cry for help.*

On one level, this is not a cry of despair, but one of triumph! 'He has not hidden His face from Him, but has listened to His cry for help!' Herein lies the first hint of the victory that will come out of this apparent disaster.

Of course, there is an important dimension of truth in His words; one that is crucial for us to understand, and this is the second reason why Jesus quotes this Scripture. For Jesus wanted us to know that, in His humanity, it *felt* like God had abandoned Him, just as it frequently does for us. It was vital for Jesus that He communicate to us that He knew what it meant to be truly human and feel like God was not there for Him. If we thought for one moment that the crucifixion was somehow not as awful as it actually was for Jesus, because of the divine aspect of his nature, its importance would be substantially diminished. We would be able to say, 'Oh, it wasn't so bad. He was God, so He didn't really suffer as a normal human being would.' But the pain of feeling that He was separated from God was far greater than the physical pain, agonising as that was. The enemy is all about separating us from God, because that makes us doubt God's goodness, and that in turn threatens our faith. And Jesus knew the pain of separation. But, at the same time, He knew that when He triggered the memory of the full lyric of the psalm, it would contain these words that tell us that, even though He felt as if God was not there with Him, in actuality, God had not hidden His face … but had listened to His cry for help.

Scripture tells us that there is nothing we experience in this life that Jesus did not also identify with and recognise from His own time on earth. (Hebrews 4:15, 'We do not have a high priest who is unable to empathise with us in our weakness, but one who was tempted in every way, just as we are, yet He did not sin.') That's really important for us to know; and this is Jesus telling us that when we feel like God isn't there and we are screaming into the darkness and receiving only silence in return, He gets it.

So, this is a really important example of why we shouldn't take verses of Scripture singly, literally or out of context. Jesus's words from the cross suggest one thing in isolation, but once we apply our knowledge of Psalm 22 and place both into the bigger picture of whom we know God to be as One who *is* love and *is* relationship, we can see that He was intending us to understand not one, but two separate truths, one of which is completely the opposite of the literal meaning we might read into His words at first glance. It is also why the ideas that God required the sacrifice of Jesus, as opposed to it being Their agreed plan of salvation from the beginning, that God was punishing Jesus in our place, as opposed to putting an end to all sacrifice, and that the Father turned His face away and abandoned Jesus to His fate, are a distortion of the truth. The theory of penal substitutionary atonement ignores, or at least forgets, Jesus's own words in John 10:17 and 18.

> The reason my Father loves me is that I lay down my life – only to take it up again. No-one takes it from me, but I lay it down of my own accord. I have authority to lay it down and authority to take it up again.

'No-one takes it from me.' That 'no-one' includes the Father. The cross is not about God taking the life of Jesus. The cross is about Jesus laying down His life in agreement with the Father. 'I have authority to lay it down.' Jesus is saying, 'Guys, you need to understand that we talked about this, Abba and I. Don't imagine that this is the Romans or the Jews or the Father or anyone else taking my life from me. I am laying it down of my own accord. I have authority, permission from my Father to do this, and this is why He loves me.'

> The fact is that the cross isn't a form of cosmic child abuse – a vengeful Father punishing His Son for an offence He has not even committed. Understandably, both people inside and outside of the church have found this twisted version of events morally dubious and a huge barrier to faith. Deeper than that, however, is that such a concept stands in total contradiction to the statement, "God is love." If the cross is a personal act of violence perpetrated by God towards humankind but borne by His Son, then it makes a mockery of Jesus's own teaching to love your enemies and to refuse to pay evil with evil. The truth is, the cross is a symbol of love. It is a demonstration of just how far God as Father and Jesus as His Son are prepared to go to prove that love. *Steve Chalke* (10)

This is the truth that we need to hear and understand, that MKs who felt abandoned by their parents needed to be told. I remember the day when, sitting in a beautiful garden near my childhood home and reflecting on my schooldays, I realised for the first time that the truth was not that my parents hadn't loved me, but that it had *felt* like they didn't love me. And the same was true of God – it wasn't that He was not there with me in my grief and pain, but that it *felt* like He was not there. Jesus wanted us to understand this and that was why He spoke the words of Psalm 22 from the cross. Yet, somehow, through an already distorted vision of who God is, allied to a failure to understand the need to reconcile the truth of who the Son is with the truth of who the Father is, a quite opposite conclusion was reached. This was conveyed to children who desperately needed the assurance that Jesus had always intended we know.

> The God whom Jesus revealed as no longer our rival, no longer threatening and vengeful, but unconditionally loving and forgiving, who needed no satisfaction by blood – this God of infinite mercy was metamorphosed by the church into the image of a wrathful God of unequalled violence, since God not only allegedly demands the blood of the victim who is closest and most precious to Him, but also holds the whole of humanity accountable for a death that God both anticipated and required. Against such an image of God, the revolt of atheism is an act of pure religion. *Walter Wink* (11)

So, many children of Christian missionaries were told of the God of love and that He was their Father – but the message did not go far enough. All they knew of fatherhood at five years old was that their often mostly absent earthly father had sent them away in the name of the God he wanted them to know as their Heavenly Father. The message they received was not, 'Here is someone who will love and protect you and be with you in every situation,' even when that was exactly what they were told, but, 'Here's the guy who asked us to send you away, so He will likely do the same because that's what fathers do.' Unable to rationalise or process their extreme feelings of abandonment, rejection and despair, they had no other place to go in their minds. Even when the child was well-loved and cared for at home, which almost all were, this only exacerbated their sense of bewilderment. The more loved a child felt in their early years at home, the less able they were to understand why they had now been sent away.

Even then, it must be conceded that, for many children, the distress was so deep-rooted that they were completely unaware of the coping strategies and survival techniques they employed at the time, which we will examine later. For some, it was only when they reached midlife, having accepted much, maybe even all, of what happened to them and having supported the justification their parents had given them that they began to realise how unhappy they were and where the root of that unhappiness lay.

> The … child who perceives that his needs are unmet may develop an obsessive coping style, anxious about every detail. When such a person fears that he is unable to control events, he experiences great stress. Unconsciously he believes that only by controlling every aspect of his life and environment will he be able to ensure the satisfaction of his needs. As he grows older, others will resent him and he will come to dislike himself for what was originally a desperate response to emotional deprivation. The drive to control is not an innate trait but a coping style. *Gabor Maté* (12)

Meanwhile, the damage had been done, caused not by deliberate neglect – though neglect it certainly was on one level – but by an acceptance of the literal meaning of some Scriptures, taken in isolation and out of context, and devoid of any critical thinking. It was a view of God that mainlined on the Old Testament presentation of an angry, violent and judgmental God and underplayed the significance of the New Testament assertion, backed up by the evidence of His teaching and ministry, that Jesus was 'the radiance of God's glory and the exact representation of His being.'

> Columnist Matt Miller wrote ironically of Evangelicals' take on John 3:16. Their all-time most quoted Bible verse: "For God so loved the world that he temporarily died to save it from himself. But none of that really matters because most people will be tortured for eternity anyways." *Wayne Northey* (13)

Danny's Story

If there was one thing you learnt growing up as the child of missionaries and going to an exclusively Christian school, it was the difference between right and wrong. It was drummed into you from an early age – this is good, this is bad, always behave like this, never behave like that. So by the time Danny was fourteen he had no doubts about how adults, and his parents in particular, expected him to behave, despite the fact that those parents were now 10,000 miles away and hadn't been meaningfully involved in his life for four years.

But, for Danny, being good had profited him nothing, so far as he could see. He had been as good as he had known how for as long as he had been alive, but it hadn't prevented his parents from sending him away to school at five years old, nor, at ten, compounding that betrayal by returning him stateside whilst they remained on the field. Now, he lived in what was to all intents and purposes a children's home, cared for by an elderly couple who had their own grown-up children, and attending a school in which he stuck out like a sore thumb – his clothes, his accent, his whole demeanour suggesting another time, another place; an apparently irresistible invitation to mockery and bullying.

Danny didn't have many clothes – his parents couldn't afford many, and certainly nothing that might remotely pass for trendy or fashionable – but he had chosen his favourite outfit for his first day at high school, only to discover that it was so dated, its fabric cheap and flimsy, its design so 'last decade' that he became an immediate target for ridicule and humiliation; as if he needed any further undermining of his already fragile confidence. Danny hadn't thought that his feelings of despair about his life could plumb further depths, but that first day at his new school soon disabused him of that notion. It seemed there was still some considerable way to go.

What Danny endured during that first term was something he never spoke about. He was a bright lad and lessons were OK. But breaks were an unceasing torment and, despite his best efforts to fit in, it seemed he was just too different to be accepted by the other children, entrenched as they were in the culture and traditions of their small, rural Texan community.

But even that was not the worst of it for Danny. As if being at school during the day was not bad enough, returning to the hostel of an evening exacerbated the hollow and empty nature of his situation. Coming home after the school day was meant to be a joy, a comfort, a returning to a safe place in which he could unburden himself of the terrors of the day, be affirmed in his value as a person, distracted from the rejections and insults of his classmates and encouraged for the morrow. On the very small number of occasions that he had been able to return home to his parents after school – and these were very few indeed, confined to a few weeks during a furlough – his mom had always been ready with a glass of milk and a cookie, asked him how his day had been, given him time to play before settling him down to his homework and preparing his favourite meals. And at bedtime, she had held him close whilst she read him a story, smoothed her hand over his forehead as she prayed with him and listened to his tales of the day as he finally shared those things that had troubled him, giving them to her to make good. She would tell him he had been brave and he was 'one of the good guys,' as she always put it, and everything would look better in the morning. It was a resetting of his equilibrium that allowed him to start each new day with a restored sense of self-worth and a new hope for what lay ahead.

But his mom was not there anymore. And the hostel house-parents had too many children and too much to do running the home to give him the kind of personal attention he had received as a pre-teen. It was not even a safe place. Once, he had confided in the house-mother that he was being bullied at school, but she had told him to be strong for his parents' sake. She had even forbidden him to tell them in his weekly letters home. 'You can't go upsetting them and distracting them from their work,' she had said. He knew then that his letters home were read for any content that might reveal the extent of his unhappiness.

Anyway, once he had turned sixteen, he had not been of a mind to confide anything to anyone. He had been forced to find his own way through life and had known for some years now that no-one was really going to help him through. He had faced everything alone – separation, loneliness, rejection, bullying, puberty – with no-one he could trust to answer his questions about his changing body and only playground gossip to fall back on in understanding the hormonal chaos that raged rampantly through him.

But now his parents were due to return, and there was at last some light at the end of the tunnel. It was only for a year of furlough, but it would at least be twelve months of respite from the hostel – maybe even the school – since his family would be living near his grandparents in Iowa. Such hope as Danny allowed himself, which was not a great deal, since he was conditioned to expect disappointment by now, gave him the courage to endure the dreadful present on the promise of a brighter future, albeit only for a while. And then the blow fell.

A letter arrived from his father, not addressed to him but to his house-parents, reporting that there was a staffing crisis on the field and his parents would not return as planned; perhaps not for another year. That was the moment the anger came and took up residence. Accustomed as Danny was to dealing with life alone, this final confirmation that he was so low down on his parents' list of priorities that they would even forego returning home and taking him back into the family was too much. The little boy in him wanted to cry as he had never cried. The adult he had been forced to become some years ago now simply sank down into the well of darkness from which he had long been forced to drink … and died.

When Larry came into his life a few weeks later, he brought with him beer and some pills that he assured Danny would make him feel better. The distraught teenager was now too careless of his own life to even ask what they were. And they worked – for a while. But then, quite suddenly, they were not enough and Danny craved something more. So Larry introduced him to Brad.

> Whatever the degree of injury, all addiction is a kind of refugee story: from intolerable feelings incurred through adversity and never processed, and into a state of temporary freedom, even if illusory. Gabor Maté (1)

There is no need for me to describe the remainder of Danny's life, suffice it to say that he spent most of it curled up on the floor of a derelict house in a pool of his own vomit wishing only for the end, which was all he had the strength to hope for now. When the phone call finally came to the hostel from the police, it might have been the smallest comfort to know that Danny was now free from his misery, if it had not been such a surprise. In fact, it was a huge shock, as if those who cared for Danny, and those who had passed his care into the hands of strangers half a world away, were completely unaware of his pain – as indeed they were, of course. They had no idea – because Danny had always had to cope alone, his survival almost entirely dependent upon the strength of his own resources. He had never confided his distress to anyone, because there was no-one to hear it. His parents were not there, his hostel parents did not want his parents upset from so far away, so they never asked, and anyway they had other children to care for. Even in primary school, his letters home had been censored for anything smacking of homesickness or any indication that he was unhappy. So he had put on a brave face, pretending he was coping, hiding his despair even from his friends, because he didn't want to be revealed as the only child who wasn't actually coping. And, since everyone else was doing the same, Danny really thought he was the only one that was bad, ungrateful, weak and – that heaviest of burdens – unlovable.

Danny never did find the faith of his parents. He never even understood it. They talked about God as a Father of love who wanted him to be sent away, which simply didn't add up. Then his earthly father, loving as he had been when he was actually around, had sent him off to school, away from that love, and that didn't add up either. What was all this love that it caused so much pain and loneliness? Who was this God that He showed His love by dividing families and taking children away from the safety and affection of their parents? Why would Danny want to believe in a God like that? It sounded more like a devil to the bewildered teenager, even though he had struggled against his feelings of rebellion for so long.

Danny's parents returned from the field, but they were too late to save their son. Too late, even, to save their own faith, once they realised how their actions had been responsible for their son's death. And so, the beliefs that had motivated them to spread the message of love and forgiveness to a people unaware of their need for God had turned full circle to become a life bereft of the love their child needed, all for God and too little for Danny, ultimately characterised by their inability to forgive themselves. In the midst of life, they had been in death, loving their God not wisely but too well, sacrificing their son on the altar of their service by offering him to God in a way and to an extent that God had never required. Such is the Jephthah Inheritance.

> Cannabis isn't a gateway drug. Alcohol isn't a gateway drug. Nicotine isn't a gateway drug. Trauma is the gateway. Child abuse is the gateway. Molestation is the gateway. Neglect is the gateway. Drug abuse, violent behaviour, hyper-sexuality and self-harm are often symptoms (not the cause) of much bigger issues. And it almost always stems from a childhood filled with trauma, absent parents and an abusive family. *Russell Brand* (2)

Laid upon the Altar

Hindsight is a wonderful thing. We have already reflected on the truth that many of the consequences of the MKs' childhood experiences were beyond any level of damage that the leadership could have been expected to anticipate, even if some may have understood them, and others might at least have anticipated them. Child psychology was either not yet a concept or in its infancy; indeed, the whole area of psychology was viewed in Christian circles with more than a little suspicion and was liable often to be dismissed, as we saw earlier.

It should also be understood that, even as the 20th century entered its second half, there was still an element of 'children should be seen and not heard' that remained embedded in the attitude of the middle and higher echelons of society from which many missionaries were drawn, and so the idea that children might have some intrinsic needs that required careful nurture and sensitive handling was alien to many. For some in leadership, children were undoubtedly seen as an encumbrance, a distraction from the important work of evangelism and one to be tactfully dispensed with at the earliest possible opportunity. All this, allied to the narrow focus characteristic of the dedicated servant of God, the default leaning towards hardship and sacrifice as essential aspects of Christian service and the tendency at times to read some Scriptures as a reinforcement of one's beliefs rather than a vehicle for transformation and change, and to misinterpret or just plain ignore others, resulted in a heady cocktail that made the marginalising of MKs inevitable, or at least likely in some circles.

So, what were these consequences? This is what we will examine in this chapter. Whilst the focus here is on the extremes of mission work overseas, the same issues, to one degree or another, often affected many of the children of full-time workers at home. The degree is not the issue; a child's suffering is their suffering and comparisons are invidious and unhelpful. None of us needs to prove that our suffering was greater than that of another. Pain is pain is pain; and it hurts whatever the cause. A person's trauma does not cease to be trauma just because it is not actually defined as post-traumatic stress disorder (PTSD). It remains trauma and its distress remains significant to the person concerned.

A Sense of Abandonment

Despite all that he suffered in the school the worst of all for him was the realisation that his mother could leave him. Even as a child he was incredulous that a mother could just leave her child; it was as if this was a taboo – he said 'this just does not happen'. But of course for him and others like him it did. *Joy Schaverien* (1)

It is difficult to describe the sense of abandonment a five-year-old feels when sent away to boarding school for the first time. Most MKs had been well prepared by their parents for the separation, though even to say so is to suggest that such preparation is possible in any meaningful sense, which many would dispute. What I mean by this is that many parents had spoken to their child of the reason they were being sent away, had explained its necessity and gone through the logistical process that would follow. Given that, for some, this would entail a journey of perhaps two or more days and involve a variety of modes of transport over perhaps a thousand miles or more, this was naturally beyond the comprehension of most children of that age; but it made the parents feel better. In an effort to make the prospect more appealing, and in part to salve their own consciences, much stress was placed on the adventure it was all going to be, the fun that would be had, the new friends that would be made and the privilege it was to attend such a wonderful school. (All of this was true, by the way, it just didn't begin to make up for the trauma and anguish that would accompany it.) Keep in mind that what a parent presented to their child as 'an adventure' was often something that in their own mind they equated with significant danger. To top it off, God was then invoked as being both the instigator and redeemer of the process as the child was first of all told that this was something that God required, then promised that He would protect, comfort and nurture them during this time of enforced separation. I do not doubt for a moment that practically every missionary who went through this often well-rehearsed speech believed every word they uttered. And so, of course, did the children. For a while, at least.

But even if the child left for school with a sense of excitement and anticipation, which was certainly true in some cases, there were two aspects of their looming separation that were simply beyond their ability to grasp – distance and time. As has already been mentioned, one determined the other, since the duration and expense of journeys to and from school necessitated that their frequency be limited, often resulting in school years of two terms rather than three. Any half-term break was characterised by only a brief suspension of lessons, replaced by a week of activities, but did not involve the children actually going home at all. Thus, many MKs found themselves separated from their families for upwards of four months – twenty weeks or more at a time.

Young children's concept of time is limited, to say the least. Next week may just about be processable, but something that is going to take place a month away is, in a child's mind, just another version of 'in a few days' time' and so just very far away. For a five-year-old to be told, 'We'll see you in the holidays,' or 'at Christmas,' was utterly meaningless and exacerbated the seemingly endless duration of their abandonment. And abandoned is how they felt – left to cope alone, away from the love, safety and reassuring predictability of family life.

> People often tell us that they remember a pre-boarding school happiness which was irretrievably lost by going away. This can be a personal calamity that affects a person's central sense of self. Some told us how they had to exchange the instinctual

> warmth of life in the colonies for the chill of an English institution. Such losses are deep and can leave an individual with a feeling of being in exile. *Nick Duffell* (2)

The consequences of this feeling of abandonment – and it's important to understand that the crucial aspect of this is not whether the child actually *was* abandoned, but that they *felt* themselves to have been abandoned – included a sense of unlovability, a poor sense of self-worth, a sense that they were bad people, and a determination not to give themselves in love to anyone ever again in order to avoid the pain of separation they were now feeling. For many MKs, this last unspoken and subconscious decision led to a lifetime of relationship failures, due to their inability to commit or their need to end relationships to minimise the pain of what they saw as inevitable – that the other person would end things at some point. One MK, having had this subconscious early childhood process explained to them in midlife told me, 'I never could understand why I got so angry with my husband whenever he went away on business. I would distance myself from him for a week or so before he left and I was really terribly unkind to him. Now I realise that what was happening was that my inner child was responding to the memory of that pain of abandonment from all those years ago and I was trying to protect myself from feeling it all over again.'

A Loss of Security

> Premature separation of the child from the continuum of life means that isolation, alienation and estrangement become the foundations on which the child's emotional life will be based. *Joseph Chilton Pearce* (3)

British psychologist Joseph Bowlby's work on attachment theory in the 1950s and '60s, simply put, proposed that the successful maturing of children from dependence upon their parents into independent adult living is predicated upon their being allowed to perform the process of detachment at their own pace. Children learn to explore by making initially small, but ever-increasing forays into their world knowing that the safety, protection and assurance of a parent is always within reach. For the youngest children, 'within reach' may have a very literal meaning, whereas for the eleven-year-old it may mean having their mum on the end of a phone during their first sleepover, or for a sixteen-year-old having their dad pick them up from their first night shift at a fast food outlet. Important to Bowlby's work is the understanding that if children are forced to detach sooner than they are naturally ready to do, significant damage can occur to their mental wellbeing.

What is actually happening throughout this process is that the child is gauging the level of risk inherent in trying out something new as being inextricably related to their certainty that, should something go wrong, their parents will be present, available and, naturally, willing to rescue them. We have likely all witnessed the kind of scene wherein a toddler stands by its mother, who is deep in conversation with a friend who has a dog with her. The child initially clings to their mother's skirt, but then begins to edge towards the dog, finally reaching out a hand to stroke the animal. Having done so, they run back to take their mother's hand, reassuring themselves of her presence, and understanding that presence to be their place of safety. The child may perform this ritual several times before finally being confident to remain by the dog, having ascertained that their attentions are well-received and the animal poses no threat. Multiply this image and increase the significance of the forays past the point where the child no longer wants to be dropped off at school by a parent and forward to the time when the very idea of a parent still being up when the child returns from their first date is a major embarrassment to them, and you will get an understanding of this process.

When this process of detachment is forced to occur before a child is ready, the child can suffer significant emotional damage. For the MK, this was inevitably the case. Sending a five-year-old away to school, perhaps for four-and-a-half months, was a massive acceleration of the detachment process and removed them from their place of safety, a state they had known all their lives, placing them into a strange and unfamiliar environment where any sense of safety was absent from the outset. Oh, it might be acquired in time, but that time would likely not be soon and, often, it would never happen at all, such was the huge loss of trust suffered by the child as a result of their treatment.

There are three particular points in a child's day when this sense of safety, or lack of it, is crucially emphasised, and needed. (I am indebted to Family Therapist Ulrika Ernvik, herself an MK, for drawing this to my attention.)

First thing in the morning, the child living at home is welcomed into the day, fed, helped to prepare for what lies ahead and taken or waved off to school by a parent. The message the child receives from this is, 'You are loved, you are safe and, whatever the day holds, I will be here for you when you come home and all will be well.'

The boarder, on the other hand, wakes to a dormitory full of other children, has to wash and dress without privacy, file into a noisy dining room for a meal that may or may not be to their liking – and if it isn't they just go hungry, or are forced to eat it anyway – and then they embark on their day, often with a sense of profound anxiety as to what it might hold and how they might cope with it. So, safety and reassurance is replaced by anxiety and fear. (Personally, I cannot overstate the degree of fear that accompanied me at the start of almost every day throughout my fourteen years of boarding school experience.)

The second crucial time comes at the end of the school day. For the child living at home, there is (for most, it is to be hoped) a parent to welcome them back, offer them a drink and a snack, ask them about their day and give them some time to relax and play before settling down to homework, for which the parent will often make themselves available should the child become stuck or just need some encouragement and motivation. The message the child receives is, 'I'm pleased to see you and happy to look after you and bring you a little comfort and joy at the end of your working day. Whatever has happened at school, you are safe now and we can talk through your day if you would like to.' Whether the child avails themselves of this opportunity is not the point. The point is, they know they can discuss any problems faced and seek advice or comfort if it is needed.

But for the MK, there is no smiling face waiting for them once classes are over. Perhaps there are organised sports, which some dread beyond anything else they can conceive, or just a seemingly endless couple of hours before anything else is scheduled; time to be filled, or not; perhaps with friends, perhaps not. But no-one with whom to process the events of the school day or in whom to confide their disappointments and distresses. The process of rebooting the child's confidence, a natural and instinctive feature in the life of the child living in the family home, is missing. And this is not just a daily omission, but an accumulation of stress from one day to the next, since the restored sense of wellbeing available to the child whose parents engage with them at these crucial times simply doesn't happen, can't happen. By bedtime, the child at boarding school can be in a state of high anxiety – and, for many, the worst is yet to come.

Bedtime, then, is the third vital moment in a child's day. This is the point of preparation for sleep, when our brains process and sort through any problems that may have occurred. For a child living at home, it is often a time of comfort and reassurance as they are settled into bed, perhaps read a story, prayed with, sometimes talked through one of the issues of the day that has hurt or confused them, and reassured that everything will be fine and tomorrow is another day. It is a parent's opportunity to gather the youngster under their wing, and the message the child receives is, 'You are safe, I am here, you are loved and cherished and valued. Whatever the problems of the day that has passed, you can start again in the morning with a fresh page on which to write the story of your life.' A reset button has been activated for the child by the parent.

But for the child away at school, it is a time of homesickness and fear. The very fact that what is described above is the norm for many children makes its loss felt even more acutely. Prior to being sent away, without having any conscious awareness that it was so, this process of resetting and reassuring at bedtime was a vital part of the child's sense of security. My own mother would often read me a story, pray with me, stroke my forehead to soothe me towards sleep and speak quietly of the events of the day and our hopes for the morrow. Her absence, added to the onset of darkness, the noises of the jungle from which wild dogs howled and small mammals could be heard scurrying about in the undergrowth by the windows, was a bereavement to me. And the things that had troubled me during the day – the unkind words, the physical abuse, the unfair punishment, the lesson in which I had struggled to understand, the lonely playtime – I had to process alone without any reassuring voice to tell me that I had done my best, I was not naughty for feeling so sad and all would be well in the morning. Neither could I share the good things that may have happened – the friendly word, the star from the teacher for a piece of work well done, the new friend who had played with me after school – all these I had to keep to myself, small gems that were hardly worth the polishing because there was no-one with whom to share them. For children who were afraid of the dark, or for those fearful of punishment who did not want to join in the after-lights-out antics and disobediences of others in the dorm, bedtime could be a daily trauma, an ordeal that was anticipated from late afternoon and was almost always an experience of high stress and anxiety. To add insult to injury, a common principle of discipline was to punish a group of children en masse in the absence of any information that might identify the culprit of any particular infringement of the rules, or of any confession, which was almost never forthcoming. So, many children ended up being regularly punished for the sins of their class or dormmates, thus increasing the sense of fear and injustice that darkened their days and nights.

> Boarding schools don't 'build character' or 'make the man,' they break the child and replace it with a coat of armour filled with fear, loneliness and alienation. *Nick Duffell* (4)

The consequences of this loss of security for a young child are deep and wide-ranging. Fear has entered their world – and it has come to stay. Without the protection and reassurance of their parents, without that safe place to run back to, the child is alone and forced to face everything the world might throw at them by themselves. For an eight- or nine-year-old, this is a terrifying ordeal; for a five-year-old it is quite simply beyond the ability of their undeveloped minds to rationalise or reconcile, and they acquire for themselves a protective shell to minimise the damage that can be done to them. Features of this coping strategy may include emotional numbness, a significant denial of reality, massively suppressed anger and resentment, recourse to dishonesty in order not to reveal the true extent of their pain, physical withdrawal from company (ironically interspersed with periods of desperate attention-seeking), suppression of tears, a distinct lack of interest in eating or maintaining standards of hygiene, sudden and uncharacteristic flashes of anger, overwhelming moments of self-pity, periods of deep depression, cynicism through loss of hope, and self-destructive behaviours. The child's emotional infrastructure has been demolished, the foundations of their security have been undermined and their sources of strength and reassurance have been removed. For an adult, to be thrown upon one's own resources can be an opportunity for growth; but for a young child, who has no resources of their own to speak of, it is an experience that is beyond their ability either to understand or cope with. Thus, any of the survival techniques they employ under these circumstances are likely to be inappropriate. And, because they are entered into subconsciously, they may stay with the child for decades, and sometimes, if unidentified or unaddressed, for the rest of their life.

> I became a strategic person, always on the lookout for danger and how to turn every situation to my best advantage. I still do it. It's exhausting. I don't know how to stop doing it. *Nick Duffell* (5)

A Lack of Self-Worth

> The situation of little children in relation to their parents may be described as one of complete dependence; children are miserable when deprived of the experience of being loved. *Abraham Heschel* (6)

Young children understand things on a very literal level. They don't yet have the tools that will allow them to consider and rationalise, nor do they have any perspective from which to make reasoned judgments. They are de facto practitioners of Occam's Razor – the principle that one should always select the solution with the fewest assumptions, or, as it is sometimes expressed, the simplest and most obvious answer is probably the correct one. So, when seeking an answer to the question, 'Why is my family sending me away?' young children gravitate to the most obvious reply: 'Because they don't want me around anymore.' There are various versions of this: 'I'm not lovable,' 'I've done something very bad,' 'I am not important to them,' 'I am not as important as their work,' but they all amount to the same thing in the child's eyes: 'I am not really wanted.' And, since a further characteristic of children during their early years is that they are very egocentric, so pretty much interpreting everything as revolving around their own needs and desires, there really aren't any alternative answers available to them.

Quite suddenly, the child is torn from an environment of love, security and affirmation into a world in which they are unknown, unloved and, as they unavoidably interpret it, insignificant. The sense of shock is palpable, visceral. It is a classic instance of a child's world being turned upside down. It is mostly not a case of the child actually asking, 'What have I done to deserve this?' but more an instinctive, default understanding that something is wrong or this would not have happened. And what is wrong? They are. 'It must be me,' they reason, 'because my parents are good people and God is a good God, so for something this terrible to have happened to me it can only be because I deserve it; I am bad.'

These thoughts and feelings are so distressing to the child that they resolve to keep their distress a secret. To reveal the extent of their grief would be also to reveal their shame. So they grieve in secret; they cry alone and away from the eyes and ears of their contemporaries, which naturally exacerbates the issue in a very significant and equally damaging way. Because when each child is concealing their pain from the rest, even when everyone is feeling the same as everyone else, they all think they are the only one! If the other children are all going somewhere quiet by themselves to cry, no-one ever sees anyone else crying. So they think, 'Everyone else is coping and I'm the only one who is not,' which naturally adds to their sense of shame and isolation. One of the most commonly heard phrases repeated over and over again at school reunions and conferences of adult MKs is, 'I thought I was the only one!' It is a complete revelation and an inexpressible relief for these folks to finally understand that their experience was shared by their contemporaries.

So, there is a double whammy here. Being sent away significantly reduces a child's sense of self-worth, so huge is the rejection they feel and so inadequate their ability to rationalise their experience. But this is lowered still further once they actually enter the world of pretence and deception in which they conceal their grief from their peers for fear of even further rejection; but, because the other students are doing the same as they are, they inevitably understand themselves to be the only one unable to cope which, in turn, confirms their feeling that they are truly bad, ungrateful children, in some cases even feeling as a result that they deserved to be banished from the family home.

The consequences that follow from this sense of rejection and worthlessness are seriously damaging to both a child's emotional and spiritual wellbeing. To be sent away from the family home, removed from an environment of love and safety, and placed into one of fear and anonymity is devasting in itself. But then to be required to process this alone, to have little or no sense of the shared grieving that could have been such a healing, to be allowed to believe that they were the only child suffering such sadness, and that they were all the worse a person for their inability to cope with the situation was a judgment so harsh as to leave them with lifelong scars gouged across the face of their self-image.

> Our acceptability is always conditional, and every human soul carries the wounds of rejection from not meeting someone's standard. How terrible when that wound is inflicted by a parent, a spouse, a community or a church. Rejection always leaves a wound – not a visible one, but a cut in our souls whose scar we may carry for the remainder of our lives. *Skye Jethani* (7)

There are many aspects of boarding schools that are intrinsically damaging, and the sense of rejection that children receive from the actions of their parents is a clear and obvious one. In a Christian setting, though, the distorted image that this presents of who God is and how His love impacts on our lives multiplies that damage several-fold. For a child to consider that they are not wanted in the family home anymore is one thing; to then take on board the idea that the God whom their parents serve, who has been declared to them as a God of love, justice, compassion and mercy, who actually supports – even initiated – this move, is utterly condemning of them as a person. How is a child meant to maintain any sense of self-worth or inherent dignity when such powerful forces are arrayed against them? Social structures dominate the lives of young children, who recognise when an adult is powerful and, in their eyes, important; almost all of them, then! So, when parents, mission leaders and even God Himself deem something to be good and right, there is no question in the child's mind that their decisions and actions might be anything other than good and right. How could there be? But they are grief-stricken, angry, betrayed, and alone. Such logic as is available to their undeveloped minds tells them that it is they who are wrong, and they are bad people for feeling the way they do. Their self-worth lies in tatters at their feet.

Even more significantly, any trust they might have had or been acquiring in God has now been holed below the waterline. As I once heard the writer William Paul Young express it, 'You want me to run to this God? I don't think so.' It is a mark of the grace of God that many MKs did come through this experience with a faith, some even returning to the mission field, and many retaining that faith throughout their lives. But it is probably also true to say that they all 'walked with a limp.' Each of us must tell our own story.

> If the enemy of our souls can convince us that God has rejected us, is upset with us or has withdrawn from us because of some sin we have committed, he knows we will hide from God and try to live our lives performing well enough to earn His love, thus increasing the depth of our guilt and shame. *Jack Frost* (8)

> When we do not feel loved by those who gave us life, we often suffer our whole life long from a low self-esteem that can easily lead to depression, despair and even suicide. *Henri Nouwen* (9)

Premature Maturation

> I was a child who was forced to confront an adult. I had to take the power position before I should have needed to and before I was ready. I paid for it in fear. *Brene Brown* (10)

Children who are sent or taken away from their families at a very young age become little adults; if not overnight, then over a short period of time. On one level, this is a generalised overstatement, being significantly more true for some children than for others. But, in essence, it is inevitable that when a child is thrown upon its own resources and into an environment where the available adults are detached, often unaware, sometimes uncaring of the child's needs, it becomes an automatic coping strategy, a survival technique for the child to take care of themselves without recourse to those adults.

Most children grow up with an instinctive sense that adults are safe people to be with – bigger, stronger, wiser and able to protect and care for them. This is part of the beautiful innocence that we love in young children. For some MKs, it was a simple enough process for them to transfer this trust onto the strangers into whose care they had been placed. I well remember visiting a mission school as an eighteen-year-old and walking across the playground from the classroom block to the main house. By the time I arrived, a distance of perhaps seventy-five metres, I had acquired two children, one in each hand. I did not know either of them, and they did not know me. They had simply walked up to me, slipped their hands into mine and walked with me for a couple of minutes; innocently trusting to the safety of my company, but also desperate for that sense of adult security, affection and reassurance that they so lacked in the absence of their parents. There were many loving, accessible, nurturing staff at mission schools who acted as surrogate parents and with whom some children developed strong bonds of attachment and affection. These adults were safe places and welcome shelters when loneliness came calling, as it so often did, loudly and persistently.

But these adults were not always around. Another memory is of a staff member at my own school who had always shown me genuine care and affection and whose presence brought me an important sense of safety. But then I learnt that she was returning home the following day for a year of furlough. My sense of betrayal was visceral. I was shocked and confused. Here was someone who had validated me and shown me some of the love I so badly missed due to the separation from my family. And now she was abandoning me too. I was perhaps eight, and my reaction to her leaving was, of course, very selfish and egocentric, disproportionate and quite unreasonable on one level. On another, it was perfectly understandable. I had been sent away by my parents and was still trying to cope with the sense of rejection that the experience had generated within me. In my effort to cope, I had transferred my affections to another, who had fulfilled my need for love and attention, and restored some of my faith in my own lovability. And now she was leaving me too – and without telling me! I was completely devastated, but quite incapable of expressing that emotion. I felt guilty about how I felt, but unable to process that feeling. I certainly wasn't going to share those emotions with anyone, because that would have been to reveal my shame, my weakness, my failure to deal with what my parents had asked of me. Also, it would have been likely to attract mockery and scorn from my contemporaries, who already thought I was a sissy and a cry-baby, though I tried very hard to conceal my tears from them.

> Unsympathetic scorn is just what the survivor fears most. *Nick Duffell* (11)

In such instances, there was no alternative but for the child to 'grow up,' as teachers were fond of saying to some of their more recalcitrant students. If being a child, with all its attendant vulnerabilities and weaknesses, was no longer a bearable option, there was nothing left but to acquire a level of maturity that most children are allowed to grow into, just as most children are allowed to detach themselves from their safe adults at their own pace. MKs were often lauded and admired by adults for their maturity and composure, but the price they paid for it was high. Too high – and it would cost them dearly in later years as they were forced to revisit their childhood issues and fill in some of the gaps.

One aspect of this early maturation was that MKs developed the ability to rationalise their experience. If contemplating the reality of their situation was too shocking for what it revealed about their parents and their parents' God, then resorting to a reasoned and calm defence of their actions at least made the child appear to be toeing the party line, as it were. Even though deep down they might still feel that they were a bad person for being so disturbed by their experience, developing a hard shell of resilience and acquiescence at least gave MKs the appearance of being at peace with the realities of their existence and – of vital importance – stopped parents and school staff from becoming concerned about them. It was a self-defence mechanism that held the world at arms' length and sent the message that the child was coping well and no-one need lift the lid to find out what might be bubbling away underneath. MKs away at boarding school learnt very early on that communicating any degree of unhappiness or homesickness was counter-productive. In the first place, it was likely to bring down the wrath of the school staff upon them, since it reflected badly on the school. But secondly, it only increased the child's despair due to the response from home, which almost always insisted that the parents' decision was for the best and one day the child would realise how blessed they were to have had such a privileged education, or something similar. And so they kept silent, wearing a mask of acceptance, or at least resignation, concealing the true nature of their despair from everyone for fear that its revealing would exacerbate the problem.

> Boarders wear survival masks, the main problem of which is that they were designed when we were young and become less workable, or even counter-productive, as we grow older. *Nick Duffell* (12)

The consequences of a child taking on an adult role before they were ready to do so were, firstly, that a substantial proportion of the essential childhood and growing up experience was removed from the child and, secondly, that they were forced into adopting a kind of character pretence which compromised their true sense of identity. The subject of identity confusion is a major one and merits a discussion of its own, so we will deal with that in due course. For now, we will just consider the issue of a stolen childhood.

Outside of the direct teaching and study environment, children learn through play, mirroring and pushing the boundaries of their existence, and exploring, experimenting and engaging with new ideas and experiences. For the child growing up without the love, assurance and safety of a family around them, in a place where fear, mistrust and grief are their companions and loneliness the soundtrack of their life, all of these are fraught with danger. You see, what lies behind the coping strategy employed when taking on an adult persona whilst still a child is the need to appear capable and in control. The message the child is trying to send to those around them is, 'I understand what is happening here, I'm OK with it, I can justify it and explain it if need be and I don't need any help, thank you very much.' (Of course, inside they are screaming, 'How can this be happening to me?! I hate it beyond my ability to find words and I just need someone to come alongside me, to help and comfort me and let me be a child again! But no-one will!') Indulging in the pursuits of childhood is dangerous because it makes the child intrinsically vulnerable. In fact, just being a child is intrinsically a vulnerable condition. 'Being a child,' the victim reasons, 'is what got me into this trouble in the first place. Someone else was in control and look what happened. If I am going to protect myself from further hurt, I need to be in control myself. So, since it is adults who are in control, I will wear the trappings of adulthood and maybe I will be trusted to live my own life without them interfering anymore.'

In order to achieve this, the child steps back from childish things and, in doing so, misses out on the learning processes necessary to acquire mature adult status. But so desperate are they to control their own lives and attempt to find a degree of emotional equilibrium, most find a way around this and play a very convincing role, often one that is admired and respected by adults. Danica Newton's blog describes her own MK experience and offers advice to parents in helping their own MKs through the experience of transition. She reflects:

> When I was sixteen, I stayed behind in Texas while my parents and younger siblings went back overseas. I remember that time as confusing and dark. But years later, adults who were close to me at the time have told me things like: "You seemed so mature," "You handled it so well," and "We had no idea it was so hard for you, you seemed fine." I seemed fine because at that point I had spent the majority of my childhood in transition. (13)

The tragedy of this forced premature maturation is that the child then goes through the rest of their life reliant on a high level of pretence and self-deceit, without the necessary tools they would have acquired for adulthood had they been able to play and engage with the world fully as children. It works at the time and, to be fair, for many it's what gets them through and allows them to survive without imploding in despair; but it lays up all kinds of troubles for them in the future.

> The boarding school child will endure and do anything to keep the heat off him. By compromising and adapting to ensure his survival. But he seals his self-betrayal.
> *Nick Duffell* (14)

The Removal of Any Sense of Belonging

There is a simple test by which you can find out if a person is a TCK or not. Just ask them where they are from. If they tell you straight out, then they have probably had a normal upbringing. But if they respond with, 'Er … ' or 'How long have you got?' or something similar, then they are probably a TCK. You see, third culture kids don't know where they are from, or where they really belong, because they have lived in so many different places and identify to some extent with all of them. In my own case, I was born in England to English parents, but taken to Singapore before I was a year old, and then on to Malaysia before I was two. So, my first memories are of South-East Asia and I didn't even visit England until I was five, by which time I had lived for nine months in Cambridge, spent another two months living in London, spent three months on board a ship, six months in Singapore, had another four homes in Malaysia and had been sent away to school somewhere else still. I then lived with relatives in England for ten months, returned to a home in Malaysia for another year, went away to school again and then returned to Singapore before being shipped back to England for my secondary education. So, where am I from? Well, it depends on what you mean by 'from.' Where is my home? Well, it depends on what you mean by 'home.' See what I mean?

Of course, this meant that there was an element of interest and adventure in my childhood which made it exciting and something of a privilege. I can certainly credit many of the values and virtues I possess today (such as they may be) with having experienced other peoples and cultures from a very early age and learnt to value them all equally. But there is a downside, because belonging is a very important foundation stone in the house of our personal security. Everyone needs to feel that they belong somewhere and to someone. To belong is to know we have value and identity as a human being and it is the frame of reference through which we look out onto the world around us. Just as importantly, to feel that we don't belong anywhere is a serious undermining of our confidence and identity and can lead to significant mental health issues.

> The absence of love, belonging and connection always leads to suffering. *Brene Brown* (15)

For the young child sent away to boarding school, all vestiges of belonging were stripped away within the first term. Even if they went to school for the first time with some sense of belonging, they quickly came to question it. The very act of being sent away undermined any sense of belonging the young child may have had. 'After all,' they reasoned, 'if home is really where I belong, why have I not been allowed to remain there?' And, after twenty weeks at school, perhaps five hundred miles away from home and with the memory of their mother's face fading with every passing day, is school where they belong now? Do they actually belong anywhere? Does it matter where they belong? All these questions are too specific to actually enter the mind of so young a child, but they linger unspoken in their subconscious and deeply affect their thoughts and sense of personal security.

> Herein lie the roots of trauma. Disconnection from our felt sense of belonging leaves our emotions floundering in a vacuum of loneliness. *Peter Levine* (16)

Belonging is about familiarity, security, safety, and trust. Each of these is either removed or undermined by taking a child away from their home and parents. In time, the school will become familiar and they may even come to love the place, as many MKs did. It may also be a place of security and safety, though this is a realisation that only comes with time and, to begin with, all sense of security and safety has been left at home by the child. Like trust, these things have to be earned. Sadly, for some, their schools were not places of security or safety at all. Some were in areas of terrorist or bandit activity, even civil wars. Occasionally, some staff were abusive or violent, making the school a place of terror and despair. In a Christian context, and given the solidarity with which the necessity of a boarding school education was presented to children by parents, school staff and mission leaders alike as being what God wanted, young children were faced with an apparently united front which meant that when a child encountered an adult who betrayed their trust, there was an assumption that this betrayal was known about and approved of by other adults. This meant there was no-one the child could trust, no-one in whom they could feel safe to confide, so they kept their fear and sadness to themselves, allowing inappropriate behaviour by school staff to go unreported and unchecked, as we will see later in Jerome's story. In some schools, this perception was reinforced by a policy of preventing the children from communicating any sense of unhappiness or reporting matters such as bullying in their letters home. In time, children interpreted this as being part of their own responsibility, obviating the need for censorship of their correspondence, since the children no longer bothered to communicate their distress. After all, there was nothing their parents could do about it, except remove them from the school. They might even have to leave the mission. And this would make the school, the mission and God angry. Such was the burden the child carried when it came to concealing the actuality of their existence.

> If my parents knew what really went on at the school, I used to think (not being the first little boy to imagine that my main job was that of protecting parental innocence), they would faint from the shock. So I would be staunch and defend them from the knowledge. *Christopher Hitchens* (17)

The consequences of growing up with no sense of belonging casts children adrift on the sea of adulthood without either an anchor or a rudder. With no firm idea of where they belong, or to whom, they exist in a permanent state of identity confusion and restlessness, always desiring to move on, as they were forced to do as children, and without any incentive to settle down, or at least any ability to hold onto any such motivation for more than a short while. Because the people they grew to love never stayed with them for more than a few years at most, these children develop a sense of intentional (if subconscious) detachment, a resignation that relationships are only temporary and hardly worthwhile because of the pain of separation that inevitably follows – and all too soon. From this comes an inability to commit and the fear that, whatever someone else may declare in respect of their own commitment, the innately unlovable essence of who the child is means that no relationship will last for more than a few years. Because that is how it has always been.

> Children who never find a place where they feel they belong carry an incapacity for attachment into their adult lives. *Tim Keller* (18)

Significantly, this it also what produces the chameleon effect in MKs; the ability to blend in with their surroundings, to fit in with any group of people by mirroring accent, body language, speech patterns, dress and even behaviour patterns.

> I became an expert fitter-in, a chameleon. And a very lonely stranger to myself. As time passed, I grew to know many of the people around me better than they knew themselves, but in that process I lost me. *Brene Brown* (19)
>
> If I chronically repress my emotional needs in order to make myself 'acceptable' to other people, I increase my risks of having to pay the price in the form of illness. *Gabor Maté* (20)

It is, on the one hand, an impressive tool for easy social interaction which gains such children admiration from adults and acceptance from groups in which they might otherwise struggle. On the other hand, it often requires such a drastic departure from their natural character, behaviours and standards that it becomes hard for them to remember who they really are, further exacerbating that lack of any sense of belonging or identity. Without the clear and unequivocal sense that where they belong is under the safe and guiding protection of parents and family, and in a home that offers them both familiarity and security, uncomforted by those whom they most love and from whose enfolding presence they have been torn, MKs drift into a life of (often desperately) searching for someone or something to replace that loss, whilst simultaneously being frightened of accepting the same for fear it will end as it always has done – with rejection and a pain so unbearable that the reward is not worth the risk.

> If the wounds of your childhood were left uncomforted by your earthly father, you may never feel comforted in God's presence. And you may spend your entire life looking for a place of safety and belonging, longing for a home. *Jack Frost* (21)

Identity Confusion

> We long to be known and we fear it like nothing else. Most people live with a subtle dread that they will one day be discovered for who they really are and the world will be appalled. *Brent Curtis and John Eldredge* (22)

The 'Where do I belong?' question and the 'Who am I?' question are inextricably linked for all of us, but perhaps at an even deeper level for the MK. Such is the need to belong, many confuse the answer to the first with their answer to the second. For example, they think, 'Because my heart is so rooted in Kenya and my love for my home there is so strong, who I am is Kenyan and I will steadfastly resist any attempt to define me as American, even though that is where my parents are from and where I was sent to school and now live.' Having been given a place in which to belong, only to be subsequently sent away from that place, we cling to our sense of belonging there with an iron grip, sometimes clothing ourselves with aspects of that culture that are important because they reinforce our identification with it even when those aspects played little or no part in our experience. So, we may study the language, prepare the national cuisine, dress in the local garb and decorate our houses with paintings and ornaments that remind us of 'home.' The place where we understand ourselves to be from and belong becomes who we are, and we wear it like a national costume: proudly, defiantly, and often – especially in our teenage years – loudly. Add to that the chameleon effect, which is no more nor less than a survival technique in an effort not to stick out from the crowd and attract unwelcome attention, and you have all the ingredients for serious identity confusion.

Where am I from? Well, I started in one place, moved to another, then another, then was sent away to school, returned 'home' to yet another strange house, returned to my parents' home country for a while to live with grandparents, then went back to the field to a fifth home, was sent away to school again …. And so it went on. Where am I from, indeed? Who knows?

Who am I? Well, when I am with my family, my accent is home counties English and I am quiet and relaxed. But when I am with my American friends, my accent is New England and my persona is more animated and excitable. But then again, when I am at work and in meetings with Asian colleagues, there is a flavour of pidgin English to my speech and I resort to verbal tics reminiscent of the country in which I was raised, if 'raised' can be used of someone who effectively raised themselves. In other words, I am relentlessly adaptable and can fit in with any group of people and deal with any situation; because I have always had to, just to survive. To be different is to be strange, feared, and risk more rejection. I will do almost anything not to endure that again. A person can only take so much rejection before they go mad. And I had filled up that particular container by the time I was ten, thank you very much.

> The awful burden of the false self is that it must be constantly maintained. *Brent Curtis and John Eldredge* (23)

A confused identity is rather like a lie. Once you have embarked upon that particular course, you are obliged to maintain it. The trouble is, adapting your persona in order to fit in with what are often wildly differing groups of people is akin to splitting your own personality. And the effort involved in maintaining that personality in a manner that is consistent enough for you not to be discovered in your deceit is huge, and a considerable strain on a person's mental resources. In fact, it is a significant threat to a person's mental health and has sometimes resulted in the kind of breakdown from which recovery is a slow and painful process. It becomes increasingly difficult for a person to remember who they really are, partly because they are always becoming someone different and partly because they were never really sure who they were in the first place.

Then there is the question of having grown up with a perception that we are not a very good or acceptable person because we have been so unhappy with what has happened to us, despite being told it was good and what God desired for us. We identified ourselves as rebellious, disobedient, and subverting our parents' faith and the God whom they served. Not to put too fine a point on it, we are going to hell for being so unaccepting of God's will for us as children. That's what happens to people who disobey God, isn't it? Even in adulthood, the childhood perception of who God is and how He works dominates our thinking and this can overwhelm our adult reasoning. Not only are we unsure of who we are, but we know that we are not a good person and, as such, undeserving of being loved, or even treated well.

The consequences of confused identity, whilst beneficial in making friends quickly and easily, and adapting well to new groups of people, situations and cultures, are deeply damaging in the long run. Consistency of thought and behaviour is a prerequisite of good mental health. Having to factor in where a person is from, who they are, and what their reaction is going to be to a given comment or situation before deciding how to behave places an enormous strain on that person. It frequently results in embarrassing social gaffes, and saying or doing something which is directly counter to their real standards or beliefs, which in turn leads to them carrying a huge level of shame which remains with them for years – sometimes a lifetime. But when you are unsure of who you are, and fitting in with others to avoid the kind of rejection that has so characterised your childhood existence has become your default behaviour, shame becomes the most constant of companions and often the only one that can be relied upon to accompany you. Many MKs struggle to acquire the levels of confidence necessary to stand on the foundation of their own identity or move out into the world from that safe place.

> Shame is the intensely painful feeling or experience of believing that we are flawed and therefore unworthy of love and belonging. *Brene Brown* (24)

For an MK, shame often starts with being sent away in the first place, though there may of course be additional preschool triggers related to early childhood events or indifferent parenting. Typically, a child reasons, albeit subconsciously, 'I am not valued, I am not wanted, all that I believed about my value as a person has now been revealed to be a lie.' The child is ashamed of having so miscalculated their value to their parents that they are shocked to be so discarded. They are unable to conceive that there may be some fault attributable to their parents, or to the mission, or to God – such a possibility is quite unthinkable. Any fault must be theirs, and theirs alone.

Not unnaturally, shame is something we work hard to conceal, sometimes even from ourselves. Shame is emotional pain, and none of us want to live with pain. But, since pain cannot be ignored, we find ways of numbing it. So, although we remain aware of the pain, the effects are dulled and masked so it becomes a feature of our lives that we can pretend for much of the time isn't there, or at least isn't completely debilitating. But, as well as being a consequence, it is also another contributory factor to our loss of identity. Since our shame is a reminder of some negative aspect of who we are, in ignoring or dulling it, we are pretending that we are not that person, so becoming someone else. There is a vicious circle of self-deceit and subconscious pretence going on which leaves us confused and bewildered – often increasing our shame! We are not sure who we are; some of who we *do* know (or imagine) ourselves to be is not someone we want to be; so, we pretend that we are not that person and forget who we truly are.

> Shamed … we forget who we are. We actually become the protective mask we adopt to shield us from the accusing fingers pointed toward us. Cut off from our spirit, we spend the rest of our life trying to prove our innocence. All of our responses to shame are replicated and significantly intensified during adolescence.
> *Joseph Chilton Pearce* (25)

For a child living at home, there are parents and extended family to help them understand who they are as they are growing up. Reminding a child, 'That's not who you are,' is an important realigning of that person's true character and identity and of the standards and beliefs they hold dear. For a child away at boarding school, there is usually no-one to perform this function, nobody who can bring that person back onto an even keel and remind them of their true self. Even when parents are around for a brief period of time during a furlough or holiday visit, they have little idea of who their child has become over the intervening years of their absence and lack the knowledge or, importantly, the relationship to perform this service. Tragically, yet another layer of this problem can be that some parents who are able to discern a youngster's needs in this respect are so resented by their offspring for their perceived lack of interest or concern in their welfare that even if such guidance is offered it is refused out of sheer resentment: 'You haven't been around for the last four/eight/twelve years – who do you think you are to come back into my life for a few weeks and imagine that you know who I am or have the right to tell me how to live?' In the child's mind, especially that of a teenager, that particular boat has sailed!

A Retreat into Secrecy

One of the features of boarding school life that is seldom recognised or understood by those who have not undergone the experience is the lack of privacy, which is both unwelcome and permanent. Today, many boarding schools provide pupils with their own study, or at least one that is shared with only one other person. But, in the UK at least, this was a change that, for the most part, began to be made only towards the end of the 20th century, and even then only in the wealthier schools that were able to charge considerable fees and were gifted with significant endowments, sponsorships and subsidies. None of these factors applied to mission schools and most MKs spent all but the final year or two of their education in dormitories of varying sizes and standards of comfort and hygiene.

There were twenty-eight beds in my first dormitory at secondary school, in a room the size of an aircraft hangar, heated by a two inch hot water pipe that ran around the walls about eight inches off the wooden floorboards, and with sash windows perhaps twelve feet above the floor that were often broken and jammed either open or shut. Depending on the time of year, you might suffocate from the heat or freeze from the cold but, either way, you could not alter the temperature one iota. The uncarpeted floors still contained the large holes that a century before had held the posts from which hammocks had been slung for the then inmates. The beds had cast iron frames and were made up with two sheets and a single blanket of dubious heritage but significant age. Each boy had a small locker and a place to hang his uniform. Personal items were not encouraged and a number of what might have been regarded as necessary comforts were, in fact, contraband and would be confiscated if discovered. Other items were frequently confiscated by older pupils anyway, just because they were something the boy wanted for himself. Anyone who was foolish enough to place a family photograph on his bedside locker was liable to be mercilessly teased or just come back one evening to find it on the floor with the glass broken.

Privacy was non-existent. You got dressed in the morning in front of twenty-seven other boys and you got undressed in the evening in front of twenty-seven other boys. You washed in a communal washroom with sinks laid out like horse troughs and you were permitted one bath a week in one of two bathrooms consisting of perhaps fifteen to twenty baths each, for which privilege you were wakened at the crack of dawn, led down two flights of stairs and across a quadrangle, come rain or snow. Everyone knew who had a scar or a birthmark, and where; who was circumcised and who was not; who was guilty of idiosyncratic peculiarities of personal hygiene; who favoured what flavour of toothpaste .... Nothing was secret, nothing was hidden, everything was open to scrutiny and subject to mockery if it fell outside the accepted norms of appearance or behaviour, according to the particular rules of the community. Boys who slept with a teddy bear did so for only one night before submitting to the scorn and ridicule of the dorm, as did any who still sucked their thumb or twirled a finger through their hair as they tried to sleep. Some would talk in their sleep, or wake sobbing or screaming, or just wet the bed. Whatever it was, no-one kept it from the rest and all had to endure the loud and joyful mockery of those who coped less well by those for whom it was a sport to be indulged in with relish at every opportunity. Often, this took a very physical form and boys were beaten in their beds, leapt upon whilst they slept by an older boy who had donned his football boots for the occasion, or just taken out onto the landing, stripped and tied to the banisters for the entertainment of some of the senior boys.

By the time a boarder left school, heaven was a single room – quiet, solitude and the right to decide for yourself how much light would filter through the darkness. There was never enough darkness in the school dormitory for anyone not to be able to see clearly across the dorm to the other side; just knowing that you were visible to all brought the fear that you were being watched, and with it the attendant discomfort that kept a child from sleep long into the small hours of the morning. As a result, many of what Nick Duffell calls boarding school survivors, a demographic with which he has worked for some years now, retained a lifelong need for privacy and solitude when it came to everything involved with sleep. Even some who were happily and successfully married chose to sleep alone, so anxious and on edge did it make them to sleep in a room with even one other person. One former boarder told me, 'The fact that our living arrangements make it impossible for me to do anything other than share a room with my wife means I am never completely relaxed at night and even a one-night stay on my own in a hotel brings me a degree of joy that is childlike in its completeness.'

So, the need for privacy is a major issue for ex-boarders, which is most MKs. And from privacy to secrecy is but a small step. Here, the twin issues of forced independence at too young an age and the shame that is intrinsic to the experience of early childhood separation join forces to torment the adult survivor. Inevitably, the child who is forced to care for themselves is going to try to accomplish tasks that are beyond them. But, thrown upon their own resources, living with a shame that is born of the certainty that they are not loved and not wanted, they protect themselves by controlling as many aspects of their life as they reasonably can. Even unreasonably, sometimes. In doing so, they make mistakes that lead to further shame, which comes from the realisation that they bit off more than they could chew and have perhaps made things worse. But, since they felt forced to do that thing, it is incredibly hard for the MK to admit that they have made a mistake. Their reasoning is thus: 'I don't have anyone to look after me properly, so I must look after myself. I have tried to do that and if it hasn't worked, that's really not my fault, because I shouldn't have to be doing these things in the first place. But I'm not going to ask anyone for help – if that were an option, I would have done it in the first place. So I will cover up my mistake, lie if I have to, find a way out of this mess and make good.' And so secrecy begets secrecy. As one survivor told Nick Duffell during research for his seminal book, *The Making of Them:*

> I became a strategic person, always on the lookout for danger and how to turn every situation to my best advantage. I still do it. It's exhausting. I don't know how to stop doing it. *Nick Duffell* (26)

Most boarding school survivors will recognise this. For it is not just due to a fear of failure that secrecy takes hold in the child's life – it is also about the fear of discovery, on the part of another, of some habit, behaviour or action, even a possession that will lead to ridicule or mockery and give that other person an opportunity to exploit an area in which the child may feel vulnerable. Boarding school life was sufficiently intolerable without someone becoming privy to information that might give them some kind of hold over you that, in turn, could lead to your public shaming or humiliation. This began with the very first shout of, 'Look who's been crying!' on the child's first night in a dormitory full of other children, resulting in a nickname that would stick for the rest of their time in the school or weeks of relentless teasing. Not a very positive first impression of boarding school life.

The survival strategies of a childhood lived on the edge, dominated by fear, high levels of anxiety, rejection, humiliation and shame, and prey to the need for control, self-protection and secrecy do not leave the child when they move into adulthood. So deeply entrenched have these survival techniques and coping strategies become, so subconsciously were they growing in the much-too-young child thrown upon their own resources before their senses of reasoning and rationale were developed, that they continue to be the default behaviours and thought processes of the adult long into later life. In fact, unless these behaviours and thought processes are revealed to the person, along with the means of addressing them, they frequently remain a source of inappropriate behaviour and deep sadness in perpetuity.

Working with midlife adults who had experienced early childhood separation and a prolonged boarding school experience, I found that many were, as I had been, quite unaware of why they behaved or responded the way they did in pressure situations. But once it was explained to them in the context of default, subconscious responses to their trauma, they recognised the connection and were immensely relieved to finally identify the root cause of their anxiety and pain, and realise that these could be lessened – even healed – as a result of that acknowledgement. Alongside that relief came a sense of disbelief at having lived for so many years imagining that they were alone in having experienced that pain and having adopted such coping strategies when, in fact, they were part of a community in which all had experienced almost identical effects and enacted similar methods of coping.

The consequences of growing up feeling the need to cover one's mistakes or keep one's plans secret for fear they might fail, led to an inability on the part of boarding school survivors to share themselves fully, even in close relationships – some might say *especially* in close relationships – for it is the fear of losing those closest to them that haunts them most. There is also a loss of the sense of reality that keeps us grounded when we are able to admit our weaknesses or inability to cope in a given area. So crucial is the need to protect themselves from the mockery or feelings of inadequacy that would follow any kind of failure as children, the adult MK continues on that road with a relentless determination that refuses help – or even counsel – in their desire and need to prove themselves to be independent, grown-up and able to lead their lives successfully without the guidance and wisdom that was unavailable to them as children. Following on from this is the absence of forgiveness for that failure that would likely be forthcoming from those closest to them, and which would naturally carry with it the healing that such words and actions bring. So, unable to share their fears and failures, and unable to forgive themselves, they live on under the sentence of their own judgment to which is added the perceived judgment of others, a judgment that they so fear. Such fear breeds more fear and is inherently destructive by nature.

> Hiding behind secrets is like walking across a frozen lake as it melts beneath your feet. Each step is filled with fear. *William Paul Young* (27)

Increased Sensitivity to Time

> I filled my time with work and my tendency to 'steal' time for pleasure, which would invariably be private and often secret. *Nick Duffell* (28)

Time passes slowly for a young child. Waiting for Christmas or a birthday, even if it is only a few days away, can seem like an eternity. For the child separated from their parents for four-and-a-half months at a time, the passing of time is so interminable as to be crushing of all hope. It is quite simply unending. Even when the final week of term comes at last, it seems to take forever before the day is reached and the journey home can begin. Then there are other children who will leave first, because their journey is longer or their transport has arrived and yours hasn't – and still you know that even once you actually get on the road, it will be many hours, perhaps two or three days, before you finally reach home.

There is a great deal of waiting that forms part of boarding school life. In primary schools, time is mostly organised for the children but in secondary schools there can be quite long periods of time when a child is left to occupy themselves, especially at weekends. The British public school's obsession with organised games notwithstanding, free afternoons were welcome times of relative liberty, once you understood the rules concerning out of bounds areas and came to terms with the limitations on entering dormitories during the days. (Disallowing the option for a child to go to their own room or study to enjoy a degree of quiet and solitude was a huge source of frustration for many.) So, it was often hard to fill these hours, particularly during the winter or on days when the weather made being outside unpleasant or impractical; the phrase 'bored to tears' might have been invented for such occasions. In my own case, the time between the end of the Sunday morning chapel service and evening roll call, punctuated as it was only by lunch and an evening meal, was an impossibly difficult space to fill satisfactorily.

That said, time was precious, especially personal time, and anything that infringed upon it was experienced with disproportionate frustration and irritation, so much at a premium was it. Such freedom to determine how to use their day as was available to the boarding school child was rare enough without that freedom being violated by some random and impromptu demand that a designated group of pupils was to go to a particular part of the school in order to put out or put away chairs or pick up litter, or whatever unpleasant task a teacher or prefect had been deputed to organise. So, just as privacy and solitude were practically non-existent and became valued out of all proportion to their worth, unstructured time took on an importance that would dominate the life of the boarding school survivor long into adulthood.

The guilty sin expressed in the quote above – the idea that time to oneself was somehow undeserved but all the more precious for that – is very recognisable for the ex-boarder. So rare was it, so precious when it did occur, that its advent brought about a sense of indulgence tinged with the fear of discovery that gave it a certain frisson. Of course, the need we all have for time that is our own is now recognised as being requisite to good mental health; the idea that there should be any kind of guilt attached to seeking after such time is faintly ridiculous. But, for the boarder, the enforced sense of guilt one was made to feel for desiring free time led to it becoming associated in the mind of the child with some kind of sin or wrongdoing. In turn, for some, this led to a sense of 'In for a penny' and increased the likelihood of infringements such as truancy. After all, the child reasoned, if I'm going to be punished for needing time to myself, I might as well be punished for a real offence.

> For a child, all time is by and large 'now time,' and apparently endless. *Frederick Buechner* (29)

The consequences of this distorted importance of time and the high level of sensitivity to it with which the boarding school survivor enters the adult world can lead to a level of obsessive compulsion that becomes a millstone around the person's neck. And, since it is accompanied by a sense of guilt, the level of distortion is magnified. Place these in the context of Christian teaching about the ethics of work and relationships and you have yet another stick with which the ex-boarder beats themselves. As with any part of our lives that we come to regard as necessary, addiction to it is but a small step away from the rational and healthy level of requirement we all need; a person can experience significant distress if alone time is not forthcoming with whatever degree of regularity they deem it to be necessary.

My own failure – or was it just an inability? – to look after myself in this respect, so sure was I that taking time for myself as a married man and a father was self-indulgent and undeserved, once led to a health scare which prompted my doctor to prescribe 'at least a week away, preferably two, and on your own!' I thought I had suffered some kind of stroke or heart attack, but it seems my body had just reached the point where it had shut me down in protest and demanded that I reduce my stress levels by doing what I desired deeply but was incapable of allowing myself because I didn't want to appear weak or selfish.

The very concept of this being an issue is allied to the fact that a pupil in a boarding school is in control of almost no aspect of their existence. Every part of their day is timetabled and controlled by someone else. They get up when the bell goes, attend a succession of lessons, eat meals that contain little or no element of choice (at least in times past – things are better now, perhaps), are forced to take part in sporting activities, often for several hours, have prescribed hours and locations for homework, and then are told when to go to bed and made to do so in a room full of people with whom they may or may not get on. And so it goes on, for days and weeks and months and, ultimately, years. By the time the student leaves school and gains the level of freedom in which they can determine how to spend their own time, there is a sense of desperation and euphoria (in equal measure) associated with such freedom that can lead to an inverse reaction, sometimes startling in its inappropriateness. I have known boarders take months to themselves before re-entering the real world and being prepared to pick up the strands of their lives. But for most, there will always be some degree of need to 'steal time,' and with it a sense of guilt with which they may never come to terms. The need to manage their own time, and especially to have guilt-free alone time, has put a massive burden on many MKs' marriages, already strained by the issues of commitment and self-worth discussed earlier in the chapter.

The irony of all this is that the child's perpetual sense of being alone to cope in a world without a safe adult presence has now become their default place of safety. Loneliness, so ever-present and so profoundly traumatic to the distressed five-year-old, has now become their companion; a companion whose solace they now seek, and with ever-increasing necessity. They have acquired the inner Stockholm Syndrome of the desperate survivor, whose coping strategies and survival techniques have morphed through the secret despair of their early teenage years to become the belligerent determination of their late adolescence; the determined resentment and two-fingered resilience that will see them into adulthood, despite everything. (Stockholm Syndrome refers to the feelings of trust, even sometimes affection, felt by victims towards their captors. It describes a psychological bond with one's oppressors.)

Alienation from Family

> People often tell us that they remember a pre-boarding school happiness which was irretrievably lost by going away. This can be a personal calamity that affects a person's central sense of self. *Nick Duffell* (30)

Perhaps what no parent realised when they first sent their child away to boarding school was the irretrievable nature of their loss. For most, the immediate sense of bereavement – and, no, that's not too strong a word – for both the parents and the child was so all-consuming that no thought was given to anything other than how to cope with the separation and when they might be reunited again. But the fact was, in most cases, it amounted not to a stretching of the ties that bound the child to its parents, but a snapping of the cord. Like a lifeline linking a rowing boat to a cruise liner that becomes snagged on a rock below the surface and snaps, there was still a visible connection between the two parties. But, inexorably, they were drifting apart. And a time would come when they would hardly be able to see each other.

Two inevitabilities occurred here. Firstly, the child was forced into a degree of independence of both thought and action that quickly became a habit. The child had to make decisions and develop coping strategies on their own, not through choice but simply because the truth was, they *were* on their own. There was no parent, no safe adult to help, support or advise them. There were exceptions, of course, but these were a rare grace for most and a complete unknown for many. Secondly, the need for the child to present a brave face and at least appear to be dealing with life meant that they quickly learnt not to reveal the full extent of their struggles or failures to their parents or anyone else. MKs understood that the consequences of disclosing their inability to cope were considerable, and way beyond the level of guilt they were prepared to take upon themselves. It was tantamount to asking a mouse to carry a horse; the burden would quite simply crush them.

So, children learnt to deal with life on their own. And, whether they liked it or not, this became a default position from which they struggled to resign when they returned to family for holiday periods. Even though their parents were now around, able and willing to pick up their role of support, teaching and guidance, the child found themselves resisting such opportunities. This was partly out of an instinctive fear of relinquishing control, partly out of a dread of what it might mean to relax their guard and then have to pick it up again when the time came to return to school, and partly out of what was becoming a growing resentment. Even quite young children understood the inherent hypocrisy and double standard of a parent who might pick up the reins, exercising control and demanding respect and obedience for the six weeks of the school holiday, only to hand them back when it came time for the child to return to school with what was perceived as a de facto shrug of the shoulders and an unspoken but all too clear, 'You're on your own again now, buddy.'

This rendered the child–parent relationship, already an uneasy one, impossibly complex and extremely confusing for both parties. Throw in an additional separation, once the child reached secondary school age, of perhaps a year or two and eight thousand miles instead of twenty weeks and eight hundred miles and the problems multiped commensurately. A boy who had bid farewell to his parents aged twelve, still with an unbroken voice and coming up to his father's shoulder, might return for the next holiday with his voice having dropped a couple of octaves and looking his father firmly in the eye. The little boy who had left one summer as an innocent and affectionate child returned eleven months later as a strapping young man, his innocence tainted and his affections, if not out of reach, certainly hidden behind a sign that read, 'Knock before entering'! The girl who had departed the family home the apple of her father's eye, clutching her favourite doll and proudly displaying the ribbons with which her mother had tied her hair, might return a year later reluctant even to hug her father and begging her mother not to have to share a room with her brother now that her periods had started. The passage of puberty undergone by the child alone and unsupported without the parents' involvement, perhaps without their awareness, left a scar of embarrassment, abandonment and resentment for the child and bewilderment, loss and bereavement for the parents.

> At some level, I never got back home again, and always felt a stranger in my family's house. *Nick Duffell* (31)

The circumstances described above were not unusual, if not universal. They left family members feeling about each other, 'I don't know who you are any more.' There was little or nothing about the experiences of the intervening year that parents were willing to ask their offspring, and even less that the children were willing or able to talk about. Besides, you can't ask a thirteen- or fourteen-year-old, 'So, who are you now?' They hardly know themselves, having spent so much of their time pretending to be someone else just to fit in and survive the trauma of being an outsider. They are so markedly different from their school contemporaries as to stick out like a sore thumb, ripe for bullying and very often shunned for their unusual level of maturity and very adult outlook. This led to holidays that had been eagerly anticipated on both sides becoming stressful periods of reacquaintance as children groped in the dark for ways of becoming a son or daughter again after a year of being a lone adolescent; and parents struggled to find the means of communicating with this almost unrecognisable creature that had suddenly invaded their home with their intrusive taste in music, bizarre clothes, radical hair and cheekily independent attitude. The generation gap, always a wide one as children enter their early and middle teens, gaped like a chasm across the living room floor, sometimes widening to the point where both parents and children heaved a huge sigh of relief when the time came to part again.

My mother still recalls the time I returned home for a summer holiday aged thirteen, appearing at the airport in Singapore wearing a woolly hat pulled down tightly over my ears – in one hundred per cent humidity and forty degrees Celsius! My reasons were flawlessly logical, naturally! I had grown my hair down to my shoulders, a style which the Singapore government of the time associated with drug use, in accordance with which they had instituted a policy of denying entry to anyone whose hair they deemed to be too long. A number of high profile celebrities had been turned back at the border or forced to undergo a short-back-and-sides before being allowed entry and I was not about to become one of them. Needless to say, my mother spectacularly failed to recognise me and, when it finally dawned on her that the winter-clad apparition standing before her was her foot-taller son and heir, her embarrassment knew no bounds. Even then, I steadfastly refused to remove the offending headgear until I was well away from the prying eyes of customs officials and safely in the car.

The consequences of this inevitable, if entirely regrettable distancing of children from parents were often terminal. The child's feeling that they were always a stranger in their family's house never quite went away. Occasionally, a child would return for a school holiday to find that one or both parents had a new friend or colleague who seemed to have a closer relationship with their parents than they themselves did. Unavoidably, the child would feel somehow supplanted by this new friend, with whom there might be 'in' jokes or coded references to times they had shared, about which the child knew nothing. It was sometimes the case that the stranger would seem more at home than the child, and treat the place as theirs, which naturally added to the child's sense of not having come home at all, but having stumbled on some kind of private arrangement into which they were being temporarily accommodated. This deepened the child's sense of alienation further, if such a thing were possible. I clearly recall the embarrassment and resentment I felt on one occasion when returning during a school holiday to find my parents had acquired a new and close friend, and having to ask this lady, a complete stranger to me, where I could find things in the home – my home! None of this was intentional, of course; it was understandable to some degree, since parents had to get on with their lives just as their children did. But it was regrettable, to say the least, if perhaps symptomatic of the lack of awareness some had when their work or ministry was all-consuming and their children an inconvenience, well as the parents believed they loved them.

I once visited my parents on the field only to have my father ask me for rent and housekeeping for the duration of my stay. From his point of view, receiving such a pitiful remittance from the mission meant he felt a significant financial pressure had been added to him by my presence. But I was aghast. I had spent barely any time at home in the previous twenty years and now he wanted money from me for the privilege? I had to pay him to live in my own home, with my own parents?! This is a good example of the kind of bind many MKs found themselves in, whereby both parents and children felt they had legitimate issues that the other should consider, yet both felt horribly let down, unvalued and disrespected due to the unnatural and seemingly unresolvable tension and awkwardness of their mutual existence, occasional as that mutuality was.

For the child's part, this kind of experience – and there were many similar ones, even if this particular example did not occur often – widened the divide that already gaped between them and their families, in turn increasing the likelihood that they would act in a similar manner. Thus, decisions that parents regarded as life-changing and which they felt entitled to be a part of, such as when to leave school, the choice of university or job, even the choice of marriage partner, were often made without reference to parents and presented as a fait accompli. Even in those instances where this was not an intentional decision born out of resentment towards their parents for being so uninvolved in their upbringing, it was still a kind of default response to the understanding the child had reached at a very early age that life had to be faced alone. Any attempt by parents to become involved in such decisions would often be met with determined resistance.

So, what happened at that first separation, when the child was sent away to boarding school at four or five, hundreds of miles away and for periods of time which were an eternity at so young an age, was not just cosmetic damage to the vehicle of family bonds, but a snapping of the cables that linked the steering column to the wheels. Too young to have a licence, the child was nonetheless left in the driver's seat to negotiate their way along life's road unaided, unqualified and unaccompanied – clueless as to how the whole thing worked. Scarcely surprising, then, that later attempts by parents to climb into the passenger seat and give advice in the manner of a backseat driver were met with strong resistance and deep resentment. Neither was it surprising that some of these children crashed, sometimes fatally.

Such breaches of relationship often proved to be irreparable. No-one dreamed, nor could they have known when they agreed to send their child away to boarding school, that it would mark the beginning of the end for their parent–child relationship. That it did not in many cases was an act of pure grace. But for some, for too many – for even one is too many – the relationship never recovered and the children grew up in an atmosphere of mutual estrangement that was never repaired. Even when a parent died, there was often little or no show of emotion, not out of any callousness on the part of the child, but simply because the loss of their mother or father had, in reality, taken place and been grieved over many years before, and their actual death was merely the final separation of many endured over the years, as Michael's story showed.

Exile

> Exile is traumatic and terrifying. Our sense of who we are is very much determined by the place we are in and the people we are with. When that changes, violently and abruptly, who are we? The accustomed ways we have of finding our worth and sensing our significance vanish. The first wave of emotion recedes and leaves us feeling worthless, meaningless. We don't fit anywhere. No-one expects us to do anything. No-one needs us. We are extra baggage. We aren't necessary. *Eugene Peterson* (32)

To embark on life as a missionary is to enter a time of uncertainty and apprehension. Of course, none of us knows what the future holds, but many of us have a pretty good idea, at least in terms of our work and home. For many people, in any walk of life, the biggest issue is one of predictability and the boredom of routine. Lives are lived out in one country, one state, sometimes even one town, with only the occasional holiday to punctuate their sense of security and assurance with a little variety and excitement. But the missionary life is often one of movement and instability, of many homes and houses (sometimes several in a single year), and of unknowing and insecurity. These go with the territory and, for a Christian, it is understood to be part of the faith experience – that we do not need to know what lies ahead, but only to trust in God that He knows and that He will bring all things together to work out for our blessing and His glory. ('A wandering Aramean was my father ….' Deuteronomy 26:5.)

> HDA was my seventeenth school. Before arriving, I had attended sixteen schools in Costa Rica and the U.S., not one of them for a two full years (sic). *Harry Strachan* (33)

There was never a promise that such a life would be easy. And the stresses of living permanently in temporary accommodation, of not knowing how long they might be in a house or a town or even a country, of living under the threat that a sudden need on the part of the mission, a political situation, even a war, might mean having to move on, sometimes at a moment's notice, were considerable. For families, there was an added dimension to these pressures, exacerbated as they were by the need to accommodate the nurture and education of their children. Parents with preschoolers faced a period of anticipation as they prepared themselves to be separated when their child reached school age. Even those who understood and supported the need for this separation nonetheless felt its pain and many mothers in particular began to deal with the grief of their loss long before it actually happened. In the same way that we begin to grieve someone with a terminal diagnosis before they leave us, the knowledge of the certainty of the parting brought much anguish and many tears, as we saw in Anna's story.

For the child, there was a similar sense of anticipation, sometimes a mixed emotion, since parents often told their child what a wonderful place they were going to and how much fun they would have. Some had older siblings or friends who were the children of fellow missionary families who had described some of the fun they had at school, and many children looked forward to the experience. Occasionally, some even begged their parents to send them, so enamoured were they of the idea because of all they had heard about the place. What they didn't know, of course, what they couldn't possibly be expected to understand, was the emotional impact the separation would have on them and the homesickness that would so engulf them in due course. Until they had been for the first time and experienced the true meaning of that separation, they were innocent of its impact and almost completely unaware of how it would affect them.

What they also did not understand was that this was only the start. The primary school might be five hundred miles away from home, and that was light years away for a five-year-old, but once the child reached secondary school age, there was an even bigger separation awaiting them – and longer, sometimes much longer. And this separation would not just be from the child's parents, but from the place in which they had grown up; for many, the only place they had ever known as home and which was, to them, where they belonged. They were to be sent to the country of their parents' home. But it was not their home. Whether eight thousand or ten thousand miles away, it might as well have been another planet. It was an alien environment, an alien culture, and an alien landscape. It was a place they did not know, often did not like and could not understand. It might be their parents' home, but it was emphatically not their home. It was another country – it was exile, banishment, uprooting. And they went alone.

> To be rooted is perhaps the most important and least recognised need of the human soul. *Simone Weil* (34)

The anticipation of this further separation was more acutely felt by both parents and children, especially now that the child had reached an age where their understanding and ability to rationalise and appreciate their situation was much more highly developed. By now, after perhaps five or six years of a primary school boarding experience, they were old hands. They knew what it meant, they had become adept at handling the issues associated with it and they had developed coping strategies and survival techniques that had become second nature. Even so, the knowledge of the increased distance that was to be placed between them and their parents, alongside the prospect that it would be at least a year, perhaps two, maybe even three or four before they could be reunited again, added to the uncertainties surrounding school holidays in the meantime, had left the children with a weight of fear and anxiety that was not dissimilar to that experienced by refugees fleeing a war zone. (Some of these children were, in fact, actually fleeing a war zone in reality.)

Again, the necessity of this separation was impressed upon the children and many assurances were given concerning their safety, happiness and the prospects for their future that were being secured by them attending a school in their native land. What few at the time appreciated were the ties that these children had formed with the country in which they had spent their lives up to that point; the country they thought of as home. Even more significantly, but entirely understandably, the children themselves didn't understand this. How could they?

So they returned to the nation of their parents and fell into a well of grief born of the bereavement they were experiencing at the loss of all they knew and loved and called home. Since the overriding fear had been the separation from their parents, they naturally attributed this grief to that loss. But, in truth, many had reconciled themselves to the absence of their parents during the years of their primary boarding experience. There was a natural equation in their minds: 'We are further away from our parents and for longer, so of course we feel more sad.' But neither the distance nor the duration were responsible for this deepening of their grief. At its heart lay the bereavement of their exile. At five, they had been forced to detach themselves from the security and love of their parents and families; a cord, a bond that would remain irreparably broken for many. Now, at eleven, twelve, thirteen, they were forced to detach themselves from the one constant to which they had clung and on which was founded their sense of belonging and identity – their home, the only land they knew, and the place they loved. It was a ruthless and harrowing compounding of their trauma at a time when these children were entering the emotional whirlpool of puberty and adolescence, already alone, but now without even the consolations that had upheld them thus far in their lives.

As one MK told me:

> I had already lost my parents and family, now I lost my home as well – the landscape, the food, the culture, the people, the sounds that consoled me in the night, the fragrances that thrilled me during the day, the sense of belonging that had been intrinsic to my everyday existence and which I didn't even know I had until it was taken away from me.

Another admitted:

> I was overwhelmed by the grief that consumed me. I thought it was because my mum and dad were so far away now and I wouldn't see them for two years. That seemed like an eternity and I just thought that was why I was so unhappy. It was only years later that I realised I had come to terms with the unhappiness of separation from my parents by the time I was eight or nine. This had been a new sadness. I was not grieving the loss of my parents, but of my home, my country, everything I had clung onto so desperately that made me who I was.

Starting big school can be an overwhelming experience in itself for a child. They move from being a big fish in a small pond to being a guppy in an ocean of giants and sophisticates who hardly notice their existence; powerful bullies and towering intellectuals, awesome athletes and beautiful young women, talented artists and musicians to be admired and envied and brainless weirdos to be pitied and avoided. It is a minefield of social mores, institutional traditions, bewilderingly new routines, timetables and linguistic anomalies that instantly define you as acceptable or an outcast. It is one of the pivotal moments in a child's process of maturation, and a difficult enough path to negotiate without also having to deal with the sense that everything inside you has died and everything you loved and cherished has been ripped away from you.

We will look more closely at this experience shortly. But for now, we will focus on the single most significant defining consequence – it begins the process of destroying any hope to which the child may have clung that life might improve, that they might at last reach a place of safety and love in which to live. After all they have endured in their early childhood, they are now faced with a new and unimagined bereavement that is beyond their ability to bear. They have been thrust into a new world of alien and unwelcome proportions, accompanied only by the sound of final nails being hammered into the coffin lids of their hope-filled innocence.

And now the context is different too. On experiencing their first separation, the child had been placed in a Christian school with a universally Christian atmosphere and environment, with Christian staff who, for better or worse, at least had a sense that they were there to reflect the love of God to the children and provide an ambience of spiritual, emotional and moral security. Now, quite suddenly, even in a secondary school which advertises a nominally Christian foundation and ethos, the reality of contemporary western society and culture means the child is exposed to issues which are not only new to them, but bewildering in their content and import.

Everything is overwhelming and much of it beyond the powers of the child to comprehend. The contrast between the primary school and the secondary establishment is so wide as to be almost unbreachable by any reasonable standards of attainment. Worse still, whereas a normal child starting big school goes home at the end of each day and is able to process their experience with and gain support and advice from their parents, for the boarding school child there is no going home, no safe adult, no support and no advice. Perhaps it might have been available for some, in time, were the child able to relate their experiences and seek help in a letter home. But any reply might take three or four weeks to arrive and, as previously mentioned, MKs had learnt not to bother their parents with their problems for fear of causing them undue anxiety. As MK Faith Cook, in her memoir *Troubled Journey*, relates:

> I had been taught never to give any impression of unhappiness or loneliness when I wrote to my parents in case it brought them distress and acted as a hindrance to the work to which they were dedicated. On one particular occasion … I had asked how to spell the word 'doleful.' When it came to light that I had actually used that word in one of my letters, it became a cause of serious concern … even a matter for special united prayer lest the use of the word should suggest that I was less than happy. (35)

For many MKs, this default response of resorting to prayer without actually addressing the situation became a source of resentment and profound irritation. It was seen as a lazy abrogation of responsibility, placing the obligation for finding the solution to problems solely upon God without understanding the need for the children's carers to respond practically in their interests to effect a resolution. It is the same failure to understand our role as believers that allows us to pray that God will supply someone's needs without bothering to ask if He may intend that we become the means of that supply.

The tradition of sending the children of missionaries home to complete their education is long-standing and dates back at least to the 19th century. In those days, once returned, the children never went back to the field, sometimes not seeing their parents again for seven or eight years. Many spoke of their fears upon meeting their parents again after such a period. Would their parents recognise them? Would they recognise their parents? Would their parents approve of the person they had become? Was there even any love remaining for these parents who had become strangers and who, when all was said and done, had removed themselves from their children's lives for the duration of their growing years?

By the end of the 20th century, the options for educating children on the field had greatly improved, not only in terms of their appropriateness to a child's future, but also in respect of affordability. The number of international schools had increased, homeschooling resources were now being made available and the advent of the internet brought online resources into homes even in remote areas. That's not to say that children were no longer sent back to their parents' homeland for schooling, but it was not the perceived necessity it had been in previous times, and many MKs were finally able to attend high school from the family home on the field and avoid the very considerable and life-changing traumas their predecessors had been forced to experience.

So, let's be clear; the issue here is not that boarding schools are a bad thing per se. There are many excellent boarding schools, and many more now than fifty or even twenty years ago. It's not that mission schools are a bad thing either. Many mission boarding schools were, educationally at least, amongst the very best in the world, as was the boast of Chefoo in China and Hebron in India. Costa Rica's Colegio Monterrey, founded in 1955 by the wife of the then Director of the Latin American Mission to provide a sound Christian education for local children and MKs alike, upholding Christian values alongside those of the indigenous culture, continues to be a beacon of educational excellence in Central America to this day. Even so, Rebecca Hopkins, in a December 2022 article in *Christianity Today*, pointed out:

> Now only 4 percent of the 170 schools accredited by the Association of Christian Schools International offer boarding options. (36)

So, perhaps the message has already got through in this respect. Certainly, Elizabeth Strachan's vision in setting up a school to educate MKs alongside indigenous children was a bold and far-sighted initiative that was way ahead of its time, especially when viewed in the light of the advice still being given elsewhere to missionaries more than a decade later to protect their children from the heathen influences surrounding them, as we saw earlier.

But there are two distinct issues to be considered when choosing a boarding school education; firstly, the age at which a child enters the school and, secondly, a recognition that this particular type of school, with all its attendant benefits and drawbacks, may or may not be the most appropriate one for the individual child. I have friends who sent their sons to boarding school in England from Germany at aged seventeen and thirteen, respectively. Both are flourishing and loving the experience, apparently, though my observation to their mother that, 'It must have been hard for you,' brought instant tears. (It works both ways and always has done. I well remember the first time I witnessed the parent–child separation from the parents' standpoint and the sense of shock I felt as I watched a group of parents smiling and waving as their children's train pulled out of the station, taking them away for another four months, only to fall on one another's necks weeping inconsolably once the train was out of sight of the platform.)

Seventeen is late but absolutely fine, of course. Thirteen is, some might suggest, on the threshold but probably OK if the decision to send is one reached in agreement with the child on the basis that the child knows they can change their mind if it proves unsuitable. Five years old is clearly not OK.

This is where the word 'appropriate' comes in. There are children who may need and will flourish in a boarding school environment because of the independence it engenders and the opportunities it provides. Often, these are children of above average intelligence with or without a special ability in a particular area for whom smaller classes and more focused attention draws out their talent and gives them access to the resources they need to fulfil their potential. Sometimes, these are children who are treading water in a local school that fails to challenge them intellectually and cannot offer them the resources and opportunities their abilities merit. Add in a disadvantaged background of, for example, poverty, racial stereotyping, a rundown neighbourhood or a dysfunctional family and it is easy to see why taking a child out of that situation and offering them stability, affirmation and a sound educational foundation is of wonderful benefit to them. In these instances, a boarding school education is a valuable asset both for the gifted and the disadvantaged.

Anne Collard is one of the co-founders of an educational youth charity in London which helps black and minority children and young people from low income families access boarding school bursary places. She told me, 'Things are very different these days. Each student goes through a rigorous selection process to ensure they are suitable for boarding. We spend at least eighteen months preparing the students academically, socially and emotionally so they are ready to board. We support them throughout their time as boarders, providing additional pastoral care, catch-up sessions during the holidays and visiting them in school during term time.'

Such preparation and support was simply not conceived as being necessary a generation ago, though, organisationally speaking, it would perhaps not have been an unreasonable expectation in the context of Christian organisations seeking to example the care and compassion of a loving God. But it is clearly a huge step forward in facilitating the boarding school experience for children, and demonstrates a sound understanding of the issues faced by children being sent away from the family home. That Anne Collard is herself an MK is no coincidence in this regard. As one of the young people who benefitted from her programme has testified, 'The experience of boarding was life-transforming. Even though I felt prepared, it still took some getting used to in the first couple of terms. But, looking back, it was worth it. My advice to anyone considering a boarding school bursary would be to seize the opportunity and enjoy it.'

Such examples of the undoubted success for some in being offered a boarding school education is encouraging and an important aspect of the wider picture when considering the subject. But it is not suitable for all children just because the school itself is good or the opportunities it offers are tempting. And it is far from being suitable at any age. That it was a sound education option for missionary organisations when choices on the field were limited was both a blessing and a curse for MKs. Many, myself included, can look back on the privileges their boarding school provided in the knowledge that the education they received set them up in ways that a day school would not have been able to offer. Unfortunately, the price those same children had to pay in respect of their mental health and emotional wellbeing was both unknown and incalculable.

The internationally recognised ACE test is a means of assessing the effects of various kinds and degrees of childhood trauma on adult health. The higher the score, the higher the health risks for adults in later life. The TCK Training website, in their article 'Caution and Hope for Missionary Kids', reports:

> Mission kids who selected Christian school, boarding school, or homeschool as their core educational experience had higher ACE scores than those who attended local school and international school. (37)

According to their survey of more than two thousand children, seventeen per cent of those from missionary families were at high risk of adverse outcomes in adult life. This figure is almost certainly a best case scenario due to the fact that self-reporting mental health issues resulting from childhood trauma is an inevitably unreliable process, due to the extreme coping strategies employed by very young children which render them largely unaware of the depth of their pain and grief. As John Eldredge states in his book *Wild at Heart:*

> There are people who have no idea what their wound is, or even what false self arose from it. Ah, how convenient that blindness is. Blissful ignorance. But a wound unfelt is a wound unhealed. *John Eldredge* (38)

But for those for whom the reality of their secondary school experience was that it had been an exile, exacerbating the issue of separation by adding the dimension of a homeland lost, removing the essence of a child's sense of identity and belonging, the die had been cast. It may not have been the final trauma – very likely it would not be – but it was the seminal one, the defining blow whose scars would take many years to heal and would be reopened many times before the wound finally closed.

> Why should I not return to mine own home? Why should I not lay my dust in the street of mine own beloved? My bosom cannot endure the sorrows of exile. *Hafiz* (39)

Esther's Story

> When we do not feel loved by those who gave us life, we often suffer our whole life long from a low self-esteem that can easily lead to depression, despair and even suicide. *Henri Nouwen* (1)

Esther was in her early thirties when I met her; an elegant, professional woman with a ready smile but sad eyes that remained devoid of any sparkle, even when she laughed, which she did not do readily or often. She was well-respected at work – well paid, too – but was bored and unfulfilled, clearly looking to move on but lacking any specific sense of ambition or direction. She was a homeowner but childless and single, neither by design, though with only one relationship of any significance or duration behind her. Her sadness and disappointment that it had not worked out was exceeded only by her frustration that it had taken her so long – eight years – to realise that this was how it was going to be. And now, just as most of her friends were settling down to married life and parenthood, she felt herself to be already on the shelf and without either prospects or hope.

She was without any faith, despite having grown up on the mission field and in a family whose reputation for the soundness of their spiritual foundations and effectiveness of their evangelism was widely known and much admired. On the surface, hers had been an ideal home with intelligent and accomplished parents and two lovely and very able children. So it was all the more bewildering to find that Esther was a woman adrift on a sea of despair in which she felt tossed and rudderless, swimming against an ever-swelling tide of rejection and loneliness. It wasn't as if no-one had ever thrown her a lifeline but, to her at least, the rope had never been long enough and it seemed only a matter of time before she stopped trying to keep afloat and gave herself up to the waters of her grief.

We sat one summer afternoon in the shade of an oak tree, sipping her homemade elderflower cordial as she told me her story. It wasn't so different from the rest of us – born on the field, sent away to school too young, then back to her parents' homeland and more boarding school, into digs at university because there was no home to go to in the holidays and the halls of residence were closed, then straight into work, where she had been ever since. She had been able to visit her parents every summer holiday, something that was not always possible for all MKs, but these times had become increasingly unsatisfactory due to the ever-widening gulf between the rapidly maturing Esther and her parents, who still imagined they were getting their little girl back and seemed reluctant to allow her any respect or recognition of her adult status. Throughout her time at university, Esther had visited her parents just twice – one of those times only because her aunt had bought a plane ticket for her. And her parents had seemed unfazed by her absence, perhaps, she wondered aloud, because they didn't really care whether she came home or not.

But there was one aspect of Esther's story that was a little unusual, if not actually unique. It seems her parents had decided to school her locally, despite her older brother having been sent away to the mission school. At four years old, Esther had been too young to understand that joining her brother was an option and she had been content to accompany her neighbour's daughter for the short walk from their home to the local kindergarten and, later, the adjacent primary school. The choice of a local school was a novel one, having only become at all realistic in the year before Esther started there, so her parents had been keen to try it out. But they had reckoned without her brother, for whom this had not been a possibility at the time he started school and to whom it was not now offered, despite it being available to him.

Esther missed her brother whilst he was away for those long terms, but was delighted to have him home when he returned for the holidays. She was even more delighted by the tales he told of the adventures he had at school – midnight feasts and pillow fights in the dorm; hikes into the jungle on a Saturday; trees climbed, monkeys encountered and butterflies caught; games played and songs around a campfire; and roasting apples and marshmallows in the embers. Of course, that was not the whole story by any means. But, just as her brother did not tell his parents of the nights of homesickness or the long and lonely hours with no-one to play with or the weeks away that seemed like months and the months that seemed like years, so he didn't tell his sister either.

And so Esther, beguiled by her brother's tales of all that was best about going away to school, begged her parents to let her join him there. At first, they refused, reluctant to give away both their children now that it was possible to keep at least one of them at home. But, eventually, the little girl's pleading did its work and finally the day came when she joined her brother in packing her bags and embarking on the long journey south to the mission school. She was full of excitement as she left and was surprised to find her brother strangely subdued as their father drove them to the railway station to catch the overnight train. She had a new and unusual feeling in the pit of her stomach, but she put it down to a mild tummy ache brought on by the many prawns she had eaten at supper and thought no more about it. Then, kissing her parents goodbye, she clambered aboard the night sleeper and settled herself by a window where she could wave to her mum and dad as the train pulled out of the station.

It was only as Esther turned away from the window once the tiny figures of her parents on the slowly receding platform had finally disappeared from view that she realised her brother was nowhere to be seen. The other children seemed unusually quiet and watched as the teacher escorting them handed around little packets of snacks.

'Where's Timothy?' she asked.

The teacher looked down at the little girl with undisguised sympathy. 'He's gone straight to his bunk, love,' she answered. 'I think he might want to be alone for a while.'

Esther frowned. It wasn't like Tim to want to be on his own, never mind missing snacks. The feeling in her stomach was becoming more pronounced now and she slipped off her seat and walked back to the sleeping car, where she had left her suitcase. Tim had chosen the bunk above hers, but the curtains were pulled tightly across and she was unable to see him. She could hear a faint sobbing coming from somewhere, but she knew it couldn't be from Tim. He loved his school and had always talked of it with such excitement.

Esther slipped onto her bunk and stared out of the window at the city lights as the train made its way south. Quite suddenly, without her being aware of it, she had begun to cry. Mummy would not be along to tuck her into bed tonight. She hadn't really thought about that part of it until now. Mummy wouldn't be tucking her in for a while.

A very long while.

She had no idea how long.

Esther paused and looked up at me for the first time since she had begun to relate her story. 'I didn't know,' she told me. 'Nobody told me how I would feel. And nobody came to comfort me.'

Tears ran unchecked down her cheeks. 'When I realised that it was Tim who was sobbing above me, I felt betrayed. He had told me he was having such a wonderful time and I had just wanted to have what he had. But it wasn't like he had said. Oh, it was all true, and he did love the fun times. He just hadn't told me the whole story. He had left out the most important part.'

Once she had recovered her composure, Esther told me of the conversations she had initiated with her parents during her sporadic visits to them at home now that they were retired. They had been home for some years, but had chosen not to live near her and it was a four hour drive if she was to see them at all, a responsibility they had placed on her rather than taken upon themselves. Several times she had asked them why they had sent her away to school and every time they had given her the same answer: 'You wanted to go with Tim. You asked us to send you.'

'But,' she had protested, 'I was six! Since when have parents changed the schooling plans for their child on the basis of what the child wants? Didn't you understand that you knew things about it that I didn't, that it might have been for my own good for you to refuse? What were you thinking?!'

Such exchanges had always ended in tears and anger, and usually with Esther throwing her things into a bag and driving home within the hour.

'They just want to know why I'm not married,' she continued. 'They keep asking me why I'm depressed and why I can't just pull myself together and get on with life, like Tim has. They have no idea how screwed up he is. He just doesn't let them see that side of him, while I can't help it. I want them to answer me properly, instead of hiding behind their decision by blaming it on a six-year-old child. They tell me they love me, but they still have no idea who I am. Or maybe they just don't like who I am and are hoping someone will wave a magic wand and I will become who they want me to be. Meanwhile, I can't even look at them sometimes. I want them to love me, but I can't bear to be with them because it just emphasises their rejection of me.'

Esther dried her eyes and smiled bravely. She would carry on. At least, she would try. 'But I can't believe in their God,' she added. 'They keep telling me He loves me, but I can't see it. Maybe He doesn't like me either.'

I knew Esther's parents. They were good, kind people, extremely bright and capable and very caring of those they had gone to serve. But, somehow, Esther had slipped through the net. She had required – demanded even – more of their love, their time, their commitment in relationship than they were prepared or able to give. It is not for me to say which, for only they know … perhaps.

And, just as she could hardly bear to be with them, they struggled to be with her, so uncomfortable were they with her brokenness and, perhaps, unable to accept that, at least in part, it was they who had broken her.

> Most parents feel unconditional love for their children, and that is what they hope to get across to them. That is important to know, but it is not what matters. What matters are the child's unconscious perceptions, based on his innermost interpretations of his interactions with the world. Those interpretations, embedded at the cellular level, constitute the biology of belief that governs much of what we feel, what we do and how we react to events. *Gabor Maté* (2)

Strangers in a Strange Land

> Humans tend to experience no greater distress than when in relationships of intentional, unqualified abandonment – abandoned physically and left out of the mind of the other. *Curt Thompson* (1)

> By the rivers of Babylon we sat down and wept when we remembered Zion. How can we sing the Lord's song in a strange land? (Psalm 137:1 and 4)

How indeed? The move from Christian mission primary school to secondary school, even a nominally Christian one, was a culture shock in itself. But the transition from what was then thought of as a third world culture to a western society environment was overwhelming for many MKs. One might as well have placed a child on Mars, for all that they were able to recognise their surroundings or understand how to respond to them or behave.

There was no more division of school clothes and play clothes, but now a uniform; often it was of almost military conformity, always of dubious style and never of comfort. For the boys, this meant wearing a tie every day and a suit made of material that itched when the weather was warm and smelt like an unswept stable when it was damp. The girls fared little better, often being forced into inelegant navy underwear and stockings, with some also obliged to wear a tie.

Thus any sense of personal character or identity was submerged beneath a very deliberate forcing of a child into the mould of the school's corporate identity. Even the worst mission schools were staffed by safe adults who had managed to maintain a knowledge of the children and offered some degree of compassion and understanding towards their sense of abandonment. But the boarding school experience, particularly in Britain, often had more in common with a gladiatorial arena than a nurturing institution, and a child might be there for two or three years before some staff even knew their name.

Even so basic a building block of a child's daily life as language was seriously compromised as they entered a world of vernacular and profanities which everyone seemed to understand and be comfortable with except them. For the MK, whose security had become based on their ability to blend in and be confident coping in new situations, this was a massive threat to their need to avoid drawing any kind of attention to themselves. Their learnt sense of expectation that they would be able to cope, which relied on their quickness of thought and ability to understand a situation, brought a return to what was, for many, a deep-rooted sense of shame and insecurity. It was bad enough being the new kid, without having to ask one's classmates what certain words or gestures meant. There were a lot to learn too, and the asking inevitably brought unbridled mockery and disdain at such a basic level of perceived ignorance. Equally inevitably, because again, this was a learnt process that lay far beneath the subconscious of the child, this led to a further withdrawal into his or her self; a determination to avoid such humiliation by never again asking such a question and therefore an enduring ignorance of terms which, in turn, led to the child misunderstanding, or worse, misusing an expression and experiencing yet more humiliation and ridicule.

Every situation, from the rising bell in the morning to the final hiding under the sheets in the hope of avoiding a beating at the end of the day, was fraught with apprehension, bewilderment and fear. Even the 'Where are you from?' question that punctuated a child's first few days at a new school came to be feared for the derision that so often would ensue when the MK revealed that they were from a country halfway around the world. This was somehow taken as showing off, or as a form of offence, that the child's native country was in some way not good enough. A child might find themselves saddled for the rest of their time at the school with a nickname that was nothing short of a derogatory term of racism sometimes applied to the inhabitants of the country in which their parents served.

The concentration and effort needed to maintain even a basic level of equilibrium under such pressure was immense. It would be true for a mature adult but for a ten- or eleven-year-old, it was crushing – and it resulted in an imperative to conform that was nothing short of a betrayal of the child's self. Denying the truth of who one is, or who one wants to or believes one should be, is an emotional trauma which leads not only to confusion and a profound lack of self-worth but, ultimately, to an abandonment of self which compounds the child's already deeply disturbing experience.

> [The boarder] has to adapt, to fit in, to survive. And to do so, he has betrayed himself. This is a terrible blow to the soul. In order to save himself he may have become his own soul-murderer, and will secretly hate himself for it. *Nick Duffell* (2)

All of this was just the start of what, for most, was seven or eight additional years of boarding school, taking them through puberty into adolescence and moulding them in significant and life-defining ways that would determine the person they would be for much or all of their adult life if they were not graced with any awareness of either the depth of their trauma or how to deal with it. In particular, the English boarding school ethos, designed to knock any sense of emotional fragility out of a child and prepare them for a career as a servant of the British Empire and, de facto, an enforcer of colonialism, violated not only the essential character of the child but also the spiritual heart that lay at the core of their being. To the absence of their parents, which by this time the child had grown accustomed to, was now added the absence of any kind of spiritual guide or mentor, save for the occasional angel some children encountered and received as, very literally, a godsend. But, in general, the reality that the child would have to exist almost exclusively without help, support, encouragement or advice was now exacerbated hugely and many children felt as though they had been parachuted into an alien landscape without the knowledge or tools to survive. That so many of them did is a miracle. That some did not is a tragedy – one that, very sadly, could have been avoided.

The child's world of cultural variety, tropical landscapes, exotic food, exploration and adventure, albeit conducted under a cloak of loneliness and abandonment, had now been exchanged for one of cultural bewilderment, alien landscapes and relentless, controlled routine. Only the loneliness and grief remained, added to now by the loss of home and all that made it so precious to the child. Just as they were beginning to understand who they were and get a handle on life, the rug was ripped out from under their feet, leaving them to climb yet another precipitous mountain on their journey into adulthood.

> Premature separation of the child from the continuum of life means that isolation, alienation and estrangement become the foundations on which the child's emotional life will be based. *Joseph Chilton Pearce* (3)

Isolation, alienation and estrangement – the three musketeers that became the personal trinity of the missionary child; one for one and all for God. Everything was multiplied – the distance from home, the time that would elapse between visits home for holidays, and the intensity of the emotions involved. Now added to the list of issues were exile, determination to survive, inappropriateness of the strategies employed .... The list went on and on.

As if school wasn't bad enough – and for some it was nothing short of a nightmare – the holidays now had to be spent in another home. For a lucky few, this was the home of a relative, perhaps an aunt or uncle, but for most it was a children's home, albeit one provided by the mission rather than a state-run institution. To some degree, this was little more than a teenage version of their primary school environment, staffed by a Christian couple, perhaps intermittently aided by a few younger adults from a missionary training college or Bible School. Some children, the luckier ones, had their own room and were able to make a small home for themselves which at least gave them a degree of privacy and freedom to be themselves; but most had to share a room, sometimes with two or even three others. This brought the boarding school dormitory experience into the holidays and meant that there was no respite at all from the unremittingly communal nature of the child's life. Living under the permanent gaze of others, who were not necessarily one's friends, compounded the tension that accompanied every daily necessity, such as getting up, washing, dressing, resting, playing music, and reading. Nothing could be done alone, and yet everything was done alone, because this was not about sharing but about being deprived of privacy. It was not about making one's self vulnerable in that important way that builds relationship, but about being placed in a vulnerable position in that destructive way that screams intrusion and violation.

Some, though by no means all, of the adults running these hostels or homes had been missionaries themselves and understood something of the concerns the children in their care were having to deal with. Mostly, these were godly, loving and compassionate people who acted in loco parentis with sensitivity and wisdom, to whom the children would later express enormous gratitude for their role in guiding them through their teenage years. But occasionally, as sometimes happened at the mission schools, couples were brought in to fill a need rather than because they had any particular calling to a role for which, in time, they proved themselves to be unsuitable. By the time this became evident, damage had been heaped upon damage, all of it at the children's expense, and none of which could be undone.

So life became a round of school, then hostel, then back to school, then back to the hostel, then back to school … but seldom home. For the fortunate ones, a summer holiday back on the field with their parents was a welcome oasis in this desert of lovelessness. For the unfortunate, a summer as one of the remnants left behind, trying to pretend that it didn't matter, followed by another year of the same, was their unwelcome destiny.

Even those who were blessed with a ticket home had much to negotiate in the minefield that family life had become. As had been the case at primary school, but even more so now, the six weeks were roughly divided into three blocks of two. The first two were spent readjusting to family life as child and parents circled each other apprehensively, trying to work out who they now were in relationship to each other, with the child testing their new boundaries and their parents trying to work out how their role might be different from when their child had last been home. There was joy at their reuniting, for sure; but there was tension too, and often very real conflict, as we have reflected already. By the middle two weeks, things had settled down, if often uneasily, and the child gave themselves up to basking in the contentment of being home, revelling in the many joys that had been so missed and so often dreamt about during the intervening months, drinking in the atmosphere of their true home. Then followed two weeks of unsought anticipation as parents and children began to deal with the relentless advance of that day when they would be separated again, and the child set their face towards their dreaded return. This was often a time of subconscious withdrawal, conflict even, as tempers frayed, resentments surfaced and relationships were adjusted to a level that would render the separation more bearable. This might mean a withholding of affection, unkind words even, disagreements provoked, time spent alone – anything that might mean the child could tolerate their parting by persuading themselves that going back and being away from their family was, in fact, the best thing and they were well out of it. It was a subconscious logic in the tradition of Mithridates VI, Greek King of Pontus who, a century before Christ, cultivated an immunity to poison by daily ingesting small, non-lethal amounts.

Neither were parents immune from these behaviour patterns. One MK recalls her mother telling her a week before she was due to return to boarding school, 'I'm not going to hug you anymore this holiday so that you will be used to it by the time you go back.' Presented as a kindness to the child, this strategy was no doubt equally born of self-protection on the part of the mother – a perhaps understandable, but nonetheless deeply troubling coping strategy that exacerbated and emphasised the agony of their separation.

Unless the parents returned home during their child's secondary education, there were seven or eight years of this routine – school, hostel, intermittent but dramatic and all-too-brief adjusting to family life, then back to school again – to be endured. It got easier with age as the children inured themselves to the pain progressively through their teens, persuading themselves that they could cope, justifying their parents' abandonment of them to all who questioned it, but burying deep the associated emotions and storing up the effects of their trauma for the future. Some parents saw what was happening and did come home. But even then, for many, it was too late; the damage had been done, and now the children bore the burden of guilt because their parents had forsaken their calling on their behalf. A no-win situation had been created and so, inevitably, no-one really benefitted from a solution that had come too late and was significantly too little.

For others, the isolation was unremitting. They left school, went to university and were rendered homeless by the mission washing their hands of responsibility for the MKs once they reached eighteen. Access to the hostels that had been their homes for the duration of their secondary education was denied. Now, they faced the choices and problems of their late teenage years alone – not that this was anything very different from what had gone before. So used were they to making such crucial decisions alone, many had become incapable of seeking advice, seeing it as a sign of weakness and an indictment of their ability to cope with life. They had become, within themselves, an extreme of contradictions; on the one hand, institutionalised by having spent three-quarters of their lives and almost the entirety of their conscious existence in boarding schools, and on the other, radically independent and survivalist through their need to identify themselves as viable, capable individuals who could cope with life without being sucked under in the sea of emotional vulnerability and trauma in which they had been forced to swim.

> "Don't be yourself, be what I want you to be," is the institutional message. However, human beings need to feel alive, to be vitally engaged in the business of living. *RJ Lifton* (4)

For as long as they could remember, 'the business of living' had been the business of surviving for the MK. Through it all they had carried the weight of their trauma and dealt with it in the only ways they knew how; ways that were mostly subconscious, almost always inappropriate and the effects of which would continue to seep like an open wound into their everyday existence until such time as they were recognised and dealt with.

Being the children of Christian parents involved in full-time ministry did not, of course, protect these children from the temptations and failings of normal teenagers. In fact, the absence of safe, wise, mentoring adults in their lives made them, if anything, more vulnerable. Even so, the fact that some of these children turned to drugs or alcohol, became victims of sexual abuse or temptation, even became abusers themselves, were expelled from school or became involved with the law in some way was still a huge shock to parents and mission leaders. On such occasions, the need for parents to return home to deal with the problem was mostly recognised and opportunities for parents to dip into their children's lives in order to set them back on the straight and narrow were made. Not that such visits were welcomed by the children, especially since no responsibility for their situation was generally recognised or expressed by the parents, and certainly not by the mission. The knowledge, the certainty in the mind of the child that the parents' visit was just that – a temporary visit and not a recognition that the child now needed their family around them more than ever – often resulted in a sullen, resentful and unresponsive reaction from the child, who understood such measures to be a sticking plaster on the gaping wound of their trauma. If their behaviour had been a cry for help, which to some degree at least it inevitably was, the cry was for permanent and lasting help, not a two-week mercy dash and then back to the real work.

In time, some would find relief from their trauma through the love of others, through counselling or therapy, through an increasing awareness of the need to deal with the ghosts of their past and, for some, through sheer bloody-minded determination not to be defeated by the system that had turned them into victims. Some even returned to their childhood homes as missionaries themselves, repeating the mistakes of their parents with their own children and, even in the face of the obvious distress of those children, insisting that their prioritising service to God over their families was good and right and, naturally, biblical. Of these, a few returned home only to find that the foundations of their faith had been seriously undermined by their experiences and they no longer believed what they thought they believed when it came to the realities of life on the field. Their determination to justify their parents' actions even to the point of repeating them simply ran out of energy and reason and, as was also true of some parents in retirement, they lost their faith, unable to deal with the reality of a God who had asked them to do the impossible and sacrifice their children to Him in the name of evangelism. Of course, He hadn't done this but the power of their indoctrination over decades of bad theology held sway.

Thus did the debit column in the leger of these missions become increasingly blotted with the names of its own children, lost to God through their own negligence and lack of care. Thus was Jephthah's inheritance realised once more.

Jerome's Story

Jerome was a real boy's boy – energetic, cheeky, with an insatiable curiosity that saw him poking his nose and hands into everything and with the readiest of grins which would spread across his face like an upside-down rainbow and make his ears twitch. Going to school in the mountains was heaven for him and after lessons had finished for the day he spent every moment he could exploring the forest paths, climbing the trees that grew along the perimeter of the playing fields or searching the little stream for small fish or freshwater crabs. He had a butterfly net which he wielded expertly, chasing the fragile specks of colour along the tops of the banks before easing them gently free, holding their fragile bodies with a delicacy that belied his strength, and clearly relishing their beauty. Then he would release them back into the sunshine to fly free once more, laughing delightedly as they fluttered away.

To all who knew him, Jerome was a happy, carefree child, seemingly unaffected by the separation from his parents and flourishing in the caring little community of his primary school. But Jerome was harbouring a dark secret. His ready smile came out with the morning sun, but it did not last into the evening. As the light faded and darkness fell around his little mountain valley, a new and bewildering fear entered the little boy's world, one of silence and secrecy which he did not understand, but knew in his heart was evil. He knew, too, that this was a secret he could never share, but that these were times he must endure for now, and surely they would end in time.

By the time he moved on to his new school, though still only eleven, Jerome was no longer the happy little boy whose smile had lit up classroom and playground alike, but a child whose innocence had been betrayed by an unsafe carer. Deep in his heart, he no longer knew what love looked like and he wore a cloak of shame that he wrapped tightly around himself in the hope that it might hide him from the world. But things were about to get even worse.

Jerome's introduction to his new school, where he was to board as he had always done, would remain seared into his memory for the rest of his life. With more than four times the number of pupils and covering ten times the acreage, it bore no resemblance to his primary school or anything he had ever experienced in his young life. He knew, too, that this was where he was destined to spend the rest of his school life as his parents returned to the mission field, leaving him to spend his holidays in a children's home provided by the mission. He would see his parents again in two years, by which time he would be a teenager, so no longer the child they had left behind. As he passed through the gates of the school that September afternoon, he carried with him a burden of bereavement and trepidation such as no child should ever have to carry.

The school's buildings were large and imposing. Met by a school prefect, Jerome was ushered with his new classmates through a courtyard and into the stairwell of a three storey, Victorian red brick building. The steps wound around the stairwell, hugging the walls and with a wrought iron railing on the inside that was punctuated at regular intervals by small metal domes painted in gold to distinguish them from the black of the railing, a discouragement to boys like Jerome who might otherwise have been tempted to slide down the narrow banister.

'Right, come in here and stand by the wall for a moment,' the prefect instructed. The obedient and overawed group of boys allowed themselves to be herded into the stairwell, gazing up at the faraway ceiling with its narrow skylight. The prefect continued.

'Before I take you up to your dorm, let me tell you a story. One of the traditions of the school is that prefects and older boys are allowed to punish the younger ones if they are cheeky or step out of line. And one of the ways this used to happen was that two boys would take a first-year boy up to the top floor and hold him upside down over this stairwell by his knees. They would then let go and catch him by his ankles. Only, one day, they lost their grip and the boy fell onto the floor, right in front of where you are standing. The story is that he managed to crawl back up to the seventh step, where he died. And if you look under the stairs here, you can see a mark indicating the spot where he breathed his last. So make sure you behave or the same thing might happen to you. OK, let's go upstairs now.'

There was an awed silence as the prefect began to move up the stairs and, for a moment, nobody moved. Then, one by one, they followed, each alone with his thoughts as he struggled to carry his suitcase up the six flights to the huge dormitory at the very top that was to be their home for the next year. It was a terrifying introduction to their new school, but perhaps it was just a story. The boys talked about it in the dorm over the next few days, but most laughed it off as an attempt to scare them, and Jerome took some comfort in this approach. Even so, tales of such cruelty and despair were a million miles from his experiences at his Christian-run primary school and Jerome was unable to avoid the hand of fear that clutched at his heart.

And then it happened.

One afternoon, after lessons had ended, Jerome was chosen to attend football practice out on one of the playing fields. But when he went to his locker, he realised he had left his games shorts in the dormitory. The dorms were out of bounds during the day, but Jerome knew he would be in trouble if he didn't wear the correct kit for practice, so he dashed up the stairs and collected his shorts. Stuffing them into his trouser pocket, he was just about to descend the stairs when a voice shouted to him from the door of the senior dormitory at the end of the landing.

'What are you doing here?! You're new, aren't you? Don't you realise you're not allowed up here during the day?'

Jerome could hardly speak, so terrified was he of the senior boy and his potential to do him harm. But he mustered the courage to answer.

'I know. But I left my games shorts in my dorm locker. I need them for football practice.' Jerome made to start back down the stairs again, but the senior boy was not finished.

'Hey, Steve,' he called, summoning his friend from the senior boy's dorm. 'Look what we have here.'

A second boy joined his friend on the landing and a cruel smile spread across his face. What happened next was a blur, so great was Jerome's fear and so fast did it all happen. Before he could move, the boys had sprinted across the landing and gathered Jerome up, whereupon one of them hoisted him over the banister, where he was hung head down and held just below his knees. Jerome had never known such fear and, despite himself, tears sprang unbidden, falling from his reddening cheeks onto the concrete floor far below. Then he felt the boy's hands loosen and let go … and he fainted.

Jerome survived his ordeal but, in some ways, only in body. In mind and spirit he was crushed and broken, all sense of hope or love beaten out of him on that September afternoon. He never told anyone what had happened whilst he remained at the school, least of all his parents. But he left as soon as he could, and the school were glad to be shot of him, frankly, so disturbing and aggressive had his behaviour become. Over time, he drifted into drug and alcohol abuse and his life became an exercise in the avoidance of the immense burden of pain and despair that had been inflicted upon him. Born into a Christian family, Jerome had been handed into the care of strangers who had abused and beaten him until he could no longer cope with life. That he eventually found a way to do so was both a grace of the God in which he could no longer now believe and a mark of his resilience and courage in the face of inexpressible torment. The energetic, cheeky, delightful little boy that had been sent away to school as a five-year-old had emerged at sixteen a frightened, resentful, bewildered and angry teenager, hopelessly ill-equipped for life, sacrificed on the altar of evangelism by parents whose rash oath to serve God at the expense of the care of their children had all but killed him. Jephthah's inheritance had come to Jerome big time.

Happily, that is not the end of Jerome's story and, in time, he married a woman who loved him through his pain and, reuniting later with some of his school friends from his primary days, he found an empathy and support that began to reach down and lift him back onto the path of recovery. It was not an easy or a short journey and, as I write, it still continues, slowly, bumpily, but bravely, despite the discovery that his best friend from those long gone days of innocence had fared no better and had eventually ended his own life, so desperate and unbearable had his pain become. But Jerome somehow found the strength to move on with a hope that is not always his own but which, in recognising it in the hearts of those who love him, energises him nonetheless. Such is mercy, such is restoration, such is grace.

But the scars remain, some healed, some healing, others seeping still; vivid, aching and beyond the erasing of mere man.

By This Will All Men Know …

> "Then why didn't … why didn't God protect me?"
>
> And there it hung, the question. Eve let it hang there, suspended and ominous, the question uttered by a billion other voices. It rose from grave sites and empty chairs, from mosque and church, from offices, prison cells and alleys. Tattered faith and battered hearts lay broken in its wake. It demanded justice and begged for miracles that never came. *William Paul Young* (1)

Many MKs were victims of the process of claiming truths about God that turned out to be without foundation, at least in respect of the circumstances to which they were applied. In such cases, a little knowledge was indeed a dangerous thing. For example, God's promise to Joshua: 'I will never leave you nor forsake you' (Joshua 1:5), was certainly true for Joshua and we can reckon it to be true for ourselves. Many MKs were given this verse to cling onto as they were sent away. It's true, but it's not enough information for a young child being forced to live away from their family and cope alone. For a child to understand the full truth of this statement, more explanation is required and the statement needs to be unwrapped.

For example, a parent would never just tell a child needing surgery, 'You have to go with the doctor and he will cut you open and make you better.' They would explain the problem and the treatment in simple words; they would talk about the anaesthetic and the fact that the child would be asleep throughout the whole process, assure the child that one of them would be there when he or she woke up and that, though they would have some pain for a while, they would be given medicine and looked after until they were better. In other words, everything would be done to inform and reassure the child.

So, when a child is being told that God will be with them, an explanation of what it looks like for God to be with them is required. Children can be very literal in their understanding and the concept of God being with them might lead to an expectation that they would actually see Him, or at least have a tangible awareness of His presence. And, as parents, this awareness is certainly something we can pray for. But it needs to be explained to the child that they may not experience anything quite so physical or tangible; in fact they might not even feel like He is there at all – an experience Jesus gave expression to from the cross. We might talk about how we can't see the sun on a cloudy day, but we know it's still there above the clouds because we can see its light, even through the rain. And at night, the sun is still there; it's just around the other side of the world shining on our friends far away. Likewise, although we can't always see

God and the world sometimes seems very dark and a little bit scary, He is always there and we can always talk to Him and listen for His answer. In the morning, we will wake up to find the sun has come back for the new day and, in the same way, God will be there waiting to walk with us into that day.

As I have spoken with adult MKs over the years, many have testified to having been told as they were dispatched to boarding school that God would be with them, but that it was not evident to any extent and they were left feeling rejected and abandoned not only by their parents, but by God as well. Looking back, some are able to say, 'I can recognise now the ways in which He was with me. But at the time, it just seemed like He wasn't there and didn't care.' Others are clear that they always felt His presence. But in most cases, it took many years of growth in grace and understanding for this recognition to dawn and become acceptable to them. For many others, it never did come.

And for a few, for whom the experience remained a deeply traumatic one, whose childhood faith had been holed below the waterline by this apparent turning of God's back on them in their infant desperation, they remained unconvinced even by the testimonies of those who were reassured in hindsight, asking, 'Even if God was with me, what was the point if I didn't know it and couldn't feel it?' For them, the mantra that 'Actions speak louder than words,' is the bottom line. If the truth that 'God is love' (1 John 4:16) is to be meaningful, they need to see that love, recognise its effect, and feel its presence. Otherwise, what's the point of being loved?

> You may say to me, 'But if He loved me so much, then why haven't I felt Him or seen Him?' It isn't God who has failed you, but those around you. Too many times we have failed to become His voice and His hands to those who do not know Him.
> *Floyd McClung* (2)

So, where was God's love when these children so badly needed it? The answer is that it was all around them in exactly the way God had intended it to be – in those to whom He had entrusted the care of His children. For God has always known it would be hard for us to be aware of and experience His love, which is why He chose to demonstrate it most powerfully through His servants, whom He had asked – indeed commanded – to pass on His love, just as He had passed it on to them through Jesus. 'By this,' said Jesus, 'everyone will know that you are my disciples; if you love one another' (John 13:35).

God was never going to appear in person to the child sent away to boarding school, nor to comfort them with words spoken out of the darkness of the lonely night. Not because He didn't care, nor because He wasn't with them, but because He had set in motion another plan – one that was infinitely more appropriate to the needs of the child. After all, the voice from heaven or the physical manifestation of the divine presence, as we know from Scripture, was always an experience that brought fear and terror before it bestowed any comfort or reassurance. Even Jesus, appearing to His disciples after the resurrection, found it necessary to declare, 'Don't be afraid,' before He said or did anything else, so aware was He of the effect of His unexpected appearance on those who nevertheless desired deeply to see Him.

It was through His servants, the staff that He had called to *be* Him to the children at these schools (assuming they were actually called and not just put there to fill in, though them too) that His love was to be available and by whom it was to be expressed. If there were a small number of Scriptures that might have justified parents in sacrificing their children in the cause of God's work, there were many more that made clear the imperative of Christ's followers to bring them His comfort and love.

> My command is this: Love each other as I have loved you. (John 15:12)
>
> Whatever you did for one of the least of these brothers and sisters of mine, you did for me. (Matthew 25:40)
>
> In everything, do to others what you would have them do to you, for this sums up the Law and the Prophets. (Matthew 7:12)

These are not just verses from God's word, they are the words of The Word – the words of Jesus. Not just to love, not just to show love, but to love with the love of the One who *is* love, to love 'as I have loved you.' The call to serve Jesus is the call to *be* Jesus in the world. The Sermon on the Mount is not just a list of ways Jesus would have us live, it is Jesus's personal CV – a testimonial that tells us, 'This is who I am, and who I am calling you to be.' And since, through Jesus, 'you died and your life is now hidden with Christ in God,' (Colossians 3:3) these are not unattainable ambitions from some kind of heavenly wish list, but evidences of the righteousness we have in Jesus, given to us by Him through His forgiveness and grace, 'not by works, so that no-one can boast.' (Ephesians 2:9) We are perceived by the Father as righteous because Jesus has 'dressed me in a robe of *His* righteousness' (Isaiah 61:10).

Paul reiterates our role as ambassadors of Christ in this respect when he writes in 2 Corinthians 1:3–4:

> Praise be to the God and Father of our Lord Jesus Christ, the Father of compassion and the God of all comfort, who comforts us in all our troubles, so that we can comfort those in any trouble with the comfort we ourselves receive from God.

So, clearly, God has provided for us to be comforted by providing us with one another so that we can share with each other the comfort 'we ourselves receive from God.' Implicit in this is the idea that adults are more able to receive and understand God's comfort, making it incumbent upon them to share that comfort with children and pass it on to them in ways that those children will understand.

> As the Father has sent me, I am sending you ....

This is what Jesus told His disciples in John 20:21. In other words, in case His disciples haven't yet picked up the thrust of the message He has been teaching and modelling over the past three years, 'I am the Way!' (John 14:6). He might also have quoted Isaiah at this point, by saying:

> This is the way; walk in it. (Isaiah 30:21)

This is what parents meant when they told their children that God would be with them and would comfort them if they were lonely, homesick or unhappy away at school. They had been taught how to pray and now they were taught to expect that those prayers would be answered. What they were not taught, for the most part, was that the way in which those prayers might be answered was probably not the way that they were expecting. So, because of their infant literalism and inability yet to rationalise their experiences, the simple process of asking God for something which they then did not receive became an equally simple process of believing God was not there for them, not hearing them, not caring about them, or just that they were undeserving of His attention. This last belief was a fear that was already lurking dangerously in their minds as a result of having been sent away at all; now it was fed by the silence that met their desperate pleas to God for help or comfort.

Their needs were to be met; the comfort and affirmation that they so needed from God was to be given through those into whose care they had been entrusted. God was not going to appear in a flash of light because that's not how He works and, anyway, such an appearance would be far from comforting. God was planning to provide comfort and affirmation to the children of His servants through those who had the access and means to comfort them. A five-year-old child away from their mother for the first time needs to be gathered up into the arms of someone who can hold them as they sob, let them express their grief, validate them in it, smooth away their tears, and assure them that they are very much loved and valued, that they have not been rejected and that they are safe. Christian people were on hand to show 'the love of God that surpasses all knowledge' (Ephesians 3:19), and to be Jesus to those children. God's solution was in place; His plan was as it had always been. But, though often it was fulfilled, and fulfilled beautifully, too often it was not; not by God, but by those through whom he had committed its fulfilment.

The idea that whatever God has planned will come to pass is a classic example of bad theology. Whatever God has *commanded* will happen. But that is not the same thing. Whatever God has *planned* may not happen because God has allowed that His plans are subject to our co-operation. The point that is being missed here is God's determination to submit to the will of man in order never to violate our free will. That means God can plan something and intend it to happen, but He leaves Himself vulnerable to the selfishness and independence that we, in our sin, so often choose.

For example, in Exodus 32 we read the story of the Israelites, bored with Moses' absence up the mountain where he is receiving the ten commandments from God, making a golden calf which they proceeded to worship. In His righteous anger, God declares that He plans to destroy them all because of their unfaithfulness. But Moses bargains with God, pointing out the damage such an action might do to His reputation amongst His enemies, and God relents. God planned something, His servant responded, and God changed His mind.

> In His sovereignty, the Lord will do all His pleasure – all that He pleases to do. If He commands something to happen, it shall happen. Nothing can thwart that which He makes determination to do! Nonetheless, concerning His determined rule – His ways with mankind – it is clear: God does not command all things to happen, nor is His 'perfect' will – that which has been put within our grasp – always accomplished. God has chosen, instead, to limit Himself and to engage in real relationships with men. *Pamela Gourley* (3)

The consequences of confused thinking over what God has commanded and what He has planned, and the difference between the two, are many. Amongst the most significant are that good, honourable, well-meaning Christian people miss out on a crucial aspect of the truth of who God is – and their children are made vulnerable to misunderstanding and disappointment. Yes, He is the all-powerful One, the almighty God. But He is also the all-vulnerable One, the meek Father who chooses to rein in His power, even as He reigns in power, and submit to our will, even as He asks us to submit to His. God planned that His servants' children sent away from their families would receive all the comfort, assurance and love that He longed to give them. But He chose to give it through those He had called to His service, rather than violate anyone's free will by forcing them to believe in Him because of some dramatic appearance or miraculous sign. Neither was necessary, since there were already so many good, kind, loving people in situ to minister to the children. That so many did not do this was neither God's fault nor any part of His plan. It was what it always is when God's plans are thwarted: a consequence of man's disobedience and determined independence; our unwillingness to seek God's will, to ask what He was doing and join in, and to bring about His kingdom on earth as it is in heaven.

Many MKs would come to view this as a dereliction of duty. Perhaps on one level it was; but, in most cases, it was a failure born of ignorance and naivety more than of malice or neglect. Sadly, it was a failure of which each of us, in our own way and on many occasions, has been guilty; perhaps we might hold back from being overly swift in our judgment.

> Let anyone ... who is without sin be the first one to throw a stone .... (John 8:7)

Perhaps too, whilst much love was indeed shown and many school staff gave all that was in them to give, what the children actually needed could never be adequately recompensed, but only mitigated.

Of course, this is not the whole story. There are many MKs who testify to having had an awareness of God during their childhood days away at school; many who did not suffer the agonies of separation as some of their contemporaries did; many who can testify to the love and care they received from parents, teachers and dorm aunties that has left them with happy memories and a very real sense of gratitude for the blessings and benefits of their education. To be fair, even those most traumatised have good and happy memories, albeit these have often become hidden under the weight of their suffering.

Understanding why there should be such a gulf in experience between those who loved their time at boarding school and those who were traumatised is a question that merits a book in itself. The combination of factors is infinitely varied and way beyond the scope of this discussion. Suffice it to say that it behoves each of us to take the experiences of our fellow MKs at face value, not seeking to trump or demean either the experience itself or their current understanding of it. That for some it was a time of adventure, privilege and joy whilst for others it was a time of loneliness, fear and distress is as worthy of our respect as it is unfathomable. For sure, these consequences are not an indicator of success or failure, of good or bad parenting or of God favouring some and ignoring others. It is what it is and our purpose here is not to devalue the positive occurrences that took place but rather to highlight that where the experience was not good – even if it may have been to some extent avoidable – by examining and discussing it, we at least give future generations the opportunity not to repeat it.

Leyla's Story

Leyla was at home with her parents when her final school exam results arrived. She was not meant to be, since it was one of those years when the mission her parents served with had not budgeted for her to come home and she had spent much of that last school year anticipating, dreading actually, another summer holiday spent in the children's hostel provided for such occasions. But a couple of the staff at her school had become aware of her situation and bought her a plane ticket so that she could return home. Naturally, she was thrilled, especially as her university term would not begin until October, giving her a few weeks longer than the normal school holiday would have offered. Thrilled until the questions started, that is.

It began the evening of her arrival home, when her father asked her what she planned to major in during the next three years. A talented artist, she had won awards for her paintings whilst still a young girl and her parents had always been proud of her work. But she was also an accomplished academic, with a particular interest in the sciences, and the process of deciding which direction she should choose during her time at university had been a long and difficult one. She had tentatively sought her parents' opinion during that final year of school, albeit through her weekly letters home, since that was the sole option available to her, and even then only in passing. She had also listened to the advice of her teachers, who were divided in their opinions and, understandably, favoured the subjects they taught. But mostly, she had listened to her heart and talked it through with her friends and, after much soul-searching, and having wrestled stoutly with her conscience, she had finally opted to study art and been offered a place at a well-respected art school in her nation's capital. She had not told her parents, thinking to keep it as a surprise, and wanting to share her joy first-hand, so delighted was she with the outcome. And now she awaited the grades from her final exams.

Leyla was unprepared for the frosty reception that greeted her news to study art, not only because it had never occurred to her that her parents might not support her decision, but because she had barely been back at home for three hours after eleven months away and she had expected there to be at least some kind of honeymoon period before any conflicts arose. Her mother managed a weak smile and, 'That's lovely, dear,' her voice just a shade too high to communicate sincerity, but Leyla had seen the glances exchanged between her parents and she knew her decision had not gone down well. Fortunately, all parties left it at that for the evening, so the matter had been shelved for the time being. But Leyla had retired to bed with a heavy heart, her joy at returning home tempered by the prospect of the future showdown that seemed to be inevitable.

So, when her exam results arrived some ten days later, she opened them with more than a little trepidation. Suppose they weren't good enough to allow her to take up her course at the art school? She couldn't bear the prospect that her disappointment might be matched by her parents' relief, rendering sympathy of any real sincerity moot, to say the least. On the other hand, if the results were as she was hoping, there was a difficult conversation ahead of her and she wasn't at all sure how she was going to deal with it.

Leyla picked up the letter from the post box in the foyer and tore open the envelope whilst she was still on the staircase leading up to the apartment. She wanted to know the results for herself before she relayed them to her parents. Opening them under the expectant gaze of her disapproving father, in particular, was not something she was about to do willingly.

They were mixed. She had gained the necessary grades to attend art school, so at least that was not an issue, and she was relieved not to have overestimated her ability in that respect. On the other hand, her science grades were better, fuelling her father's case that she should attend what he called 'a proper university' to study a subject which, in his eyes, increased both her future career prospects and her earning potential. In other words, the results gave both Leyla and her father backing for their opposing positions, so it was going to come down to a question of judgment and which of them respected the opinions and desires of the other enough to give way.

Looking back, Leyla would reflect that it was her deeply-rooted resentment towards her father that had formed the foundation for her insistence on doing what she wanted and rejecting his advice. She recalled her tearful, if fiery, response to his persuasions: 'Maybe if you had shown any interest in my life before now I would be more ready to listen to you! But since you have left me to make every decision for the last thirteen years by myself, how dare you try and make this one for me?! I thought you might at least respect me for knowing what I want to do with my life. But no, you think that, even though you have effectively orphaned me for your damn mission, you still have the right to order me around! Well, you don't!'

Leyla had packed her bags that night and was gone before her parents got up the next morning. An accomplished and seasoned traveller, she journeyed north to stay with friends for a while, swearing them to secrecy as to her whereabouts. She had left a note, instructing her parents not to search for her; she would be safe, so they had no cause to worry. But, since they had driven her away ….

She left the sentence unfinished. She felt sorry for her mother, but her dad would have to deal with that. After all, it was mostly his fault she had left. But then, as she told her friends when she arrived to stay with them on their plantation, he would probably be more embarrassed at having to explain her absence to his fellow missionaries than concerned about the future of their relationship. She knew this was harsh; but she also felt that her harshness was merited, understandable at the very least.

Upon returning to the country of her parents, the hostel where Leyla had spent her school holidays for the previous seven years informed her that she would not be able to return at Christmas, so she would have to find living accommodation near her college. She would not be able to take a room in their halls of residence because these closed over the holidays, so she would need somewhere to stay that would allow her to remain when each term ended. But, now that she was eighteen, the mission would no longer support her – at all. She didn't know whether she was more angry at being made homeless or that no-one had thought to inform her until two weeks before the university term started; but she was incandescent, and felt utterly betrayed.

By the time I met Leyla she was an accomplished professional artist, earning a living as a teacher and selling the occasional painting through a local gallery. She mostly confined herself to landscapes and the occasional pet portrait when commissioned, but her portraits of people are distinctive and memorable. She has a particular ability to convey emotion through facial expression and especially through the eyes. That her men are placed at a distance in her paintings and seem to be universally angry is an embarrassment to her, though few notice – any more than they notice the vulnerability she captures in the expressions of the women she paints, placing them more in the foreground, though still at a distance. It is why she is happier painting places than people. She smiled weakly at my observing this, remarking, 'Well, at least I don't have to explain that to you.'

Leyla was confident, capable and gregarious, but thrice divorced, alone and in therapy. She did not try to hide why. She told me, 'It's the ghosts – the ghosts of my past. They haunt my dreams, determine my waking thoughts and inhabit my paintings. I can't seem to shake them off.'

Eventually, Leyla attended a conference whose intention was to provide an opportunity for MKs to share with their erstwhile contemporaries and receive education, support and counselling to help them understand and address the trauma of their early childhood. She leapt at the chance, actually, and was not disappointed, finally receiving validation for what she had always understood to be a childhood emotional response of which she should feel guilty, and beginning a journey out of her grief and sense of abandonment, towards a life of more appropriate responses and decisions, and some sense of adult equilibrium. She even made an effort to be reconciled with her parents, though she received a cool reception. Leyla was at least able to apologise for her teenage rebellion – not for her decision, but for her reaction to her father's criticism of it – which brought her some comfort and resolution; as it turned out, not a moment too soon.

Fourteen months later, Leyla died, taken by cancer just as she was rediscovering the faith that her parents had both taught her and of which they later robbed her, 'their actions so spectacularly failing to live up to their words' – her expression, not mine – that it took most of her adult life even to bear to consider trusting in the God who, she had believed, destroyed her family and brought her such distress when she was a little girl. She left this world unsure of the welcome she would receive on the other side, perhaps even unsure of whether there was another side to be received into.

It was and is my personal belief, and I told her so on the last occasion that we were together, that she was in for a lovely surprise.

> If we do not hold our children close to us, the ultimate cost is the loss of their ability to hold on to their own truest selves. *Gordon Neufeld* (1)

The Land of Lost Content

> If you treat children well, they are going to be OK. If you don't treat children well, they are not going to be OK. That's the whole science. That's all there is to it. Nobody needs to know anything else. *Gabor Maté* (1)

It was in the late 1970s that a British charity called The Dogs Trust came up with the slogan, 'A dog is for life, not just for Christmas' in an effort to put a stop to the practice of dogs being given as Christmas presents then dumped as unwanted gifts. The evangelical Christian version of this might have been, 'A child is for life, not just until you get a ministry.' In both cases, it is the fact that such a line might have been deemed necessary at all that is disappointing, shocking even. Of course, the second of these wasn't considered necessary and so never saw the light of day. Whether you regard that fact as even more shocking than the slogan itself will depend on the extent to which you recognise or accept the problem of Christian workers prioritising their work over their families to the point where they handed their children's education and upbringing into the care of strangers from the age of four or five and left them there throughout the remainder of their childhood and adolescence. Some still don't.

But, as the eminent Hungarian–Canadian physician and expert in child development and trauma Gabor Maté points out in the quote above, an intentionally stark and simplistic bottom line that underwrites and underpins every case he has ever encountered, 'If you don't treat children well, they are not going to be OK.' To which I might add the profound response of that equally eminent millennial philosopher and role model, Homer Simpson, 'Duh!'

The problem is, not being OK covers a multitude of traumas, anxieties, addictions, inappropriate behaviours, excesses, default responses, self-harming events, relationship disasters, suicide attempts and more, that do not end with childhood but are carried over into adult life and haunt the victims, to one degree or another, for the rest of their lives. Frequently, and often for a significant length of time, these yet-bleeding wounds go undressed and un**ad**dressed for many years, so deeply embedded are their roots in the subconscious. Decisions reached as a very young child are almost impossible to identify unless and until the events of those years are brought to mind in the context of a journey towards healing and resolution. Even that journey itself is often not recognised as being necessary by many, so determined are they that they have survived the experience relatively unscathed and therefore have no need to revisit those times.

> Part of the dynamic of trauma is that it cuts us off from our internal experience as a way of protecting our organisms from sensations and emotions that could be overwhelming. *Peter Levine* (2)

> Every man carries a wound. I have never met a man without one. No matter how good your life may have seemed to you, you live in a broken world full of broken people. *John Eldredge* (3)

A number of MKs and pastor's children crashed and burned in their teenage years – expelled from school, flunking their exams (despite undoubted intellect, in most cases), numbing their pain with drugs or alcohol, engaging in defiantly promiscuous sexual behaviour and thoroughly rejecting the God of their parents. Of course, these are paths they might well have gone down anyway, as many children from families with normal backgrounds do. But when damaged children manifest damaging behaviours leading to damaging consequences, it is to suspend reality beyond the bounds of acceptable reason to suggest in such cases that two and two does not equal four.

Looking back, some MKs are more than prepared to be quite open about the self-destructive nature of their behaviours. The requirement of the environment in which they had grown up to be good, subservient and accepting of all that was heaped upon them yet still to honour the loving God in whose name these things had been done became too much. As one put it to me, 'Being a good girl and accepting my fate had brought me only anger, resentment and deep depression. Finally, something inside me snapped and I decided that if being good felt this bad I might as well be bad and enjoy myself. I told God that if He wanted to destroy me, now was His chance. He could punish me, kill me if He wanted. At least I would be out of my misery and pain. I didn't care anymore.' Another told me, 'If anyone knew what I had been doing in my twenties I would still be in prison to this day.'

> Compulsive, perverse, promiscuous and inhibited sexual behaviours are common symptoms of trauma. *Peter Levine* (4)

Common symptoms they may be, but, when nobody has ever identified your experience as trauma – and it goes against the naturally resilient, stoic, faith-based attitude of most children raised in Christian homes to even consider being so labelled – it can be hard to accept. Many simply weren't aware of what was going on under the surface of their heavily rationalised existence once they reached adulthood. Even as the extent of the damage was being brought to light, it was the default response of most MKs to resist a diagnosis as extreme as post-traumatic stress disorder (PTSD). I myself shied away from the suggestion until faced with the opportunity of asking a professional psychologist well versed in the issues faced by missionary children for their opinion. Even then, I was tentative in my enquiry and prepared to be told that any such suggestion was overstating the problem.

But, much to my surprise, the response was unequivocal. 'There is absolutely no doubt,' I was told, 'that the consequences of their early childhood separation can be described for most MKs as being a form of PTSD.' (Developmental Trauma Disorder (DTD) or Relational Trauma.) The psychologist went on to clarify the care that needs to be taken in bandying around such a diagnosis, but was clear that the level of trauma is exactly that serious and they reassured me that I need not have feared that I was exaggerating. In communicating this to our fellow attendees at the conference of MKs at which we were both present, there was a stunned silence, followed by widespread sighs of relief. It was a huge validation of the pain and distress we had all tried to minimise and conceal over the years, and a platform from which to construct a way forward on our journey of healing. It was also an unpleasant shock for some, who had resisted any suggestion that smacked of failure or an inability to cope, so invested were they – as were we all – in our determination to prove that we *could* cope and would not allow ourselves to be defeated by what had been well-intentioned and spiritually-based mission policies.

That MKs had also been made vulnerable to a borderline personality disorder (BPD) was a further step in a direction none of us wanted to consider. But many would recognise Elinor Greenberg's statement in her seminal work on the subject:

> [Abandoned children] fear being abandoned and are ultrasensitive to signs of rejection. They may imagine that they are being rejected, even when they are not. Then their fears lead them prematurely to flee the situation or to terminate the relationship. Or, because they long for the nurturing that they missed, they may attach themselves to inappropriate people whom they imagine will take care of them. *Elinor Greenberg* (5)

Constant fear of further rejection, ending relationships before others ended them because it hurt less to end it oneself than to suffer yet another bereavement, and seeking out intense but inappropriate relationships in order to fulfil our need to be loved and cared for as we had been in our earliest years but perhaps not satisfactorily since, are all recognisable symptoms that have dogged many MKs throughout their lives. When, at a gathering of MKs to discuss their coping strategies and survival techniques, it was suggested that many of us may recognise that we had moved away from relationships after four or five years, feeling that they couldn't possibly last and that we would be better ending them ourselves than risk another rejection, you could see the light bulbs coming on in people's brains all around the room. 'Oh, my God, that's me!' was a common response. It was a pattern of behaviour that had gone unnoticed until someone had pointed it out, but which suddenly became clear and obvious when it was revealed. Personality disorders are wide-ranging and difficult to diagnose and, it must be said, by no means inevitable under these circumstances. But early childhood separation is a classic breeding ground for such a condition and it would not be surprising were it found to be a common consequence for the children of missionaries.

One symptom of BPD is what psychologists call 'splitting.' This is when someone divides their understanding, and consequently their acceptance, of a situation or relationship into two contradictory parts whilst remaining quite unaware that they are doing so. For example, a typical view taken by many MKs was to maintain that their parents and the mission were good even though their treatment at the hands of both was so traumatic. Splitting was what allowed them to hold these two opposites simultaneously and defend their treatment. It was what kept them from the critical thinking that might have allowed them to see that good people and good organisations generally do not remain good whilst causing pain and distress to children.

Keep in mind that such reasoning is a subconscious response to the extreme level of trauma being suffered by a very young child and does not represent any process of adult rationalisation as we might recognise it. For the child, there is an innate contradiction in what is happening to them and how it is being explained to them. Splitting is how they deal with this contradiction. If it is extreme, it is also perhaps inevitable. Many MKs are shocked and angry to have it suggested in midlife that perhaps what the mission did was not right, even if it was the best they could manage at the time and under the circumstances. They have convinced themselves throughout their lives that the mission's policy was good, that they had an idyllic childhood and that they have suffered no ill effects as a result of it. Even thirty or forty years on, they are still managing the contradictions inherent in their upbringing within a faith organisation by refusing to accept that there was any aspect of their childhood experience that might have been better managed.

In seeking to create opportunities for MKs in midlife to understand and deal with the issues of their childhood trauma, I received a number of extremely angry messages from MKs who, now in their forties, fifties and sixties sought to defend their treatment unquestioningly and were outraged by any suggestion that they may have been let down or mistreated in any way. A number were furious that I was inviting a mission to participate in a healing process for MKs, claiming that the mission had no case to answer and that holding them responsible to any degree was a malicious and irresponsible form of blackmail. (Fortunately, the mission did not feel this way.) They protested loud and long that they had suffered no ill effects from being separated from their parents and refused to have anything to do with any process of healing. A small number even attended the events organised for this purpose with the express intention of proving that they were absolutely unaffected and did not require any kind of help in understanding their past or need healing because of it. They viewed these gatherings as a type of reunion and attended only to meet up with their friends. Some returned home still defiant and happy in their self-assured contentment with their lives, flaunting their cognitive dissonance. Perhaps they were right, at least for themselves. But others crumpled spectacularly, returned despite themselves to being sobbing children overwhelmed by the realisation that within them lay a well of grief and abandonment that they had never acknowledged, so complete had been their ability up until that point to suppress their feelings on the matter, and so unaware were they of their acceptance of its contradictions. (See Mark's Story.)

Such an experience is a trauma in itself – an unmaking of the resilient adult who has endured so many years of burying their pain, sleepwalking through those nights when it was necessary to return to the coffin and hammer down the lid once more, only to awake in the morning as if nothing had happened, the clamouring voice of their inner child reinterred until … well, until the next time. Some become so adept at ignoring the symptoms of their inner agony that they move through life like a Sawau tribesman walking on hot coals, seemingly oblivious to the pain and determined to prove their courage and resistance to fires which, once acknowledged, may yet destroy.

But when such a realisation dawns upon a person, it is not only their resilience and self-assurance which unravel; for many, it is their faith as well. Built on the foundations of their mission's flawed theology and their parents' acquiescence to it – or at least submission to it – upon which they have based their lifelong justification and support for what happened to them, they find themselves standing on a truth that has disappeared into thin air. Their splitting strategy falls apart as they finally realise that there were alternatives after all; being separated from their parents was not something that God had necessarily ever intended or wanted for them; mistakes were made and, perhaps most significantly, they were not bad children for feeling as they did. The relief of no longer having to carry the guilt that accompanied the bereavement of their abandonment, and the certainty of their sin in so feeling, is huge. It more than compensates for the prospect of having to pick up the pieces of such faith as they may have had in order to reconstruct it on more solid foundations. But it is a bewildering experience, and a long and difficult process.

As one MK put it, 'I came here to find myself, not lose my faith.' Sadly, the two are often inextricably entwined and the unhealthy and misconstrued aspects of our faith have to be burnt off in the fires that refine it into the pure gold that will endure forever. Just the understanding that God is good, and if someone treats us in a way that is not good then it is unlikely to be anything God wants, is a piece of critical thinking in which many MKs refused to indulge or allow themselves to contemplate. To do so would have brought the fragile tower of their received faith crashing down, along with the risk that their thus-far rationalised existence would disappear also.

> When faith ends, the journey ends – either in death … or in the living death of those who believe themselves to be without hope. *Frederick Buechner* (6)

The upside of this experience is that rebuilding one's faith on firm foundations can be an exciting and rewarding experience, as many MKs have discovered. Living a faith life that ignores the difficult truths of Scripture usually ends up with a person believing something that is not only untrue (or at best an incomplete truth), it also denies that person a full relationship with God. For so many MKs, the truth that God is good clashed powerfully and dramatically with the experience of their upbringing. No-one ever explained to us that God is always good and therefore the question is not, 'Why is God doing this bad thing to me?' but 'Since God is always good, how am I to recognise and find His goodness in this experience?' Because the truth is, God doesn't do bad things to us. He sometimes allows bad things to happen to us because He refuses to violate our free will; He is committed to the meekness we see in Jesus that means He too has submitted to the ways of the world, just for now, though His final victory and perfecting of all that He has created is assured; He understands that we grow through hardship and suffering and so refines us through the difficult times; and He works even those bad things together for good for those who love Him.

But none of this means He ever intended that those who serve Him in obedience to His calling should lay aside their parental duties and favour a ministry of evangelism over the care of their children. That was never a divine imperative, but always a human construct based on a misreading of Scripture allied to cultural, philosophical and theological attitudes, and misplaced priorities and ambitions. As many MKs have admitted since: there, but for the grace of God, go I.

We may not return to our childhoods, though we can go back to the places where we experienced them and, in doing so, some have established a new and startling relationship with their inner child that has led them to a place of peace and resolution they could never have imagined. It is as if a breeze has wafted across our faces, bringing a fragrance of memories that has drawn us back to a time and place that was once loved but long-forgotten, more out of the necessity of survival than desire. For those of us who have breathed in that fragrance, the words of AE Housman, from which is taken the heading for this chapter, have a particular resonance.

> Into my heart an air that kills from yon far country blows:
> What are those blue remembered hills, what spires, what farms are those?
> That is the land of lost content, I see it shining plain,
> The happy highways where I went and cannot come again. (7)

My own mission school was set in mountains whose jungle canopy takes on a bluish hue in certain lights, so 'blue remembered hills' is a particularly evocative description of the place where I spent the first half of my childhood. But it was not a land of content so much as a land of loneliness and despair. There were happy highways, though, thrilling and exciting times as well as days and nights of inexpressible sadness and loneliness.

But is it really true that I 'cannot come again'? Could I not at least revisit what remains of those places that were so integral a part of my experience, to suck out such catharsis as that experience might offer me? It was surely worth a try.

So, try I did, returning to the land of my ‘lost content’ and walking once more those ‘happy highways where I went’. It became a powerful factor in triggering a stage of the healing process that has now seen many MKs move on from a life lived under the weight of grief and abandonment to begin discovering some of that ‘lost content.’

> What children fear more than anything, including physical harm, is getting lost. To them, being lost means losing contact with their compass point. *Gordon Neufeld* (8)

Mark's Story

For Mark, receiving a letter from his parents' mission apologising for the distress he may have felt at being separated from his parents as a five-year-old, at the mission's instigation, came as something of a surprise. To be honest, now in his early sixties, it was not something he had thought about for decades, except for a brief period of reflection when his father had died, accompanied by some regret that they had never really been close. A part of him had wanted to ask his father why he had done it, allowed it, supported it – he wasn't sure which description was most appropriate. But that was a conversation they had never had, and now it was too late. To make matters worse, his mother, though still alive, had dementia, rendering a conversation about almost anything difficult, and placing a subject as emotive as her justification for abandoning him as a child well beyond the bounds of possibility.

It was true that Mark had always been aware of a barely suppressed resentment towards the mission for effectively having been forced to bring himself up and for the ensuing degree of estrangement from his parents, but he had never directly apportioned blame. It certainly would never have occurred to him to ask for an apology, or even to expect any particular awareness on the mission's part of what he had endured as a child. After all, the leaders of his 'great sadness', as one of his latter-day mentors had described it, were long gone. Mission policies had changed for the better, he hoped, though his curiosity as to what they were doing now barely registered on his scale of interests and priorities.

Still, the letter was of passing interest and he read it with a detached air, acknowledging its philosophical reasoning, noting its theological volte-face but, when he stopped to think about it, doubting its full sincerity. One section did catch his eye, though – the notice of a forthcoming gathering at the old school for anyone interested in addressing the issues caused by their enforced early childhood separation. TCK experts and counsellors would be on hand to talk about what they had gone through as children all those years ago and perhaps offer some ideas that might bring a degree of healing and resolution to those who felt they needed it. Mark was not one of those, but there was a stirring in his heart at the prospect of revisiting the place, and plenty of opportunities were being promised to explore the mountains and jungle in which he had grown up as well as to meet schoolfriends with whom he had lost touch almost half a century before. These last two factors were all that stayed his hand from depositing the letter in the waste paper basket by his desk. But, almost immediately, he dismissed the idea as little more than a pipe dream. Despite the mission subsidising the event, it would not be a cheap trip, especially if his wife accompanied him, which he wasn't sure she would want to do. Actually, he wasn't even sure he would want her to go, since it was such a far-distant time of his life and one he had never fully shared with her – with anyone, come to that.

He placed the letter in the carved wooden rack on his desk, the one he had brought back from his last visit to his sister, and thought no more about it. And there it remained … until the phone call came.

The caller identified himself as Ross and greeted Mark with enthusiasm, though, for the life of him, Mark couldn't place the voice. He knew of no Ross amongst his circle of friends and colleagues and, apologising for the shortfall in his memory, and slightly embarrassed at having to do so, he requested the caller to identify himself more fully.

'It's Ross – Ross McAlpine,' the caller elaborated, the enthusiasm in his voice undiminished. 'You remember. We were in a dorm together at Highmount back in the day. You called me Scotty in those days. Well, everyone did.'

'Scotty! You should have said!' Mark sighed with relief at this mystery solved, simultaneously understanding the timing of this blast from the past. 'Have you had a letter from the mission?'

'Yes. That's why I'm calling,' replied Ross. 'I'm thinking of going back and I wondered if you are planning to be there. It would be great to see you again, especially as they are going to organise hikes up the mountains and a trip to the Iskandar Falls. I can't wait.'

Mark hesitated, not wanting to be swayed by his erstwhile friend's eagerness, but feeling the spark of his interest fanned into flames nonetheless.

'Well, I only got the letter yesterday,' he replied, noncommittally, 'so I'm still mulling it through. What did you think of the letter, by the way?'

'Bizarre,' Ross replied. 'Twenty-first century political correctness gone mad, if you ask me. I would love an apology, but not from them so much as from that bastard who kept a leather strap hanging behind his study door and thrashed me twice a week for daring to be homesick. But he's been dead twenty years now, so I'm not going to hear from him.'

'I agree,' responded Mark. 'But I suppose it's all they can do now.'

'Yes, well, it would have been more meaningful if they had done it forty years ago when Larry died, poor sod. You would think that a sixteen-year-old putting a bullet through his brain would make them pause to consider if maybe they weren't a teeny bit responsible. But, no. As far as I'm concerned, this is too little, too late. Still, it's an opportunity to revisit the place – and if they're going to pay for my accommodation, it brings the trip into the realms of financial possibility, so I don't intend to look this particular gift horse in the mouth. I won't go to any of the navel-gazing sessions, though. A shot of jungle, a crate of local beer and some late nights with old friends is all the healing I need.'

Mark would not perhaps have expressed his sentiments quite so starkly, but he had to admit that Ross's analysis matched his own pretty well.

'Well, I need to talk to Cindy,' Mark concluded. 'Give me your number and I'll call when you when I've made a decision. I'm tempted, though, I will admit.'

Despite his misgivings, Mark could not ignore the mounting sense of excitement as he considered the opportunity to return to the land of his childhood and the school where, although he had been grief-stricken and lonely, and had even run away on one occasion, he had nonetheless had many happy times and still viewed the location, if not the experience itself, as a kind of childhood Eden.

And so it was that several months after receiving the mission's letter and the phone call from Ross, Mark boarded a plane with his wife and set off halfway around the world, a mixture of anticipation and apprehension battling for supremacy in his heart and mind.

It was the anticipation that won out. The prospect of seeing Ross and a number of his other former schoolmates after so many years was an exciting one and there had been regular messages and calls exchanged amongst his contemporaries from those years as they planned the things they wanted to do and the places they wanted to go together. Mark had no real concerns about 'facing his ghosts,' as one of them had put it, since his passage through life had proved relatively untroubled by the issues of his formative years. He was aware that some others had struggled with their mental health and were setting a considerable store by this opportunity to gain a measure of resolution during the visit. But he was not one of those and his focus was on being reunited with old friends and revisiting memories that had lain dormant for many years now.

The journey was a long one and it was thirty-nine hours and late in the evening before Mark and his wife reached their hotel a couple of miles away from the school, and a further twelve hours before they finally walked up and stood before the gates, where Mark took Cindy's arm and motioned for her to stop.

'Are you OK?' she asked, hitching her bag back up onto her shoulder and raising a questioning eyebrow.

Mark stood in silence for a moment, looking around.

'It's very beautiful,' Cindy observed. 'The birdsong is amazing. And the cicadas – they're so noisy.' The sounds of the jungle orchestra echoed down the valley above the faint rippling of the stream that wound through the grounds, enhanced by the fragrance of eucalyptus and pine, and the visual feast of purple morning glory, scarlet hibiscus and rainbow passion flower. All of this was new to her. But to Mark, it was a familiar yet quite unexpected fusion of sensual delights that was triggering in him a response for which he was totally unprepared.

'I'm fine,' he answered, after a moment. 'Come on.' And, together, they passed through the stone gate posts that bore the name of the school and began to stroll up the driveway.

That was when it hit him – 'like an express train,' Mark would later admit. He had taken no more than half a dozen steps when he was overwhelmed by a confusion of emotions and memories which buckled his legs and sent him tumbling onto his knees, his face contorted with grief, and torrents of tears streaming down his face. The shock and bewilderment was evident as he looked up into the face of his astonished wife, her eyes wide in amazement, one hand clamped across her mouth.

'What on earth happened?!' she cried, her confusion no less than Mark's own. He shook his head and covered his face with his hands, as if attempting to stem the tears through sheer physical force. But it was several minutes before he was able to recover his composure sufficiently to speak. Even then, he had no idea what to say, no clue how to convey what had happened to him. Grateful that no-one else had come along whilst he was getting himself together, Mark finally stood up, and the still-shaken pair made their way up the drive to where the school stood, looking just as he had remembered it … and the tears began again.

It was only that evening, when Mark related his experience to one of the counsellors assigned for just that purpose, that the events of his return and the dramatic impact of him walking back through the school gates after almost fifty years' absence were explained to him as the bursting through of decades of suppressed emotions – anger, grief, resentment, denial. The powerful effect of all those sensual triggers as he and Cindy had stood by the gate, the sights and sounds and smells that had wallpapered his childhood, had raised from the dead the child he once was, and who still lived on within him, denied a voice over the intervening years through sheer willpower and a refusal to confront the immense pain that, subconsciously, Mark had feared would overwhelm and destroy him were he to acknowledge it. That afternoon, nature had overridden his defences and, quite literally, thrown him sobbing to the ground, unmanning him in an ambush so unexpected, so complete, that his whole purpose in returning had been upended.

'I only came to see my friends,' Mark protested. 'I thought I was fine. I had no idea all that stuff was lurking hidden away inside of me.'

The counsellor shot him a sympathetic look and winked at Cindy.

'Well, you may have to revise your plans,' he said, with massive understatement. 'I think your body, mind and spirit have just sent you a quite different message. And you will ignore it at your peril.'

Mark flashed a weak smile and took Cindy's hand.

'Sorry, love,' he said. 'This isn't really what you signed up for, is it?'

Cindy smiled. 'It's not what *you* signed up for, more to the point. But I think this is important. Good, even. So, don't worry. We will do this together.'

Looking back, Mark would later confess to that week being one of the most significant of his entire life. Not perhaps the most fun he had ever had, but probably the most growth and change he had ever been able to accomplish. Even so, it was only the start of a journey that would last for the rest of his life as he sought to face up to the issues of his childhood, confront the negative emotions, release and restore the positive ones and rebuild the faith that had for many years sat uncomfortably alongside his experience of his parents' God that now needed to become his own.

In time, Mark would acknowledge some important truths that would offer him a firmer foundation than he had ever possessed before. That even though he had felt abandoned, he had not been abandoned; even though he had felt unloved and unlovable, he was neither of those things; even though he had not known the presence of God with him, God had been present in every moment; even though God had been marked out as approving of, even initiating, the separation from his family, it had not been anything God had wanted; and the God he had been brought up to believe was good, but had experienced as bad, was indeed good – always good – and that all the questions pertaining to how the trauma of his childhood had been allowed to happen could find their answer and ultimate resolution in the truth of the submission of an all-vulnerable God to the so-called good ideas of man.

Mark still got to visit the places he and Ross had discussed in the months leading up to the journey back to school. They climbed the mountains, visited the waterfalls, recalled those halcyon days with relish over uncounted bottles of the local beer, and caught up on each other's lives. Mark also attended every session to hear the TCK experts and professional counsellors offer a perspective on the MKs' experiences, determined to resolve as much as he could and restore some equilibrium to his life after his shattering experience at the school gate. To his deep regret, Ross did not join him, unwilling to accept that he had any issues at all, and intent to the end on simply enjoying the company of his old schoolmates and basking in the memories of a childhood that he was unable, perhaps even refused, to recognise as anything other than idyllic.

'Each to his own,' was Ross's comment on Mark's change of mind.

But Mark's life had changed forever. There were more tears before he and Cindy boarded the plane home a week later. Even so, Mark's final reflection was a powerful testimony to the importance of the event and the work that Mark himself had done, ably supported by Cindy but also by the community of MKs who had embraced, comforted and validated him in the courage and determination of his search for the wholeness he hadn't even realised he needed when he had arrived. In summing up his experience that week, he wrote:

> *For me, one of the benefits of getting together is to see what our past has done to us all. I can see better in others the effects of childhood separations than I can see in myself. I laugh now when I read my initial response to the invitation: "I don't need it; I have resilience." Rubbish! Of course, I changed my opinion after the event. I am just starting to realise how we are all damaged, even when we have skilful defence mechanisms in place. Saw a psychologist today and it was eye-opening to understand my layered shells. Let's keep on with this extraordinary journey!*

As for Ross ... well, perhaps he was fine, unwounded by the events of his childhood, unscarred by the separation he experienced. Or perhaps his coping strategy of burying his pain had been so successful that he was simply unable to see it, even when others were uncovering their own years of suppression in front of him. As John Eldredge wrote:

> Brennan Manning said, 'The spiritual life begins with the acceptance of our wounded self.' Really? How can that be? The reason is simple: 'Whatever is denied cannot be healed.' But that's the problem, you see. Most men deny their wound – deny that it happened, deny that it hurt, certainly deny that it's shaping the way they live today. (1)

All Things Reconsidered

> For people who have survived boarding school and who want to put their life back on more natural footings, recognising the problem and acknowledging the way they survived is terribly important. *Nick Duffell* (1)

The alumni of a number of mission schools have organised events for their members to help them address the issues of early childhood separation and their mission/boarding school experience. The responses, both from the missions and the MKs themselves, have covered a broad spectrum. One or two missions reacted rather defensively and declined to become involved, whilst others wished their alumni well, but held back from getting involved in any practical ways. At the other end of the spectrum, one or two accepted a degree of responsibility for the damage that had been done to their members' children, offering limited support, financially and logistically, to the ventures.

Similarly, there were a number of alumni organisations or communities who were quite firm in their determination not to involve their mission, most of them understandably presuming that their members would not respond well to an event in which the mission's involvement might risk leading to some manipulation of the truth or just inhibit the participation of their MKs. Neither did they want to feel beholden to an organisation that had caused them so much distress. Even those who went ahead in concert with their missions faced a permanent battle to convince their community that their events would not be compromised by the mission's involvement and were forced to place stringent limits on the presence and participation of mission personnel.

Mission involvement in these events was a two-sided coin, for sure. On the one hand, it was understood to be absolutely essential that participants could express themselves fully and freely, which some would simply feel unable to do were mission representatives present. On the other hand, some MKs were very clear that they wanted mission staff there to hear their stories and fully appreciate the extent of their suffering, albeit it under a previous regime. Those missions which did get involved were mostly respectful of these feelings, but were also keen to hear the views and experiences of their MKs in order to understand the kinds of problems about which their predecessors had been unaware, and have the opportunity to put in place measures to prevent any repeat in the future.

Sadly, if understandably, one of the most decisive factors for missions in deciding the extent to which they might co-operate with their alumni was the question of legal redress. Many of the missions concerned had, by the end of the second decade of the 21st century, been the subject of sexual or physical abuse accusations against some of their school staff, which held considerable and complex legal implications. Issues such as the statute of limitations laws that existed in many countries, which meant that legal prosecutions were disallowed once a certain period had elapsed since the alleged crime took place, were further complicated by matters of national and international jurisdiction. For example, a mission that had its headquarters in one country, its school in a second, an accused perpetrator from a third and an alleged victim from a fourth was forced to deal with laws from four different nations, not to mention ascertaining which of the four had precedence when their laws did not match up. So, there were complex logistical issues that drew out both the legal and, consequently, the healing processes, most of which were unavoidable.

Regrettably, it was also true that missions, pretty much without exception, were extremely reluctant to accept culpability, slow to deal with the accusations levelled against their members, and institutionally obstructive when it came to acknowledging the extent of their duty of care to their MKs. As a result, many of the cases brought against missions floundered or were simply thwarted by the confusion and complexity that ensued. MKs were left feeling doubly abused, made victims all over again in a situation in which they had dared to hope that Christian morality and compassionate integrity might come to the fore. But in vain.

So, by the time MKs began to approach their missions for assistance in providing healing opportunities for their alumni communities, there was already a certain wariness that any such involvement, or any admission that past policies and processes had been in some way neglectful, might result in legal actions at a huge cost to the missions concerned, both to their finances and to their reputations. (The mission that sent out the letter of accountability referred to in Mark's story took a year just to finalise the wording of that letter, having had to seek approval from the legal departments in each of the countries from which it received missionaries.)

This was matched by the wariness of MKs that missions might seek to minimise the effects of their past policies and fail to respect their full impact. As a result, the process of bringing MKs together to share their experiences and seek healing was a minefield of extreme emotions, opposing positions and conflicting beliefs which not everyone involved was always willing to hold in balance. Even a fundamental acceptance that things had been done with the best of intentions, were of their time and could perhaps not be judged fairly in hindsight, was not something on which all could agree. As with any attempt to resolve issues of emotional damage caused by long-term abuse that began in childhood, the heat is turned up high before it even begins. It requires a willingness on both sides to accept what may for some start out as unacceptable and work through their issues for the sake of others, if not for themselves. Where that acceptance was too insurmountable a barrier, there were many on both sides who stood apart from the process, often jeering from the sidelines, their pain at contemplating the issues too raw to even consider any process that might lead to healing or resolution. Some feel that hanging onto their pain and anger is all they have left.

But for those who were able to participate, these events became seminal and integral to their healing journey. The following are examples of comments that poured out from the participants as they reflected on their time together.

> I cannot put into words what this week has meant for me.
>
> I came back feeling empowered, and with a whole new set of tools to work with.
>
> Now we can process what we never got to process as kids.
>
> I came to finally understand why my understanding of God had been so wrong.
>
> This week has allowed me to recognise my losses, grieve for them, and revisit the memories which allowed the happy ones to resurface. In addition, new joyful moments were pasted onto those former ones.
>
> Thank you! This week has been a lifesaver. If I hadn't been able to come, I don't know if I could have carried on.
>
> This has been the happiest week of my life.

The very act of regathering as a community of MKs as opposed to undergoing some form of personal or private therapy produced outcomes few had anticipated. As we saw from Mark's story, the location of the event – returning to the actual scene of the crime, as it were – was a powerful trigger in allowing long-hidden emotions to surface and long-forgotten memories, good and bad, to be revisited. If Mark had simply gone to a local therapist, which he was unaware might be necessary or desirable, it might have taken years to uncover the deep well of grief and abandonment that lay within him. Instead, its lid was taken off by the simple process of walking through the school gates. And there were countless other examples of feelings and memories that had lain dormant for decades being triggered by nothing more than just being back in a place they had loved, with its sights, sounds and smells, but had experienced through a haze of pain and distress.

Indeed, one of the most important discoveries of these events was that it wasn't just the bad memories that MKs had suppressed. But, so complete was their desire to put the experience out of their minds, many good memories had been buried alongside the bad. Now, as they finally allowed the bad to resurface so that they could be exposed for what they were, and faced and processed within the safety of a community that shared and understood their pain, these adults, whose physical bodies hid such damaged and vulnerable inner children, began to recall the joys and pleasures of their childhood. This was the unseen dichotomy of their experience. For much had been good and lovely; many times had been full of excitement and deep joy. Sadly, such was the weight of the cloak of abandonment and loneliness under which they had experienced these joys, they too had become invisible. When the cloak was thrown aside and stored away in the back of the wardrobe, many of the good memories were put away with it.

Another powerful and deeply healing aspect of gathering together, as previously mentioned, was that, in sharing how each of us had felt and dealt with our adult lives, many discovered that what they had imagined was an emotion or experience unique to them was, in fact, practically universal within the community. The cries of, 'Oh, my God – that's me!' or, 'Me, too, but I had no idea anyone else felt that way!' were frequently heard as people shared some secret fear or coping strategy that they had never before had the courage to reveal but which now, sensing the safety engendered by being in the company of others whose experience had also been theirs, they felt free to speak of.

For example, many MKs are prone to what psychologists call 'catastrophising'. This means imagining that the worst possible thing has happened based on little or no evidence, an experience embarked on as a result of a deeply held fear, often of finally and irrevocably being left alone. So, many MKs, not without some justification in many instances, feared the death of their parents. It was bad enough to be separated from them for such long periods and, for children brought up under more normal circumstances, it might have been the fear of separation that predominated. But for those for whom the separation had actually happened, their attention was now focused on the prospect of final separation. This fear was exacerbated by the knowledge that some of their contemporaries at the mission schools had indeed lost parents during their time on the field; victims of war, tribal clashes, violent robberies or religious violence, amongst other reasons. So, if a period of time elapsed without a letter from home, or if perhaps a child knew that their parents were travelling to a dangerous area or even a war zone, catastrophising was a common experience.

It was just one area in which many MKs found themselves unable to cope with their runaway imaginations, fuelling their fears in extreme and unnecessary ways, but powerless to stop doing so. When one MK shared at an alumni gathering that they had 'planned the funeral of everyone I've ever loved,' there were gasps of recognition and astonishment from around the room. Many of those present had done exactly that, projecting a worst case scenario onto the canvas of their future lives in an effort to control and minimise the fear that gripped them. But each had thought that this was something unique to them, which of course had added to their guilt. The relief that they were not alone was palpable and thoroughly cathartic. Countless examples of such secret hopes and fears emerged throughout these times of sharing. One person described the experience as:

> …that combination of being at home and also loved for being me with so many wonderful people who understood!

Just being with people who, even if you had never met them before, did not require you to explain who you were or where you were from, but understood that you were bound to them by cords that, in your childhood, had felt like fetters, but now could be seen as connectors with an almost umbilical resonance, was akin to a caged bird being set free to fly. Many MKs spend their whole lives despairing of anyone ever understanding who they are, but suddenly here was a whole community of people who needed no explanations, required no apologies, but wept and laughed and sang and shared and danced and played in ways so profound that, by the time it was over, it was actually hard to leave. As one lady put it:

> I feel as if someone let me out of a box and now I don't want to climb back in the box and close the door.

Another reflected:

> I felt so loved, so understood. I guess that´s the reason for all my tears when it was time to leave. You don´t want to leave a place where you feel so much of a connection to the people you have met!

These weeks worked because they combined five crucial and equally important ingredients.

Firstly, the location – returning, where possible, to the actual school where the attendees had spent their childhood was, for many, a key that unlocked the feelings that needed to be accessed if any healing work was to be done. This wasn't a universal truth, naturally, and everyone responded in their own very personal way. We saw how Mark received an instant hit of extreme emotion as he walked through the gates of his school. But when I returned to mine for the first time, I spent a week in the place before I was able to penetrate the numbness that had characterised the entirety of my stay up to that point. Others came and went untouched, perhaps immune, perhaps resistant – who knows? But for each, it was a deeply personal and unique experience. Nevertheless, the location was a vital piece of the jigsaw, albeit not one that was available to every mission alumni, since some schools had long since closed.

Secondly, the presence of TCK professionals and counsellors provided opportunities both for educational input – understanding what had happened, what the effects were, how those effects persisted into midlife and how they might be addressed – and for personal support and encouragement. All of this was available, but not compulsory, so that those who wished to take advantage of the opportunity could do so to the fullest extent they required. Those who wanted none of the therapy did not have to go anywhere near it. Thus, the individual rights of each attendee were respected, whilst everyone's needs were catered for.

Thirdly, there were specific and well-boundaried opportunities for alumni to engage with representatives of their mission should they wish. For some, being heard, being able to tell their story and being allowed to do so face to face with the freedom to express their grief and anger was crucial to the success and progress of their personal healing journey. The potential for this to go wrong was considerable and there were a number of conversations between organisers and mission representatives that began, 'On no account say … ' as they sought to protect the often fragile mental health of those who were already distressed and abused, and for whom giving voice to that distress – many for the first time in their lives – was an act of considerable courage. Most importantly, suggesting that God was the answer to MKs' problems was emphasised as being self-defeating in the extreme and, in some cases, missions were told that any such insensitivity on the part of mission delegates would bring an immediate end to proceedings. Even so, some missions were unable to resist a defensive posture that demonstrated a significant failure to grasp the trauma their MKs had been forced to deal with, reinforcing the truth that whilst their evangelistic endeavours were admirable, their pastoral awareness and sensitivity was considerably lacking.

Fourthly, provision in the timetable for those attending to revisit their childhood haunts proved to be an essential ingredient for everyone. A characteristic of the mission boarding school experience was that, despite the emotional trauma of long and drawn-out separation, many mission schools were located in beautiful settings and surrounded by exotic landscapes and fascinating wildlife. Days off from school had often included hikes through jungles and forests or up mountains, mini safaris to nearby wildlife reserves, trips to lakes and waterfalls, and shopping expeditions into the local towns. These had been opportunities briefly to forget the sadness the children wore like a cloak – but the cloak had been there, nonetheless. Now, in revisiting such places as adults, the MKs were able to repeat the delights of these outings, and so redeem them from the strictures of the past, enjoying the pleasure of the experience without the weight of abandonment that had pressed down on them all those years ago. The opportunity to relive these adventures completed a circle for many and even brought out the child in them as they leapt over streams, clambered over rocks and swung on vines. An added benefit was the very basic need for time away from the classroom, as it were, to process or lay aside the understandable intensity of the formal sessions, to just have fun, and to have it together.

Lastly, but perhaps in some ways most importantly, as many of the testimonies quoted above demonstrate, the value of being in a gathering of people who understood and accepted one another without the need to explain, justify or apologise for who they were, was immeasurably treasured. As one person described it, those present could:

> …examine our feelings in a safe place among safe people.

'A safe place among safe people' was what so many of us had lacked as children. So, returning to the place where our trauma had begun and discovering that it was a safe place, and the people with whom we were sharing it were safe people, was a kind of miracle.

And this is where the most effective work of such events was achieved. Not in the formal sessions with experts and counsellors, not even, perhaps, in the personal sessions with therapists, but in the informal conversations with friends and strangers, where experiences and emotions were shared, validated, supported, laughed and wept over. The regular affirmation, 'You are not alone,' was such a new and moving truth for most, having lived their entire lives under the misapprehension that they were uniquely flawed by their failure to deal well with their situation, that in itself would have made the trip worthwhile for many. These were conversations in which failures as well as 'Here's what worked for me' solutions were exchanged, lifelong-held secrets were shared and fears expressed, many for the first time.

Speaking of those who boarding school survivors approach for help in dealing with their experiences, Nick Duffell says:

> Unsympathetic scorn is just what the survivor fears most. (2)

This is one reason why MKs have traditionally been so reluctant to speak of their experiences. But here, at last, was a community of people with whom these times could be shared, safe in the knowledge that scorn was off the agenda and only empathic reassurance would be offered. Here's Nick Duffell again.

> Getting better from the emotional, physical and sexual abuse takes a lot of work, a lot of courage and, above all, a lot of trust. Yet trust is what such a survivor has lost in the first place, so it is no wonder that many do not begin, and settle for the compromise of not allowing themselves to recognise that there is anything wrong. (3)

Trust was what we lost as very young children. Some MKs would say that their trust was betrayed. But here was trust, tucked comfortably in alongside the safety.

And so the weight of sadness began to lift. Slowly, almost imperceptibly for many. Some even felt that they had taken a step backwards in order to give themselves the opportunity to move forward, in time. But the powerful combination of returning to the school, redeeming the good things that had gone on, guidance by experts through the bad things, hope that healing and resolution was not just a pipe dream but eminently possible, and, above all, the restoration of tribal family relationship within the community of MKs that provided a place of safety, trust, empathy and understanding, all of these came together to build a platform from which these still damaged adults could begin to grow up their inner children and move on into the remainder of their lives.

> We begin to build a façade. And that façade is something we paint as fast as we can pick up people's expectations. We become performers from the outside in because we don't think anything on the inside is worth enough. But it's our soul – that's the problem. You can't run away from it. You can try to bury it, you can try to

> disassociate from it, you can try to cover it up. But at some point, you're going to have to go back into the places that created the damage, that broke you apart, in order for your heart to be restored. *William Paul Young* (4)

These were not times for restoring faith – that would come later for those who wished it. Some did find that resolution through their personal experience during these weeks. But they were times for restoring hope – a hope that had been absent for many, its return long ago despaired of and no longer even considered. Now it was back. And, somehow, the road ahead seemed not only clearer, but more attractive, populated as it now was with like-minded folk who would provide the support, encouragement and companionship that had been absent from so many lives for so long.

Jenna's Story

Jenna was a typical missionary kid, at least in terms of her experience. Born into a loving and affectionate family, she had been sent away to boarding school just two weeks after her fifth birthday. It was a lovely school, set in a beautiful location and with kind staff and good teachers. In later years, Jenna would look back on the place with genuine affection, longing even. But at the time, she was bereft and, despite the many good things she was able to enjoy and the privileges and freedoms she would come to treasure, she could not shake off the grief that shadowed her through every moment of every day.

On the surface, Jenna was outgoing, friendly, bright and capable. Inside, she was deeply distressed, vulnerable, insecure and perpetually in fear. She was simultaneously everyone's friend, and yet somehow friendless. She was popular and admired, but had no idea that this was so and, though she buried it with practiced expertise, she was lonely beyond words. Dispatched to the sending country of her parents at the age of ten to what *they* called home, but which to Jenna was a place of bewilderment and confusion akin to her being parachuted onto the surface of the moon, she grieved the loss of the only country she had ever really known, travelling there nightly in her dreams, but denied the return for which she constantly longed because the mission's finances did not permit her to rejoin her family, except for six short weeks during a single summer of each four-year term of service.

Teased for her mid-Atlantic accent, mocked for her sophisticated worldview, bullied for her ignorance of local and contemporary culture and laughed at for her naïvety, strict sense of morality and conservative spiritual beliefs, Jenna denied the very substance of her identity in a desperate effort to survive in this new jungle of western middle class mores and social norms, conforming to the point where she had finally betrayed herself so completely that she no longer knew who she was at all. When a classmate encouraged her to visit the local shop and steal some sweets and a packet of cigarettes, she went along, postponing the inevitable guilt she knew would dog her for weeks just to be included. When another girl kissed her in the dorm in a lingering embrace that both thrilled and repelled her, she pushed away the shame she knew would nag at her for months, so desperate was she just to be held, regardless of who might be doing the holding or what they might require in return. When a group of boys began bragging about concerts they had been to and singers they had met, she related how she had once bumped into a film star in the toilets at a gig who had autographed her hand, which she had then refused to wash for weeks – despite never having been to a pop concert in her life and having very little recollection of what the person she had mentioned even looked like. It was a barefaced lie, but it trumped the boys' other stories and gained her a few days of much-needed credibility, even though she despised the culture and social pressures that rewarded it.

Despite these lapses from her own once-cherished moral standards, Jenna's unhappiness and desperate need for the love and support of her parents, which had been at best distant, often just plain absent for years now, was her best-kept secret. She was never going to tell anyone about the stealing or the sexual encounter or about lying to impress, all of which she thoroughly deprecated in herself, and none of which she was able to place in any kind of perspective in respect of the experimental journey that defines adolescence for most of us. But even less was she going to reveal her sadness, loneliness, confusion and distress to her parents. They were five thousand miles away now, so what difference could they make? It would only upset them. Or, worse, one of them would get on a plane, at huge expense to the mission, and fly back to put things right. Even at twelve, Jenna knew that nothing could make up for what she had already lost; no-one could put right what had gone so badly wrong.

At fourteen, Jenna had her first sexual experience with a boy whilst on a Christian Union weekend. At sixteen, she ran away from her boarding school but returned before her absence was discovered, when her courage failed her two miles down the road and it began to rain. At seventeen, she was put in detention for four consecutive Saturdays for being found in the common room with three cans of beer and a cigarette lighter. Actually, they weren't hers, but she was too smart to defend herself and refuse the kudos she would gain once the story got round the school.

At eighteen, she began university, but dropped out fifteen months later. No-one had ever explained to her how university worked or what was required of her and, by the time she had worked it all out for herself, she was too far behind in her course to have any motivation to continue. So she wrote a series of letters to her parents in which she described becoming gradually more ill, making her continued presence on her course untenable, and got a job as a waitress in a nightclub. She told her parents she was working in the hospitality industry and hoped they wouldn't ask too many questions about exactly what that meant.

At nineteen, she met a thirty-one-year-old entrepreneur called Joe, who ran a sports car showroom and had a spare room in his apartment, which he offered Jenna in return for some light work delivering packages to customers around the city a couple of evenings a week before she started work. He seemed nice and the room he was offering was twice the size of her current bedsit, so Jenna moved in. She took with her the few belongings she possessed and a significant amount of additional baggage marked 'Guilt,' 'Shame' and 'Rejection.' These she tucked into the back of a cupboard and tried to pretend she couldn't hear them when they began to protest their presence in their usual unsubtle way.

By the time the police came to Joe's apartment and arrested Jenna for possession and distribution of drugs, Joe had vanished, and Jenna herself had long ago realised what it was she had been doing. She hated and despised drugs and had never taken them herself. But she hated and despised herself and her life even more and, when Joe told her he had to go abroad for six months and was leaving her to carry on the business, she had agreed – not because she wanted to be a drugs mule but because she no longer cared what happened to her and was hopeful that somehow she would be caught and imprisoned, or perhaps even killed. She did not have the courage, moral or physical, to end her own life. But she had long been on the slippery slope that was leading her inexorably to the point where she would be content for someone else to do the deed on her behalf. Placing herself at huge risk by continuing in her courier role, and keeping Joe sweet at the same time seemed like an elegant way of bringing things to a head without her actually taking responsibility for the consequences.

Jenna admitted everything at her trial and was sentenced to four years, which in reality meant two, if she behaved. No-one, not even the prison psychiatrist, ever asked her about her childhood or inquired into her mental health. Even after everything she had been through, it was still one of the worst experiences of her life but she survived and, at twenty-three, she found herself starting over again, determined now to realise her potential, face the traumas and deal with the emotions that had brought her to such a low point in her life. Somewhat to her surprise, her parents had been compassionate and understanding through the whole process, though her mother had not stopped short of letting Jenna know how embarrassing the whole thing was for a family who had brought her up as a Christian and always tried to teach her right from wrong. Jenna had bitten her tongue at this and refrained from the kind of resentful and impassioned outburst she had so often rehearsed as she had lain alone in the darkness of her prison cell. In reality, she thought, all she had done was exchange one prison for another, and at least this was one her parents could not deny – and where they would actually visit her!

The mission had not been quite so forgiving or merciful, though, and when, some years later, Jenna asked for permission to stay at their guest house whilst on what she called her therapy trip, they refused, wishing her well, but stopping short of actually being seen to sit at their table with sinners! In time, Jenna recovered her sense of identity. She forgave the mission, her parents and herself, and even rediscovered the faith she had lost under the tsunami of grief and abandonment that had overwhelmed her as a young girl. She was even able to find time to counsel and support other MKs whose journey, whilst not as dramatic as her own, was nevertheless fraught with destructive potential that her own experiences allowed her to foresee. Such is grace.

Today, as I write, Jenna is married and settled and she happily testifies that her worst days are now behind her. But her journey of healing and restoration continues and she daily faces issues and situations which require courage, resilience and the wisdom and support of those around her to retain her newfound equilibrium. Her parents' mission continues to hold her at arm's length, more anxious not to be tainted by association than they are to offer her the forgiveness and compassion exampled by the Lord in whose name they serve. For Jenna, this is perhaps harder than anything, and demonstrates that even though many missions have acknowledged intellectually their culpability in damaging the lives of their members' children, their actions have yet to match the carefully worded legalese of such written apologies as they have made. When it comes to forgiveness and grace, they remain on the shore, unwilling to hold out their staff to part the sea and allow everyone to pass over, but instead using it to draw their lines in the sand.

I will leave the last word with Jenna. Asked how she dealt with the absence of God in her childhood and later restored her faith, she told me this:

> The truth of our abandonment as children was not that God was not there to console, reassure and parent us, but that we, with our undeveloped minds, immature spirits and broken hearts, were not able to know Him to be there. Now, I know that He was. Now, I know that He is.

From Nowhere to 'Now Where?'

> Sometimes the reason people have a problem accepting the gospel is that they sense that the God lurking behind Jesus isn't safe or loving or good. *Rob Bell* (1)

That question so disturbing to the TCK – 'Where are you from?' – is one to which some have been tempted to answer, 'Nowhere.' If not perhaps the truth, the whole truth and nothing but the truth, it is at least a fair representation of how many feel when they are unable to achieve any sense of belonging to a place, or even to a family. Finding a place where they can feel they truly belong, finding a person and a community in which they can feel they are safe to be themselves – both important factors in anyone's life – are often lifelong struggles for the missionary child, sent from their home and family before they are even close to being ready to detach themselves, then later exiled to a country and culture that is alien and unwelcome.

The sense that they are unloved and unlovable instilled in them by the actions of their parents is an almost impossible perception to face up to whilst they are still children; even as adults, able to rationalise somewhat their experience, the effects linger, often late into life. Very sadly and ironically, though inevitably, it is the lacuna created between the words and actions of their parents concerning the God they serve that is as damaging as anything. That sense that Rob Bell describes, 'that the God lurking behind Jesus isn't safe or loving or good,' is a by-product of the reality of their childhoods. Many Christians manage to achieve the splitting described in a previous chapter that allows a person to simultaneously believe that someone is good whilst undergoing experiences that suggest they are cruel or unkind, and ignore the reality of such a dichotomy. In fact, many MKs, regardless of whether or not they have a faith, do the same, unquestioning in their defence of their parents' actions and minimising or even denying outright the effects on their lives – some in the face of their mental suffering, others denying and suppressing even that, so fearful are they of facing the truth.

> Many people are blocked from self-knowledge and personal growth by the myth they feel compelled to hold on to of having had a 'happy childhood.' *Gabor Maté* (2)

For those in either camp, the problem is the same – who we were told God is and who He seems to be are not one and the same. Such are the consequences of a theology that chooses which aspects of God's character we want to highlight and which to ignore; which verses of Scripture we are going to prioritise and which to lay aside; which nuances of doctrine we are going to hold onto and which we will pretend aren't there.

> If you take one passage of Scripture and hold it up while ignoring others, you will come to absurd conclusions. *John Eldredge* (3)

'Twas ever thus, it might be said, and perhaps we are all guilty of this adjusting of the lens through which we perceive and understand the One who is not to be fully perceived and cannot be fully understood; at least not in this life. The truth and power of the saying that 'Actions speak louder than words' is something we underestimate at our peril. And our failure to pay attention to the extent to which one reflects the other places us in danger of peddling snake oil in place of the healing remedy we persuade ourselves we are selling.

Therefore, anyone who removes your basic familial support base in this life and then tells you that God will compensate you, if not in this life then in the next, has perhaps misunderstood much of the purpose of this life. Children, perhaps especially the children of believing parents, take what their parents tell them as the gospel truth. So, when a crack opens up, which in time becomes a canyon, between the truth and the actuality, this is not just confusing, but deeply bewildering for a child. MKs start out belonging to a family and to God, and then to their mission family. But very soon their family has become distant, literally; God seems not to be there, at least not in the way or to the degree that it was promised He would be, and the mission is all that is left to belong to. When that happens, the child has become part of an institution, and, as history has shown, institutions are self-serving and self-preserving in their policies and pragmatisms, and swiftly develop practices that control their members rather than nurture them. In such instances, children first of all become invisible, then disappear altogether.

This is what allowed missions to disown their children once they reached eighteen, effectively washing their hands of them, despite the fact that their parents remained active on the field, where they had been throughout the whole of the youngster's schooling. By doing so, they were rendering the missionaries' children homeless, without any visible means of support. Bluntly, it might be said that what missions had done was prevent parents from raising their children in a way that might prepare them for adult life, substitute themselves in the parents' place, then drop the young person purely on the basis that they were now an adult, which allowed missions to make a secular, legal case, if not actually a spiritual or moral one, for completing the child's abandonment.

The resistance, often even antagonism, of faith communities to the increasingly accepted science of child psychology allowed missions to ignore the growing clamour of voices indicating that they were visiting significant and lasting damage on their children. Psychology, the thinking went, undermined faith by placing an undue emphasis on the effects of a secular society which was irrelevant to those who were being raised in Christian families or communities, within which God could be trusted to protect children from the alleged effects of such matters as early childhood separation or abandonment.

> In the first half of the twentieth century, and despite the influence of Freudian theories, the dominant behaviourist school argued that relations between parents and children were shaped by material feedback; that children needed mainly food, shelter and medical care; and that children bonded with their parents simply because the latter provide these material needs. Children who demanded warmth, hugs and kisses were thought to be 'spoiled'. Childcare experts warned that children who were hugged and kissed by their parents would grow up to be needy, egotistical and insecure adults. Only in the 1950s and 1960s did a growing consensus of experts abandon these strict behaviourist theories and acknowledge the central importance of emotional needs. *Yuval Noah Harari* (4)

So, what began as a Spirit-inspired venture to fulfil a divine calling through obedience to the commission of Christ, morphed into a human construct in which missionary endeavour and a heart for evangelism absorbed, almost without realising it, fundamental tenets of colonialism, elitism, white privilege, ethnic pride and a societal or institutional siege mentality that turned the demands of pragmatic logistics and survival necessities into controlling policies and legalistic rules; in turn, this meant that if you were not for them, you were against them. The desire for unity became a need for conformity, wearing a mask of pious acceptability that saw such detractors as may have seen through to what lay behind the eyes marginalised and, often, silenced. Instead of being open to reconsidering their policies, many missions retreated into self-defence mode, reinforcing the validity of their methodologies because to admit that they might have been wrong would have been to devalue the sacrifice their past members had made over the years. It's one thing to recognise and confess to errors of interpretation or judgment, but it would have been a betrayal of the trust that members had placed in their leadership to change direction and reveal that the sacrifices and suffering they and their children had undergone had been unnecessary and perhaps in vain. Here's Yuval Harari again.

> The more sacrifices we make for an imaginary story, the more tenaciously we hold on to it, because we desperately want to give meaning to these sacrifices and to the suffering we have caused. (5)

Such is the Jephthah inheritance; the traumatic consequence of a promise made which was never required, an oath taken which God did not request and a commitment undertaken which undermined the very essence of who God is. Sure, there were plenty of Scriptures that could be used, and were indeed used, to justify this; similarly, there were plenty of Scriptures that could be and were used by 19th century Confederates to justify slavery, 20th century Catholics to ban the use of contraceptives or 21st century Conservative American Evangelicals to elect a president whose words and actions were so blatantly and spectacularly contrary to the teachings of Jesus that the rest of the world stood open-mouthed in astonishment and wide-eyed in horror.

But the story of missions and their children has not ended. There are roads yet to be travelled by those called to service overseas in the name of Jesus, and many of those who heed that call will take their children along for the ride. So, what are the positives that we can take from the experiences of their predecessors? What are the lessons that have been learnt, or that remain to be learnt? Are there stories of redemption and hope, just as there are stories of brokenness and distress? Are there any signs that God has stepped in to redeem the actions of the past, many of which, as has already been stressed, were done in good faith, with the best of intentions and due, at least in part, to the knowledge, wisdom and pragmatism of the time?

Most MKs are well aware of the privileges of their upbringing. The schools they attended were often in the cool of the mountains and allowed for a level of excitement and adventure in everyday life that many children at home in western schools could only ever read about. My own experience included frequent trips into virgin rainforest or up mountains where only indigenous tribes and some curious locals had ever ventured; a school situated in a valley surrounded by jungle and later found to hold the highest concentration of venomous snakes in the country; a school dog, a wonderful and popular Alsatian, lost to a tiger which was later shot and put on display in the local town; many hours spent chasing and collecting exotic butterflies and a range of colourful insects; visits to an abandoned airfield where we collected bullet shells, some of them still live, that had just been left by departing forces; barbecues and breakfasts cooked over an open fire on the mountain ridge above the school; and a final journey home that was made in a British Army convoy necessitated by the presence of mercenary bandits eager to subvert the political status quo, guarded by a battalion of Gurkha soldiers armed only with knives. (Today's teachers' minds are doubtless boggling at the thought of risk assessing that little lot!)

So, MKs were educated into a wide-ranging and mature worldview that equipped them with a level of knowledge and understanding of life way beyond that of their contemporaries once they entered their secondary school back in their parents' home. It was one of the reasons they struggled to fit in and were often teased and bullied for being different, or for what was interpreted as arrogance when they revealed the extent of their knowledge or related their experiences. It was also what made life so hard, returning as they did from the exotic beauty of their third world home to what they often perceived as the drab boredom of provincial western life, with its comforts and predictabilities.

Spiritually, MKs had received a mostly sound and comprehensive training in the contents of Scripture, albeit some of the ways in which it was interpreted were, as we have discussed, self-serving and manipulative in the extreme. But the concept of living by faith and, in particular, trusting God to supply our needs, having absolute confidence in His saving power, was deeply ingrained in many MKs, who possessed a high degree of spiritual maturity, even if much of it would prove to be rather fragile, ultimately. In truth, many MKs were, if anything, more signed up to the concept of living by faith than were their parents or even their mission. It was a profound shock to many when, much later in life, they discovered that the reason they had not been able to return home to their parents during boarding school holidays was not simply that God had not provided the means for them to make the journey, but that their mission had not deemed it a sufficient priority to budget for them to do so and therefore had not even sought God for the provision. 'Ask and you will receive.' Don't ask and ....

It is perhaps not for me to suggest what lessons have been learnt from the experiences of MKs over recent decades, not least because each mission is different and each has addressed (or not) its own shortcomings to the extent that it has been able to accept them. But the fact that many MKs and alumni of missions schools have taken steps to face up to the issues of their early childhood separation, and that some have invited their missions to participate in this process, has meant that missions have at least been made aware that their past policies and actions were responsible for significant mental health problems in those now adult children. How this came about and how each mission reacted describes a broad spectrum of responses – from the ultra-defensive stance of those being sued in the courts for dereliction of duty, to the empathic reactions of some who have taken the time and trouble to listen to the stories of their MKs, see for themselves the distress their victims have felt and even, in some cases, provide counselling opportunities for their members' children.

The march of progress has also been a factor in this process. The advent of the internet has made homeschooling a realistic option and removed the restrictions placed upon every mission by distance, and the demands of the proper and appropriate allocation of finances. The very nature of mission work has changed of course and, where fifty years ago a couple might join a mission and remain in one area for the next thirty or forty years, many of today's missionary designations are short-term, perhaps only one, two or three years, making the considerations regarding the raising and educating of children significantly easier. Feminism and the liberal ethics of contemporary society have also had their say. Where once missions employed exclusively men in leadership, leaving their wives to find a ministry of their own where and how they could, today many missions employ couples in leadership positions where they share the role and duties, and enjoy equal recognition for and fulfilment in their work. Travel and communication are now hugely easier, if still costly, and both of these factors have dramatically shrunk the world to a size manageable in respect of keeping families in touch with each other and allowing a more normal family life. What a difference free video calls home could have made to so many of us!

Child psychology is now widely accepted and, though it was not a swift process, the pastoral care of members by their missions is now greatly improved. Where once a single Medical Officer was responsible for the physical and mental wellbeing of the entire mission – perhaps up to a thousand members – today, every mission has staff appointed to member care in each of their home countries. Additionally, there is an increased awareness that missionaries are not immune from spiritual crises or work-related stresses, and the need for mentoring and guidance of members by senior missionaries and independent counsellors is no longer overlooked to the extent that it once was. The age-old question, 'Who pastors the pastors?' used to be received as an accusation, any acknowledgement of which was seen as demonstrating a degree of weakness that was neither acceptable nor even considered feasible on the mission field. Again, no longer – happily.

That said, there remain issues to be addressed and not all missions possess the self-awareness to understand the full implications of their policies even in the light of the revelations made by their own MKs. Some remain in denial. As was mentioned previously, at least one mission categorically assured me that they no longer used boarding as an option for their MKs, despite the fact that not only were they doing so, but they were even allowing some of their members to keep their children in school over Christmas. It seems unlikely that the mission concerned was unaware of this, and there were certain cultural issues in play in this instance. The same mission once described the limitations of their support in addressing their MKs' issues as being due to their 'business plan,' even, in as many words, suggesting that simply trusting that God would provide the necessary resources for His work was 'perhaps a little outdated.' This from an avowed faith mission. So, although many good things have been done and are still being achieved, there remains some way to go. Many long-held attitudes remain deeply entrenched in some organisations, and there is a degree of resistance to considering the significant changes that still need to be made if MKs are to be properly cared for.

Are there stories of redemption and hope? Well, Jenna's story is just such a tale, albeit much of her journey was made close to the edge of a dangerous precipice. Mark's too; and there are many others. On the one hand, the very fact that so few MKs' lives ended in premature death at their own hands, and that some were seemingly untouched and did not see their ambitions and opportunities destroyed by the pernicious and persistent effects of childhood trauma that endured into adult life, is in itself a sign of redemption, if one chooses to view it that way. On the other hand, the courage and determination of those who have sought to confront their missions with the evidence of those effects and invite them to become involved in the healing journeys of their MKs has also resulted in many journeying through a process of understanding, healing and restoration, as the testimonies quoted in a previous chapter reveal. Therein was found hope and many have spoken of being able to move forward in their lives and in their faith as a result of having been given the opportunity to work through their childhood traumas. But, it is important to reiterate here that such journeys continue and their travellers face daily challenges in overcoming the deep-seated griefs and resentments caused by their experiences. As William Paul Young, author of *The Shack* and himself an MK who remains on such a journey, is fond of saying, 'We live in the grace of the day.'

Meanwhile, when books such as *Sent*,(6) documenting the experiences of MKs of the China Inland Mission and OMF International, and Ruth van Reken's literary memoir of her childhood in Liberia, *Letters Never Sent*,(7) amongst others, become required reading in missionary training colleges, Bible schools and theological colleges, we will perhaps then know that these concerns are being taken seriously by all those involved in Christian ministry, including church leaders. Ulrika Ernvik's *Third Culture Kids: A Gift to Care For*,(8) though not specifically about MKs, is also a welcome addition to mission resources in defining quality care for children in transition.

And what of God Himself? Where does He stand in all this? Is He unhappy that the rightness of the decisions made by his good and faithful servants of years gone by should be brought into question long after they have left this world? Is He part of the healing process described here, or is He content to stand back and leave it to the counsellors and therapists? Is He perhaps angry about the neglect and suffering of His children in the past? We return to the question that was being asked from the very start by missions, missionaries and their children: 'Where is God in all this?'

Interesting as these questions may be, they are, on one level, no different from those asked by Job; I will not presume to answer either on God's behalf or on behalf of those whose personal experience and understanding of God alone will fashion their perception of the truth. That is not to say that these are not questions we should try to answer, or at least consider such answers as may be available to us. Indeed, these are subjects that have been actively discussed by theologians, mission leaders and MKs for many years now. Hopefully, such talks are leading faith communities and organisations towards a deeper awareness of the issues of, and possible solutions to, practical questions of Christian ministry and a more complete understanding of how we might move forward in the future. What I will do is share a few thoughts from my own experience which will perhaps throw some small light on recent progress in this area.

For me, the principle that undergirds how we are to understand these issues is the nature of the character of God. That God is love means that love is the motivating force behind His actions: the means by which He works out those actions and the goal of their completion. God does not – cannot – act outside of love. As the Living Bible translation of 2 Timothy 2:13 puts it:

> [God] cannot disown us who are a part of Himself and He will always carry out His promises to us.

And as we read in Proverbs 16:4:

> The Lord works out everything to its proper end ….

He is 'the pioneer and perfecter of our faith' (Hebrews 12:2) and He is the one who 'in all things … works for the good of those who love Him,' (Romans 8:28). In other words, God knows what He is doing; He doesn't make mistakes; He doesn't cause us problems in our lives; and He doesn't encourage or even dictate processes which violate loving, familial relationships. It follows, therefore, that He is always interested in healing our hurts, restoring our brokenness and resolving our conflicts. So, when we invite Him to participate in the process of understanding our childhood pain and facing up to its consequences, He jumps at the chance. Just as Jesus Himself pointed out:

> If you, then, though you are evil, know how to give good gifts to your children, how much more will your Father in heaven give good gifts to those who ask Him.' (Matthew 7:11)

So, we may believe that God is eager to be part of our healing journey and that we only need to ask Him to become involved in quite tangible and visible ways.

How He reflects on the past falls into the category of His right to judge us, which in turn should be seen within the frame of His omniscience. He knows the context and perspective that governed the decisions of His servants in the past and Scripture encourages us to leave such judgment to Him. We cannot know the full facts, nor see the complete picture, so we must be content that because He can, He can also be trusted to act appropriately and in accordance with His own standards of justice, love, compassion and mercy.

But, importantly, God is always concerned about the present, because He *IS*. He *IS* love, He *IS* with us, He *IS* transforming us into His likeness, He *IS* the One who heals, restores, forgives and raises up.

> He lifted me out of the slimy pit, out of the mud and mire. He set my feet upon a rock and gave me a firm place on which to stand. He put a new song in my mouth, a hymn of praise to our God. (Psalm 40: 2–3)

At the same time, He knows about our past, about our traumas and hurts, and He is not content to leave us in a place of pain. One of the most important truths I learnt during my own journey towards healing and resolution was God's ability to backfill our lives. Herein, I believe, lies at least a part of the truth of those words of Matthew 19:29, which were so blithely used by parents seeking to comfort their children and themselves as they entered the black hole of early childhood separation that would traumatise so many. I found, as did many, that in facing up to the grief and abandonment of the past, not only did God meet me where I was, validating those destructive childhood emotions that lingered into adulthood (whose validity we ourselves had continually denied), but also, He began to pour into my life the assurances and consolations I had so desired from Him as a child. And with these came an awareness of His love 'that surpasses knowledge' (Ephesians 3:19). It was as if my life was a vase filled with pebbles, each of which was an experience of hardness and dryness; a place where flowers could not bloom and flourish, but into which He poured His living water, reaching to the bottom and filling 'to the measure' all the spaces in between those pebbles to create a place of renewal, life and nourishment, and of beauty and growth filled 'with all the fulness of God'.

My journey towards spiritual and emotional healing was born of an awareness that within me was a well of anger and grief that was deeper than I could imagine, that was destroying my ability to conduct mature and appropriate relationships or gain any pleasure from life, since I lived with an ever-present sense of rejection and abandonment. My faith was strong, but I knew it to have insecure foundations and I had rejected much of what I had been taught as a child at my mission school as being oversimplified and based on doctrines of dubious veracity and unsustainable (not to say unnecessary) levels of certainty. I went in search of the true God, the God who IS love; and I went in search of the little boy I had left behind in that beautiful but grief-filled place where I had both grown up too fast and yet never grown up at all.

There, after a long period of numbness during which I almost despaired, I found him; wise beyond his years, as so many of us had been forced to become, but eager to access the emotions that he and I had suppressed and to find together a way of removing the pressure valve that, if it remained, would sooner or later explode, to who knew what disastrous effect. At the behest of some of my MK colleagues, keen to know how successful I might be in my venture, I blogged my journey. Here is a brief excerpt.

> Night is falling now, the rain has just returned and soon the jungle's night orchestra will start up. I sat on the wall outside the old classrooms, now my bedroom, with some sticks of satay, and watched the darkness descend. An owl, who had been hooting up in the jungle below the ridge, flew across the playground in front of me and settled in a tree by the stream.
>
> But there is an elephant in the room. How has it all taken me? As I started out from Tapah, I could feel my body responding to the conditioning of all those years ago, preparing for and fighting against the car sickness that we so feared on the journey, which thankfully I was spared. It was a very strange feeling, but it helped me to understand what happened next. Because the closer I got to Chefoo, the less interested I became. All the old coping strategies and self-protecting measures just kicked in, despite myself, leaving me feeling numb. I feel nothing. And if that is how I leave here, I will have failed in my task.
>
> I have done the easy bit in coming back here. But without the children, this place is soulless. And without my own inner child, I am an empty shell. Somehow, I have to find him, here in this place, where first he was lost to me.

One week into my visit, having been staying at the old school, I moved to the mission's holiday home on the other side of the mountain. There I found the piano on which I had learnt to play and which I had thought was no longer present.

> Tonight, for the first time in several years, I sat down and played the piano for my own pleasure. It is a joy that has been lost to me for too long now and the fact that I was able to do it was evidence of some healing having begun to take place. I am becoming myself again. The little boy who used to play his heart out in the main house at Chefoo (when he was supposed to be practising!) is returning to me. I will have to be gentle and patient with him, but at last he has stepped out from behind the curtain of grief and the beginnings of a smile can be seen beneath his still sad eyes. I'm taking him out for a walk tomorrow and we will begin to talk.
>
> Today, we walked together in the jungle, the boy and I.
>
> And we talked.
>
> The morning sun shone through the rainforest canopy like a thousand spotlights, picking out the ferns, the mosses and the carpet of leaves, some of them as big as a frying pan. A tree shrew scampered from branch to branch, his bushy tail swinging this way and that, like a rudder to balance his body as he flew through the air. And we smiled.
>
> He has a ready smile, though his eyes do not join in.
>
> 'Did you come back to get me?'
>
> 'I did.'
>
> 'I'm glad. I wanted someone to find me and only you knew where I was.
>
> But ...'
>
> 'Yes?'
>
> He looked up at me with the eyes of an old man in the face of a child. He smiled, though his eyes did not join in, and he took me by the hand.
>
> 'Come on.'
>
> Today, we walked together in the jungle, the boy and I.
>
> And we talked.
>
> Clouds rolled down the valley to mask Jasar's face, but still the sun shone down on us as we walked through the trees. A golden lizard basked, sparkling, on a bank, glistening as if newly smelted in the dawn that had birthed this glorious day. Suddenly, we were surrounded by a flock of birds – fantails, bee-eaters, sunbirds, all chirruping and fluttering so that you didn't know where to look next. For a few moments, I quite lost myself in the excitement and, when they had gone, I turned, half expecting him to have left too. But there he was, perched on the stone wall by a roadside drain, sitting on his hands, swinging his legs and waiting. He had always

been good at waiting – by the gym, playing with his koala bear, by the dorm, one ear cocked for the sound of an approaching car engine, by the drive, by the stream … always waiting, waiting, waiting.

'Why do even you not love me?'

'What?'

'You love who I was, but not who I have become.'

'But you have become …. Oh. I see.'

He smiled, though his eyes did not join in.

Today, we walked together in the jungle, the boy and I.

And we talked.

We heard the silver-eared meesias before we saw them, even above the roar of Robinson Falls. They flashed green and orange amongst the leaves, calling to each other as they flew. Then the iridescent royal blue of the mountain minivet darted across our way. A fantail sat on a branch by the path, black as night, upright, elegant. And all the while the muddy waters of the Bertam River hurled themselves across the rocks of the small ravine, shouting their fury as they tumbled down the valley.

'You may not take me with you, you know.'

'But … I've come all this way. How can I now leave you behind?'

'You must leave me behind. I must always remain here. Soon, you will grieve your loss of me, though not quite yet. For now, we are together and that makes us both happy. And, if you should ever return to this place, you will find me again. For I will always be here. But you must leave me one more time.'

He smiled, though his eyes did not join in.

This evening, we walked together in the jungle, the boy and I.

And we wept.

Wept the tears of the years that have kept us from each other. Tears of such pain that I thought my heart would break and my chest ached from the effort. He held my hand until the tears had subsided.

'We are one now. All that I am will stay with you forever.'

'But … I don't understand. I thought I couldn't take you with me.'

'You can't. This is where I shall always be, must always be. But all that I am will go with you now. I must remain here, but you will not be leaving me behind. You have many more tears to shed, but they will not all be for me.'

And once again the tears flowed freely. He wrapped his small hands around mine and smiled. And his eyes sparkled with laughter-light at our oneness.

Today, we walked together in the jungle, the boy and I ….

I had not known when last I left him when I might see the boy again. But as I started up the path towards Parit Falls this morning, there he was waiting for me. And so once again we walked together in the jungle, the boy and I. And we talked.

'Come and play. We have not played for a long time and I have missed it.'

And he ran up the path, skipping lightly over the tangled roots, stopping occasionally to watch a butterfly find a place to land. I had never seen him so happy. A bright sun shone from a clear, blue sky as we followed the path by the river up to the falls. The birds were quiet, but another golden lizard scuttled up the path and into the undergrowth. The ground gave gently under our feet, lush with moss and layers of fallen leaves. Seemingly endless vines draped the trees and the boy swung them happily to and fro as we passed.

'I know where we should go!'

He ran ahead of me, ducking and scrambling over fallen trees and around rocks in the pathway. Suddenly, he stopped and pointed. And there, fallen across the river like a natural bridge, was the tree we used to play on as children, shinning over the brown waters beneath to the other side, then swinging back across the river on a vine. We stood for some minutes, each quiet with his own thoughts. An eagle flew up into a nearby tree and vanished from sight. It was I who broke the silence.

'Are there things you still have to tell me?'

'Yes.'

He paused, letting the silence ring through the treetops.

'Bringing us together again has restored to you the goodness you thought you had lost.'

He paused again and the silence crowded in, as if to listen more closely.

'You have found again the peace you could not find. These things are not of you, but they lie deep within you and you must search for them. If you lose them again, I will not be able to restore them to you a second time.'

He took my hand.

'Be happy. For both of us.'

After lunch, I explored the old shortcut from the bungalow down to the road. But the boy was not with me.

I returned to drongo territory, where we had spent such a happy morning yesterday, and here he joined me once again, the boy, and we walked through the jungle together. He slipped his hand gently into mine as he fell into step beside me. It was rest hour for the birds, but a tree frog was sitting obligingly on a whitewashed wall, elegantly painted in green and brown. We sat down by the track each lost in his own thoughts, then resumed our walking.

'Is there anything else?'

He stopped and held out his hands, cupped together, as if holding something precious.

'I have something for you.'

I held out my palms and into them he placed a small bird, so light I could hardly feel it there at all.

'Here are your dreams of all the years we have been kept apart. You are ready to let them go now.'

For what seemed like ages I stood there, looking him in the eyes as he held my gaze. Then, slowly, I lifted my palms up and watched the little bird flutter away into the forest. The boy flung his arms around my waist and held me tight as the tears flowed once again. And when I could weep no more, he again took my hand and we walked together back along the track.

'The time for words is past.'

I nodded. For deep in my heart, I had known.

And so, for a second day, we walked together in the jungle, the boy and I. And now only one thing remains. Tomorrow we will walk for one last time … at Chefoo.

Today was my last day in the Camerons and I would visit a number of the places that had provided special memories for me on this trip, walking the road to the Lutheran Bungalow, watching for drongos on the back road to Tanah Rata, ambling down Robinson Falls. And I sat in the garden at the OMF Bungalow as the white witch drifted in and out of the valleys, resting for a while in the rainforest's canopy before moving on. But there was really only one place for me to be today.

Today, we walked together for one last time, at Chefoo, the boy and I. And neither of us spoke a single word. The time for words was past. Our communion was absolute and required no voicing. But his hand never left mine the whole time we were there.

I felt his grip tighten as we walked in through the gates and his eyes darkened as the sadness resurfaced. I had barely taken ten steps before the tears returned unbidden and I could no longer see where I was walking. As we stood there on the drive, he rested his head against me and rubbed his hand in a circular motion above my heart, as if to soothe the pain. When I had regained my composure, we resumed our walk, almost imperceptibly at first, so slowly did we move, taking in every last detail of the banks and jungle.

I was not ready for the buildings yet, so we made our way down the red steps opposite the old ridge shortcut to the area where we would sometimes chase fireflies in the early evening. This was the closest I was going to come to the stream and we stood there for some minutes, listening to the burbling waters that for so many years had been the last sound we had heard each night.

We climbed back up onto the drive and resumed our gentle progress; past the playing field, past the past and on towards the future. But for now, the present … and the boy were still with me.

We sat for a while in front of the new block, behind the old dining room, and listened to the chatter of the Malay girls in the kitchen. And I recalled how quiet the school would be during lesson time, the playground empty in the brilliant sunshine, only the sounds of the cicadas and the kitchen staff chattering merrily echoing around our little valley.

Again, we sat together, this time at the back of the main house, where once a covered way had protected us from the rain as we waited to go in to morning assembly or queued to see Aunty Betty, the nurse, in the clinic. We remembered the monsoon season, the boy and I, when, donning a sweater against the chill, we would stand beside the dorms and watch the rain sheeting across the valley and pounding onto the tarmac. And we smiled.

We walked on round to what had once been the smallest boys' dorm, where the house-parents had lived in the room on the end in the days before the Headmaster's house was built. This had been our first dorm, and once more the boy tightened his grip as we approached. Here too, by the wall overlooking the playing field, we had been made to stand alone at night as a punishment. The boy stood in front of me and wrapped his arms around me. But neither of us spoke a word. None were needed.

We sat on the steps above the cottage, which had at various times been both staff quarters and a sick bay. And we recalled the lonely silence of the long, long days when we had been unwell and bored literally to tears.

So much of who I am now was shaped in this place – a childhood splendoured by unimaginable beauty and serenity, immersed in our little valley in the inexpressible delights of the very best of God's creation. And yet, a childhood spent walking in the valley of the shadow of grief, twisted by the weight of sadness on our so young shoulders that gouged its way down into the very depths of our soul. It is a sadness that will always remain in the eyes of the little boy who sat beside me, grasping me tightly with one hand, the other rubbing lightly across my chest, still soothing, still comforting. But I cannot take him home with me. And maybe at least some of the sadness will be left behind as well.

We walked back down the drive, pausing at the bend for one last look back. And then on to the gate, our reluctant footsteps dragging on the tarmac. Suddenly, quite without warning, I was overwhelmed by a black and all-consuming grief and I fell to my knees on the grass, wracked with uncontrollable sobs.

> Knowing I would not be able to bear leaving him at the gates of the school, the boy had gone. For three days he had been my consolation. And, knowing we would not be together again on this trip, I was inconsolable. But this was a grief for which I could weep tears of healing balm. This was a grief that would not last forever. And, through his gentle, ever-loving presence, the boy had guided me to a new place in my life. One where I hope I may begin again to live and love as he had shown me once I had meant to do. His place is here, and I may not take him with me. But all that he is and was is now a part of me. And if I should one day return to this beloved place, I know that I shall see him once again. And together, we will walk in the jungle … and talk.

My story is, of course, uniquely mine. And my journey is not one anyone else can or should make. It is for each of us to follow our own path. Mine had led me to this extraordinary, visceral experience of walking and talking with my inner child in a way that had made him visible, audible, tangible. It was what I needed, perhaps and, though I didn't know it, God did. For some who read this account at the time, I had lost my mind. For others, it brought tears and even, in some, inspired a small sense of envy, as they expressed later. I knew as I wrote it that there would be some who did not understand, and I took the mockery that ensued with a quiet smile. I didn't need them to understand. I had been there and those days had been amongst the most beautiful and seminal of my life. For they were not the end of my journey, but the end of its beginning. From there I would move on, have moved on, taking many others with me. (I did return, and he was there.) There were many difficult years that still lay ahead of me and, ultimately, even some of those who had walked with me in those early days would discard me as being too damaged, too broken to accompany them any further.

That my personal experience should have been so unusual, and extreme in its way, was an encouragement to many that nothing was impossible or beyond the boundaries of what could be granted to us when we sought the healing power of the God we had thought for so many years had not been there. But it was also a discouragement to some, since it was obviously a potentially uncomfortable, even perhaps scary situation and a place many did not want to go at any price. But, for me, that is the grace of God. My experience was as perfectly tailored to my needs as it would have been inappropriate for most others. My purpose in sharing my story is not to say, 'This is how it works,' but to testify that how it works for each individual can be exactly what is right for them, however different that experience might be. And different it certainly will be.

Sure, we need courage to face our ghosts and stare our grief and rejection in the face, to allow ourselves to feel emotions that we have buried for decades, and to relinquish the coping strategies that have served us so well (or so we imagine) for so long. But when we find that courage, we also find that out of it comes the means of growth and grace that moves us on in our lives in ways we never dreamed were possible, and in which we had perhaps given up hope.

A crucial part of this journey is re-imaging God to conform to the person of Jesus rather than the distorted and received caricature presented to us in our childhood. It is about trusting the truth that 'The Son is the radiance of God's glory and the exact representation of His being' (Hebrews 1:3), setting in context the wrathful and avenging portraits of the Old Testament and receiving the image not of the God some of our mission leaders declared Him to be but of who Jesus reveals Him to be. This is a process of courage and relinquishment, but one that leads to a sense of the beauty and grace that the Father always intended us to find in the love, compassion, mercy and justice of the Son. Herein lies the truth of Jeremiah 29:13.

> You will seek me and find me if you seek me with all your heart.

And 1 Chronicles 28:9.

> If you seek Him, He will be found by you.

Not, 'you will find Him,' but 'He will be found by you.' He will be found. Like a four-year-old playing hide-and-seek with his father who starts making little coughing and squeaking noises because he wants to be found, so God wants to be found by us. He will be found. He only desires that we seek, and then He will be found.

Sadly, for some MKs, the toxic theology peddled by their mission damaged them so severely that they have been quite unable to consider God as anything other than cruel and angry, if He exists at all. One of the most difficult conversations I have ever had was on the morning I was obliged to take William Paul Young, whom I had invited to speak at one of our week-long events for MKs, for a pre-breakfast walk with the sole purpose of asking him please to consider speaking a little less evangelistically and with fewer references to Jesus in his session later that morning. (I wince even to recall it.) If he couldn't do that, I told him, some of our MKs would simply leave – not just the session but possibly the entire event, so antagonistic were they to any mention of God. In fact, I had been obliged during the organisation process to promise no-one would preach at them, that being the only basis on which they were willing to attend; I considered it more important that they had access to whatever support they might need than that we offer them our version of a solution that had already caused them so much heartbreak.

Poor Paul, having been dragged halfway around the world to share his experiences and testimony was, almost certainly for the first time in his life, being asked to find a way of delivering that testimony without speaking of Jesus and thereby offending those of our MKs who would terminate their presence if further threatened by having God presented to them as even a part of the solution to their problems. Later, he would reflect that our alumni were probably the most triggered group he had ever encountered. This remark was not, I believe, intended as any kind of criticism but a compassionate assessment of the extent to which some had been damaged by having God misrepresented to them as children. Of course, he was gracious, generous and understanding and, because of his sensitivity, no-one left the event. It is not an occasion I recall with any pleasure, and I mention it only to demonstrate how very serious were the effects of their upbringing on the faith prospects of some MKs.

We should not expect that such deeply rooted and long-standing trauma might be healed without there being significant obstacles to overcome on the way and, for many MKs, the issues surrounding the outworking of their parents' faith exacerbated the effects of their experience considerably. There are serious psychological consequences for any child being sent away to boarding school at an early age or without their consent. But when you add to that the spiritual imperative that declares to the child that it is God's will that they be sent away, you are heaping sulphur onto an already flaming fire. The burden that we carried as young children of the declared rightness of what was happening to us, of the goodness of God and His desire that we be so treated over against the reality of our despair and loneliness, our sense of rejection and abandonment, was a crushing one, and a completely inappropriate burden to place onto the shoulders of so small a frame and so undeveloped a mind. The years so many of us spent growing up alone and largely unsupported, dealing with all the confusions and dramas intrinsic to the process of being birthed from childhood through adolescence and on into adulthood were unspeakably hard.

Through those years, and despite its agonies, most MKs remained loyal to their parents, the mission and the image of God that had been presented to them. This made what followed even more difficult, as we began to realise that our loyalty, laudable and honourable as it may have been in its own way, had been misplaced and we had lacked the critical thinking and mature wisdom to critique and question our treatment. For many, the shock of finding out that there had been another way, that all we had gone through was perhaps unnecessary, whatever benefits may have accrued, was huge. Hindsight, though it can be a wonderful thing, can also be a terrible thing when it reveals waste, and fuels regret on so massive a scale.

But, just as it is necessary for us to reflect that the policies and actions of those years were of their time and so perhaps unavoidable at least in some respects, so we must accept that what is done is done and it need not define us for the rest of our lives. There were many awful experiences that wounded us deeply, the scars of which we will have to bear for the rest of our lives. But there were many joys and privileges too and, though there is no benefit in weighing one against the other, we can certainly celebrate the good things and acknowledge the ways in which they have made us strong and given us an understanding of life and the world that is denied to many whose childhood is perhaps not quite so disrupted. Research carried out by Cengiz, Ergun and Cakici in 2019 even suggests that there was perhaps a degree of growth for some MKs, whose survival increased their ability to cope with all that life would throw at them as an adult; not that this should be regarded as in any way providing adequate compensation for the trauma.

> Although there are many negative effects of trauma, there are some possible positive effects of experiencing trauma. Some individuals who have experienced trauma gain higher levels of emotional intelligence and experience post-traumatic growth. (9)

The process of confronting our trauma has also meant for many MKs a process of confronting our parents. For some, that has not been possible because they are no longer with us, leaving us with mixed feelings: grateful that we don't need to have those difficult conversations but frustrated, too, that we can never know the answers to the many questions we have. Others amongst us have had to choose whether to let sleeping dogs lie and deal with our continuing problems alone, as we have always done, or initiate those difficult conversations, understanding the inherent risk that we might further damage an already fragile parent–child relationship, but hoping that we perhaps might be able to deepen it. All of these positions are well represented within the MK community and each of us has had to choose our own path.

Some have taken on the task and heard their parents continue to justify their actions and declare that if they had their time over again they would not do anything differently. The pain associated with such a response, not to mention the shock and bewilderment that a Christian parent could take such a position, is beyond conceiving.

Others have received a compassionate and gracious response, as exampled by the mother in the film *All God's Children* who, faced with the revelations of her children's trauma, said:

> We acted like we loved them. But then we sent them away. And you looked at yourself and you said, you know … "Who was I? What was I thinking of?" You would pray and ask God to take care of them. And they would cry themselves to sleep and you'd cry yourself to sleep. (10)

Discovering the truth of what their children were actually going through brought some parents home from the field. Others, finding out too late for any action on their part to make a difference, found themselves questioning their own faith, not just in their mission but also in God, the foundations of their own beliefs being grounded on the same distorted image of God that had been taught to their children. Some parents resorted to defence mode, still entrenched in their belief that God would cause everyone to live happily ever after however they behaved, and that they bore no real responsibility for their actions. An MK speaking in *All God's Children*, which details the horrific abuse suffered by children at Mamou, relates how her father said, on hearing of her abuse, 'Honey, you know we prayed for you every day.' To which she responded, 'Yes, Dad. But it wasn't prayer that I needed. I needed you.' This is Hope's story, repeated many times over around the mission world.

Brene Brown teaches:

> In the absence of love and belonging there is always suffering. (11)

And the life of missionary children was, for many decades, one characterised by the absence of love and belonging. I met up with a man who, as a teenager, had been led to Christ through the work of my parents. My father had gone on to counsel him through some very difficult times in his life and this man, by now in his sixties, spoke warmly of him as having been 'like a father to me.' Then he paused and added, 'But I realise he was much more of a father to me than he ever was to you.' Such is the dichotomy that surrounds the life of the MK and often, too, the pastor's child. Born into a loving, dedicated, Christian family, all should have been well. But instead, that love and dedication became focused firstly upon God, as He indeed asks of us, but secondly on those they felt called to serve, which God had not asked of them.

This is the Jephthah inheritance – a commitment made to a sacrifice God had not required; the sacrifice of a child.

As I write, a number of missions remain defensive of their past policies and unwilling to engage with their MKs, mostly out of a combination of fear and shame, but none out of a desire to honour God. Here's Brene Brown again.

> When the culture of [an organisation] mandates that it is more important to protect the reputation of that system and those in power than it is to protect the basic human dignity of individuals or communities, you can be sure of the following problems: Shame is systemic. Complicity is part of the culture. Money and power trump ethics. Accountability is dead. Control and fear are management tools. And there's a trail of devastation and pain. (12)

In such instances, calls for forgiveness from missions reveal the extent to which they have missed the point and failed to even begin to comprehend the extent of the suffering caused by their past policies. As one MK has put it:

> I call forgiveness 'the F word' for the evangelical community, because of how they use forgiveness. It's not that victims are against forgiveness. Victims are against forgiveness as the solution to the problem. (13)

Mission policies have changed radically since the turn of the millennium, and these changes have resolved many of the concerns that seemed insurmountable during my own childhood. There are many practical aspects of mission life that have made the matter of raising children on the mission field a considerably easier task than ever it used to be, and MKs today are cared for and educated to a much higher standard. Missions deserve much respect and credit for these changes and they bode well for the future.

But, even as I am delighted to be able to offer missions that respect and credit, I would not be fulfilling my remit in bringing this matter to a close were I not to warn that technological advances and more liberal-minded policies of equality and pragmatism are not sufficient to guarantee that future generations of MKs will be adequately cared for. It has been mentioned more than once that the policies of missions in the past were of their time, in the same way that the advances mentioned above are of this time. Times will change and no doubt there will be further progress to make it easier for missions to care well for their children. But that is not the point.

The point is, and the problem always was, that many missions acted out of a colonial, imperialist and conservatively theological mindset which viewed God as being more interested in judging His children than loving them, and prioritised the evangelising of the nations over the care of their children. Their words were drowned out by their actions and, as is almost always the way with large organisations, many morphed into dysfunctional, self-serving and inward-looking systems that ultimately lost sight of their true mission and set about controlling their members and defending their policies rather than seeking first His kingdom and His righteousness. Of course, it is easily done, and I speak out of sadness rather than in judgment. I cannot place my hand on my heart and say that I would not have been similarly guilty had my own path followed a different course.

What is important now is that the future must reflect the lessons of the past.

We are not required, as Jephthah failed to understand, to promise God things which He has not asked of us. We are not required to sacrifice our children to Him as a mark of our devotion, because He has declared:

> I require mercy, not sacrifice, and acknowledgment of God rather than burnt offerings. (Hosea 6:6)

We are not required to go because we have been called without asking God if now is the right time. How might Paul have fared if he had left Damascus after his sight was restored and ploughed ahead into Asia Minor without taking those seven years to allow God to prepare him for his venture? How might Jesus Himself have fared had he left his father's workshop at eighteen to do his Father's will without first devoting Himself to the discipline of learning how to do that will? Perhaps part of the right time to go will be defined by consideration of the consequences for the children who have not themselves been called but are going to be taken anyway.

We are not required to abrogate responsibility for the children God has given us by handing them over into the care of strangers, particularly if we know nothing about those strangers or cannot verify both their appropriateness for the role and the strength of their calling to that role.

> Many of the people who eventually became house-parents were people that didn't fit the qualifications for doing missionary work. They were not good at language learning, they did not relate well to Africans, in some instances, so, 'Let's put them down to take care of the children' (14)

We are not required to put aside secular wisdom and knowledge, as happened with the advances in child psychology, and rely exclusively on our own understanding, having faith that God will sort everything out for us. Ultimately, that is not faith in God so much as a kind of 'fingers crossed' superstition that allows us to continue along our own path without pausing to consider that perhaps there are areas of wisdom and understanding of which we are unaware, but maybe should make an effort to comprehend.

Most importantly, we are not required to preach a God of love to the unsaved without demonstrating and outworking that love amongst ourselves, and especially within our own families. After all, why should anyone listen to us when our words are drowned out by our actions? We can speak about a God of love until we are blue in the face, but unless we example and model that love to those to whom we have been sent, our words are empty and we witness only to the extent of our own unbelief and failure to understand the true nature of God.

That's a lot of 'we are nots.' So, what of the 'we ares'?

Well, only one, perhaps. In John 5:19, Jesus said:

> The Son can do nothing by Himself. He can only do what He sees His father doing.

The original sin of man in the Garden of Eden was to say to God, 'I don't trust you, I don't need you and I can do this by myself.' And every sin that has been committed ever since has been rooted in this attitude of arrogance and independence. Jesus never succumbed to an original thought in His life. To have done so would have been to have sinned. And He never sinned. Jesus looked to the Father in everything. Everything; He only ever did what He saw His father doing. He only ever said what His father told Him to say. He never did or said anything by Himself.

So, I could make a list here of all the things we are required to do but that's neither necessary nor desirable. We commit to intimate relationship with the Father, Son and Spirit and give ourselves to listening to Them and seeking first God's kingdom and His righteousness, and then we do what we see the Father doing. Anything beyond that is sin.

> Everything that does not come from faith is sin. (Romans 14:23)

So, there it is. That is the Jephthah inheritance, and it is time we put an end to this particular sin of the fathers being visited upon the children.

Afterword

These are stories that need to be told. So we don't forget. So we don't do the same again. Stories about little children left in boarding schools without the safety and security they desperately needed to develop into safe and secure adults; stories about older children and teenagers who were left on their own to deal with the hardship and evil of life without the support and love of their parents; stories about parents, many of them acting totally against their hearts but still leaving their children, being too far away from them, geographically, but sometimes also emotionally; and stories about the systems and the organisations which forced and taught, and sometimes even believed, that the best for the parents and even the children was to break families apart.

There is so much in this we can never understand. There is no way we can grasp what these children and teenagers experienced that affected them for the rest of their lives. But what we know is that this was not the best for these children. This was not God's intention and will. Research over recent decades shows us clearly that God created the human brain plastic, which means that the brain develops from our experiences. The most important experience for healthy development is the experience of loving, protecting and nurturing relationships with caregivers who are physically and emotionally present, not only during the first years, but throughout childhood. These children did not receive that.

Reading the stories of these now adult missionary kids doesn't leave us emotionless. Andrew is offering us a beautiful piece of art as he is weaving together these emotion-filled stories with reminders of how we as humans, in our search to honour God, stopped listening to ourselves, our children and even God. Maybe you are one of these children who was left on your own way too early. Maybe you are a parent who sent your child away with mixed emotions. Maybe you are one of those who received and tried to be there for a child who needed their parents. Maybe you were, or are, one of those who, with or without understanding of the consequences, was involved in the teaching and decisions that made this all happen. Whoever you are, you might by now be filled with emotions. Grief, huge grief. Anger … guilt … shame … confusion. Or numbness because it is too heavy to take in.

But in the midst of all these overwhelming emotions, this brokenness, there is beauty and hope. I have never been so surrounded by beauty and hope as at these reunions of adult MKs; strong, weak, struggling, longing people. People of integrity, caring so much for each other. Carrying grief, fear, anger, confusion and shame but with living fountains of joy just waiting to get through the lids and walls. The beauty and hope is also about the plasticity of the brain, because this plasticity means that healing can happen; healing of wounds and experiences; healing of lives and relationships. What we visualise in our imagination activates the same neurological pathways as if we had experienced it in reality. This means that there is still time to hug, comfort and love the little child. It is still possible to protect and stand up for the child and teenager, to stop the abuse and bullying. In and through our imagination, deep healing can happen. I have seen this happen again and again. It doesn't take away what happened. The memories of the hardship and traumatising events and life situations will remain, but they will no longer disturb and destroy.

This piece of art is a gift for each one of us to receive and reflect upon: How does this text resonate with me? What is touched, moved and awakened within me? What are the emotions that need to be listened to and taken care of? What are the thoughts that are stirred up, coming with messages that need to be heard and evaluated? What fears and longings are trying to get out of chambers long since closed? And what are the actions that this book invites me to take?

No child should have to experience the hardship of life without the security of their parents being within reach. This is a book about missionary kids, but there are plenty of kids of all sorts out there who need safe adults to be present in their lives. Let's continue to make sure that every child and every teenager has someone who sees them, hears them, is there with them, understands them and loves them. Let's be a safe presence for the children within us, and the children around us.

Ulrika Ernvik
MSW, Licensed Psychotherapist and author
Originator and developer of SafetyStories®
MK, mom of five MKs, and MK counsellor

Acknowledgements

My heartfelt and grateful thanks go to the following, without whom this book would not have been possible and because of whom it is all the richer.

Firstly, to my mother, whose grace and patience as I have journeyed through my pain have made my way so much easier. Her acknowledgement of her part in acquiescing to the will of her husband and the mission has taken her back into many dark places and forced her to relive her own grief at the loss of her children. That she has borne that grief and listened to so many truths from which I had protected her for so many years is a mark of her resilience no less than her humility and, inasmuch as it was necessary, we have been completely reconciled in our relationship as mother and son, the lost years returned to us as fully as may be possible in this life.

My father, who left us whilst I was still journeying out of the darkness of my troubled past to enter his own dark world of Alzheimer's and with whom I look forward to being reunited and reconciled in the embrace of the Lord he served with all his heart and in whose presence all our tears will be wiped away.

Ruth van Reken, who has upheld and supported me through some very tough years, generously encouraging and affirming me in my desire to serve the MK community as God has led and guided me. Her presence in my life is a priceless gem of wisdom, love, mercy and grace.

Ulrika Ernvik, whose wholehearted commitment to my own tribe of MKs secured forever her place in our mission family and whose invaluable teaching, loving encouragement and gentle presence won our love and admiration in a special way. Her wise and sensitive contribution to this book is beyond measure.

William Paul Young, whose generous and immeasurable support to our community of MKs, as well as to me personally, drawing as he did, to our immense benefit, on his own MK upbringing and journey of faith, has left me greatly and forever in his debt.

David Dykema, Kirsten Leed, David Houliston and Barry McKessar, whose belief in the rightness of our venture when first it began was the engine that has driven the work of healing for so many MKs, bringing them new hope and changing lives forever. Their teamwork and shared vision fanned the flames of what seemed a feeble spark, but which has now seen many brought to a place of resolution. Their contribution is simply not possible to quantify, but without it, the seed from which this book has grown would never have been planted.

John Chenoweth, whose wise counsel and patient feedback have improved and refined the text and whose friendship, unwavering support and encouragement persuaded me of its enduring worth.

Dr Freek Bakker, whose own research into and concern for the issues of MKs has done much to bring the impact of their experiences to a wider audience and whose validation, advice and constructive criticism have been of immense value.

Gill Henn, whose wealth of experience and unswerving affirmation of my writing have allowed me to push the boundaries of such talent as I have been blessed with in this area and whose editing skills have taught me more than I can say.

Merle Williams, whose interest in and experience of the issues considered in these pages provided welcome validation and whose professional advice was a significant support to me on the journey towards publication.

Isobel Strang, whose hospitality in providing for me a safe and quiet place in which to complete and refine the finished manuscript brought me great joy and peace, along with a depth of spiritual discernment and support that I treasure.

My fellow MKs, who, whether or not they have understood or supported my efforts to hold our missions to account and provide opportunities for healing, have nonetheless blessed me by their input and whose stories have provided the foundation for the experiences related herein.

My editor, Paul Bendor-Samuel, and the team at Regnum Books for their wise counsel and gentle guidance. Their determination that this book should be published and assurance that they wanted my voice to be heard has been a most encouraging validation of this project.

Finally, my wife and sons, who lived alongside me through the unhealed years, unknowingly bearing the weight of my trauma and living with the consequences of my many mistakes, and who have endured my long absences before the computer with patience, understanding and grace.

Notes

Introduction

1. John Eldredge, *Wild at Heart*. (Nashville, TN: Thomas Nelson), p. 165.
2. Gabor Maté, *The Myth of Normal*. (London: Vermilion), p. 436.
3. Brian Zahnd, *What to Do on the Worst Day of Your Life*. (Lake Mary, FL: Charisma House), p. 8.

Jephthah's Story

1. Richard Rohr, *Immortal Diamond*. (London: SPCK Publishing), p. 46.
2. Miles Van Pelt. https://www.thegospelcoalition.org/article/rethinking-jephthah-foolish-vow/
3. Kenneth Bailey, *Jesus Through Middle Eastern Eyes*. (London: SPCK Publishing), pp. 28–30.

A Good Idea Is Not Necessarily a God Idea

1. CS Lewis, *The Problem Of Pain*. (London: Collins), p. 90.
2. Ibid.
3. William Paul Young, *The Shack*. (London: Hodder & Stoughton), p. 136.
4. Gerald May, *Addiction and Grace*. (New York, NY: HarperOne), p. 139.
5. CS Lewis, *The Screwtape Letters*.(London: Collins), p. 60.
6. Hugh Nibley, *Approaching Zion*. (New York. NY: Barnes & Noble), https://www.goodreads.com/work/quotes/388657-approaching-zion-the-collected-works-of-hugh-nibley-vol-9
7. Jon D Levenson, *The Death and Resurrection of the Beloved Son*. (New Haven, CT and London: Yale University Press), pp.1-14.

Suffer the Little Children

1. Curt Thompson, *The Soul of Shame*. (Downers Grove, IL: IVP), p. 72.
2. Thomas Verny, quoted by Gabor Maté: *The Myth of Normal*. (London: Vermilion), p. 139.
3. Gabor Maté, *The Myth of Normal*. (London: Vermilion), p. 141.

Hope's Story

1. Gabor Maté, *The Myth of Normal*. (London: Vermilion), p. 112.

An Ever-Present Help

1. William Paul Young, *The Shack*. (London: Hodder and Stoughton), p. 93.
2. Marcus Borg. 'Female Images of God in the Bible', *Radical Grace,* vol. 24, no. 1 (Cincinnati, OH: St Anthony Messenger Press, 2011), p. 4.
3. National Fatherhood Initiative and US Census Bureau statistic. https://www.fatherhood.org/father-absence-statistic
4. Gabor Maté, *The Myth of Normal*. (London: Vermilion), p. 126.

Michael's Story

1. Gabor Maté, *When the Body Says No*. (London: Vermilion), p. 250–251.
2. Gordon Neufeld, *Hold On to Your Kids*. (London: Vermilion), p. 271.

From Great Commission to Great Omission

1. Mark Galli, *Jesus Mean and Wild*. (Grand Rapids, MI: Baker Books), p. 57.
2. Richard Rohr, *Falling Upward*. (London: SPCK Publishing), p. 26.
3. Joy Schaverien, *Boarding School Syndrome*. (Abingdon-on-Thames, Oxfordshire: Routledge).
4. Nick Duffell/Katherine Whitehorn, *The Making of Them*. (London: Lone Arrow Press), p. 43.
5. Nick Duffell, *The Making of Them*. (London: Lone Arrow Press), p. 4.
6. I do not wish to attribute this quote directly in order to preserve the anonymity of the individual and mission concerned and by doing so avoid unnecessary opprobrium.
7. Yuval Noah Harari, *Sapiens*. (London: Penguin Random House (Vintage Popular Science)), p. 303.
8. Nick Duffell/George Monbiot, *The Making of Them*. (London: Lone Arrow Press), p. 27.
9. Gordon Neufeld, *Hold On to Your Kids*. (London: Vermilion), p. 10–11.

Marianne's Story

1. Gabor Maté, *The Myth of Normal*. (London: Vermilion), p. 444.

Justified by Fate

1. Gabor Maté, *When the Body Says No*. (London: Vermilion), p. 255.
2. Mark Galli, *Jesus Mean and Wild*. (Grand Rapids, MI: Baker Books), p. 15.
3. Gabor Maté, *The Myth of Normal*. (London: Vermilion), p. 445.

4. Lindsay E Stone, *Missionary Kids and Trauma.* https://scholarworks.waldenu.edu/cgi/viewcontent.cgi?article=11168&context=dissertations
5. Brad Jersak, *A More Christlike God.* (Pasadena, CA: CWR Press), p. 38.
6. John White, *Changing on the Inside.* (Glasgow: Harper Collins), p. 48.
7. Richard Rohr, *The Divine Dance.* (London: SPCK Publishing), p. 161.
8. James Hudson Taylor, https://dotheword.org/2009/10/14/beware-gods-work-done-gods-way-will-never-lack-gods-supply/
9. CS Lewis, *The Screwtape Letters.* (London: Collins), p. 16.
10. Brad Jersak, *Can You Hear Me?* (Abbotsford, BC: Fresh Wind Press), p. 214.
11. Jack Frost, *Experiencing Father's Embrace.* (Conway, SC: Father's House Productions), p. 16.
12. Mark Galli, *Jesus Mean and Wild.* (Grand Rapids, MI: Baker Books), p. 57.
13. Pete Grieg, *Dirty Glory.* (London: Hodder Faith), p. 142.
14. CS Lewis, *The Four Loves.* (London: Collins), p. 37.
15. George MacDonald, *Creation in Christ.* (Vancouver, BC: Regent College Publishing), p. 102.

Anna's Story

1. Gabor Maté, *When the Body Says No.* (London: Vermilion), p. 188.

Father, But Not Far Enough

1. Brad Jersak, *A More Christlike God.* (Pasadena, CA: CWR Press), p. 58.
2. Jomo Kenyatta, https://quotepark.com/quotes/760996-jomo-kenyatta-when-the-missionaries-arrived-the-africans-had-th/
3. Richard Rohr, *The Universal Christ.* (London: SPCK), p. 32.
4. Henri Nouwen, *The Way of the Heart.* (New York, NY: HarperOne), p. 42.
5. Joy Schaverein, *Lost for Words.* https://www.boardingrecovery.com/docs/lostforwords.pdf
6. Brian Zahnd, *Sinners in the Hands of a Loving God.* (Random House, New York, NY: Penguin), p. 87.
7. Richard Rohr, https://cac.org/substitutionary-atonement-2017-07-23/
8. William Paul Young, in a conversation with friends.
9. TF Torrance, *Incarnation.* (Milton Keynes: Paternoster), p. 190.
10. Steve Chalke, *The Lost Message of Jesus.* (Burr Ridge, IL: Oasis).
11. Walter Wink, *Engaging the Powers.* (Minneapolis, MN: Fortress Press).
12. Gabor Maté, *When the Body Says No.* (London: Vermilion), p. 128.

13. Wayne Northey, *Stricken by God?* (Grand Rapids, MI: Eerdmans), p. 361.

Danny's Story

1. Gabor Maté, *The Myth of Normal*.(London: Vermilion), p. 229.
2. Russell Brand, http://absentofi.org/2019/07/russel-brand-trauma-is-the-gateway/

Laid upon the Altar

1. Joy Schaverien, https://www.therapyroute.com/article/boarding-school-syndrome-the-psychological-trauma-of-the-privileged-child-by-j-schaverien
2. Nick Duffell, *The Making of Them*. (London: Lone Arrow Press), p.41.
3. Joseph Chilton Pearce, *The Biology of Transcendence*. (Rochester, VT: Park Street Press), p. 138.
4. Nick Duffell, *The Making of Them*. (London: Lone Arrow Press), p. 31.
5. Ibid. p. 10.
6. Abraham Heschel, *The Prophets*. (New York, NY: HarperPerennial), p. 377.
7. Skye Jethani, *The Divine Commodity*. (Grand Rapids, MI: Zondervan), p. 153.
8. Jack Frost, *Experiencing Father's Embrace*. (Conway, SC: Father's House Productions), p. 24.
9. Henri Nouwen, *Life of the Beloved*. (London: Hodder), p. 36.
10. Brene Brown, *Braving the Wilderness*. (London: Vermilion), p. 85.
11. Nick Duffell, *The Making of Them*. (London: Lone Arrow Press), p.29.
12. Ibid, p. 240.
13. Danica Newton, https://www.alifeoverseas.com/an-open-letter-to-parents-of-missionary-kids/
14. Nick Duffell, *The Making of Them*. Page 29. (London: Lone Arrow Press), p. 29.
15. Brene Brown, *Daring Greatly*. (New York, NY: Penguin (Life) Random House), p. 11.
16. Peter Levine, *Waking the Tiger*. (Berkeley, CA: North Atlantic Books), p. 266.
17. Christopher Hitchens, https://slate.com/news-and-politics/2010/06/fragments-from-an- education.html
18. Tim Keller, *The Prodigal God*. (London: Hodder), p. 91.
19. Brene Brown, *Braving the Wilderness*. (London: Vermilion),p. 16.
20. Gabor Maté, *When the Body Says No*. (London: Vermilion), p. 197.

21. Jack Frost, *Experiencing Father's Embrace*. (Conway, SC: Father's House Productions), p.98.
22. Curtis & Eldredge, *The Sacred Romance*. (Nashville, TN: Thomas Nelson), p. 84.
23. Ibid, p. 88.
24. Brene Brown, *Daring Greatly*. (New York, NY: Penguin (Life) Random House), p. 69.
25. Joseph Chilton Pearce, *The Biology of Transcendence*. (Rochester, VT: Park Street Press), p. 149.
26. Nick Duffell, *The Making of Them*. (London: Lone Arrow Press), p. 10.
27. William Paul Young, *Eve*. (London: Simon & Schuster), p. 149.
28. Nick Duffell, *The Making of Them*. (London: Lone Arrow Press), p. 10.
29. Frederick Buechner, https://friendsofsilence.net/quote/author/frederick-buechner
30. Nick Duffell, *The Making of Them*. (London: Lone Arrow Press), p. 41.
31. Ibid, p. 142.
32. Eugene Peterson, *Run with the Horses*. (Downers Grove, IL: IV Press), p. 142.
33. Harry Strachan, https://static1.squarespace.com/static/5ff51d2d1fb0c35798605075/t/5ff7b27c63f2691ba9920337/1610068611450/Finding+a+Path+w+Pics.pdf
34. Simone Weil, https://www.atlasofplaces.com/essays/uprootedness/
35. Faith Cook, *Troubled Journey*. (Edinburgh: Banner of Truth), p. 105.
36. Rebecca Hopkins, https://www.christianitytoday.com/ct/2022/december/missionary-kid-buse-statistics-safeguard-prevention.html
37. TCK Training, https://www.tcktraining.com/blog/2022815caution-and-hope-for-missionary-kids
38. John Eldredge, *Wild at Heart*. (Nashville, TN: Thomas Nelson), p.114.
39. Hafiz, *The Garden of Heaven*. (Mineola, NY: Dover Publications Inc), p. 10.

Esther's Story

1. Henri Nouwen, *Life of the Beloved*. (London: Hodder), p. 36.
2. Gabor Maté, *When the Body Says No*. (London: Vermilion), p. 238–239.

Strangers in a Strange Land

1. Curt Thompson, *The Soul of Shame*. (Downers Grove, IL: IVP), p. 72.

2. Nick Duffell, *The Making of Them*. (London: Lone Arrow Press), p. 235.
3. Joseph Chilton Pearce, *The Biology of Transcendence*. (Rochester, VT: Park Street Press), p. 138.
4. RJ Lifton, *The Life of the Self.* Quoted in *Gestalt Therapy: Practice and Theory,* by Korb, Gorrell and Van de Riet. (Gouldsboro, ME: Gestalt Journal Press), p. 75.

By This Will All Men Know…

1. William Paul Young, *Eve*. (London: Simon & Schuster), p. 150.
2. Floyd McClung, *The Father Heart of God.* (Colorado Springs, CO: David C Cook), p. 25.
3. Pamela Gourley, *God's Sovereignty and Our Responsibility*. (Fredericksburg, VA: Plainfocus Books), p. 177.

Leyla's Story

1. Gordon Neufeld, *Hold On to Your Kids*. (London: Vermilion), p. 109.

The Land of Lost Content

1. Gabor Maté, https://hydro-ease.co.uk/gabor-mate-in-conversation-with-vivian-mckinnon/dr-gabor-mate-in-conversation-with-vivan-mckinnon-part-six/
2. Peter Levine, *Waking the Tiger*. (Berkeley, CA: North Atlantic Books), p. 73.
3. John Eldredge, *Wild at Heart*. (Nashville, TN: Thomas Nelson), p. 67.
4. Peter Levine, *Waking the Tiger*. (Berkeley, CA: North Atlantic Books), p. 73.
5. Elinor Greenberg, *Borderline, Narcissistic and Schizoid Adaptations*. (New York, NY: Greenbrooke Press), p. 166.
6. Frederick Buechner, *A Crazy Holy Grace*. (Grand Rapids, MI: Zondervan), p. 52.
7. AE Housman, *A Shropshire Lad.* (Ludlow, Shropshire: Palmers Press), p. 59.
8. Gordon Neufeld, *Hold On to Your Kids*. Page 19. (London: Vermilion), p. 19.

Mark's Story

1. John Eldredge, *Wild at Heart*. (Nashville, TN: Thomas Nelson), p. 67.

All Things Reconsidered

1. Nick Duffell, *The Making of Them*. (London: Lone Arrow Press), p. 39.
2. Ibid, p. 29.
3. Ibid, p. 55.

4. William Paul Young, https://www.youtube.com/watch?v=geLPmDN99pg&ab_channel=CCLI

From Nowhere to 'Now Where?'

1. Rob Bell, *Love Wins*. (London: Collins), p. 175.
2. Gabor Maté, *When the Body Says No*. (London: Vermilion), p. 247.
3. John Eldredge, *Wild at Heart*. (Nashville, TN: Thomas Nelson), p. 72.
4. Yuval Noah Harari, *Homo Deus*. (London: Penguin Random House (Vintage Popular Science)), p. 103.
5. Ibid, p. 349.
6. *Sent: Reflections on Missions, Boarding School and Childhood*. Mixed authorship (Bisbane: John Chenoweth Publisher, 2020), https://sent-stories.com
7. Ruth van Reken, *Letters Never Sent*. (Elgin, IL: LifeJourney Books).
8. Ulrika Ernvik, *Third Culture Kids: A Gift to Care For*. (Sweden: Familjeglädje).
9. Lindsay E Stone, *Missionary Kids and Trauma*. https://scholarworks.waldenu.edu/cgi/viewcontent.cgi?article=11168&context=dissertations
10. *All God's Children*. C&MA. https://www.youtube.com/watch?v=V3KMa8sVGqY&ab_channel=GHWP
11. Brene Brown, *Atlas of the Heart*. (London: Vermilion), p. 154.
12. Ibid.
13. *All God's Children*. C&MA. https://www.youtube.com/watch?v=V3KMa8sVGqY&ab_channel=GHWP
14. Ibid.

Bibliography

Bailey, Kenneth. *Jesus Through Middle-Eastern Eyes.*
Bell, Rob. *Love Wins.*
Borg, Marcus. *Female Images of God in the Bible.*
Brown, Brene. *Atlas of the Heart.*
Brown, Brene. *Braving the Wilderness.*
Brown, Brene. *Daring Greatly.*
Buechner, Frederick. *A Crazy, Holy Grace.*
Chalke, Steve. *The Lost Message of Jesus.*
Chilton Pearce, Joseph. *The Biology of Transcendence.*
Cook, Faith. *Troubled Journey.*
Curtis, Brent and Eldredge, John. *The Sacred Romance.*
Duffell, Nick. *The Making of Them.*
Eldredge, John. *Wild at Heart.*
Frost, Jack. *Experiencing Father's Embrace.*
Galli, Mark. *Jesus Mean and Wild.*
Gourley, Pamela. *God's Sovereignty and Our Responsibility.*
Greenberg, Elinor. *Borderline, Narcissistic and Schizoid Adaptations.*
Grieg, Pete. *Dirty Glory.*
Harari, Yuval Noah. *Homo Deus.*
Harari, Yuval Noah. *Sapiens.*
Heschel, Abraham. *The Prophets.*
Housman, AE. *A Shropshire Lad.*
Jersak, Brad. *A More Christlike God.*
Jersak, Brad. *Can You Hear Me?*
Jethani, Skye. *The Divine Commodity.*
Keller, Tim. *The Prodigal God.*
Korb, Margaret; Gorrell, Jeffrey; Van de Riet, Vernon. *Gestalt Therapy.*
Levenson, Jon D. *The Death and Resurrection of the Beloved Son.*
Levine, Peter. *Waking the Tiger.*
Lewis, CS. The Four Loves
Lewis, CS. The Problem of Pain.
Lewis, CS. The Screwtape Letters.
MacDonald, George. *Creation in Christ.*
Maté, Gabor. *The Myth of Normal.*
Maté, Gabor. *When the Body Says No.*
May, Gerald. *Addiction and Grace.*
McClung, Floyd. *The Father Heart of God.*

Mixed Authorship. *Sent.*
Northey, Wayne. *Stricken by God.*
Nouwen, Henri. *The Way of the Heart.*
Nouwen, Henri. *Life of the Beloved.*
Neufeld, Gordon & Maté, Gabor. *Hold On to Your Kids.*
Peterson, Eugene. *Run with the Horses.*
Rohr, Richard. *Falling Upward.*
Rohr, Richard. *Immortal Diamond.*
Rohr, Richard. *The Divine Dance.*
Rohr, Richard. *The Universal Christ.*
Schaverien, Joy. *Boarding School Syndrome.*
Schaverien, Joy. *Lost for Words.*
Thompson, Curt. *The Soul of Shame.*
Torrance, TF. *Incarnation.*
van Reken, Ruth. *Letters Never Sent.*
White, John. *Changing on the Inside.*
Wink, Walter. *Engaging the Powers.*
Young, William Paul. *Eve.*
Young, William Paul. *The Shack.*
Zahnd, Brian. *Sinners in the Hands of a Loving God.*
Zahnd, Brian. *What to Do on the Worst Day of Your Life.*